9/76

A.Ay

095034546b

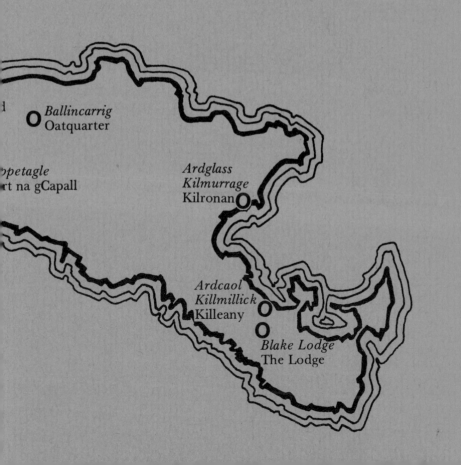

Ballincarrig
Oatquarter

ppetagle
t na gCapall

Ardglass
Kilmurrage
Kilronan

Ardcaol
Killmillick
Killeany

Blake Lodge
The Lodge

The Novels of Liam O'Flaherty

The Novels
of Liam O'Flaherty

A Study in Romantic Realism

Part I: Background & Profile
Part II: Analysis

Patrick F Sheeran

WOLFHOUND PRESS

First published 1976
Wolfhound Press, Dublin

ISBN 0 9503454 6 6

Printed and bound in the Republic of Ireland

CONTENTS

Part I Background and Profile

Part II The Novels

Acknowledgements
Quotations from the works of Liam O'Flaherty
and other writers which are used to illustrate
the text are copyright of the individual
authors and publishers concerned; the original
sources are cited in the notes on the text, and
are gratefully acknowledged.

PREFACE

This is the first study devoted exclusively to the novels of Liam O'Flaherty within the context of Anglo-Irish literature and life.

Part I, Background and Profile, concentrates on O'Flaherty's early life, in particular his youth on the Aran Islands. The proximity of Galway to the islands facilitated this study; contact with older inhabitants and research in local newspapers and government files dealing with the region revealed a picture of island life which is very different from the more generally accepted one. Familiarity with the history and folklore of Galway revealed too that O'Flaherty based a number of his novels on actual events and persons.

Part II is devoted to a detailed examination of O'Flaherty's novels. *Hollywood Cemetery* and *The Return of the Brute* have not been treated as they do not merit serious critical attention.

I would like to express my gratitude to Professor Lorna Reynolds, of University College, Galway, for her advice and personal interest throughout the course of this work. My thanks are also due to the staff of the Library and Secretariat, U.C.G. for their unfailing help and courtesy.

Finally, I wish to acknowledge, with thanks, a grant to assist towards the publication of this book from the National University of Ireland.

PART I: BACKGROUND AND PROFILE

INTRODUCTION

Liam O'Flaherty concludes his principal autobiographical volume, *Shame the Devil*,[1] with a caveat to future biographers: '. . . should I be considered worth a biography, I have robbed grave-robbers of their beastly loot.' The melodramatic tone is significant, the assertion hardly justified. The facts of his life related in the three volumes *Two Years*,[2] *Shame the Devil*, and *I Went to Russia*[3] are far from clear and are often contradictory. There is a recurring tendency to dissolve the facts in wild fantasy, or to constrain them to fit a pose. The autobiographical volumes are none the less important as projections of his own image of himself, his 'life-illusion' and the record of that illusion. They are particularly important in that the problems and views presented more directly in the autobiographies have a close bearing on O'Flaherty's fiction. In novel after novel he projected himself or part of himself into fictional characters and thus created an immense problem, seldom resolved, of artistic detachment, for the critic of his works. The purpose of this chapter, then, is to assess, as far as possible, the relationship between the man and the masks and to site the study in a broad consideration of the relevant background. The background, particularly of his early years, will be considered not simply as a backcloth but rather as a dynamic force which helped to shape the whole course of his fiction. Two periods of O'Flaherty's life are of the first importance for an understanding of his work: his youthful experience on the Aran Islands and the later years spent in London and Dublin. To simplify — the first provided him with his subject matter, the second, a point of view.

It is invidious to see a novel either as purely autobiographical or as shaped solely by social forces. This is not the intention of the present writer. Rather is it to point out those elements of character and social context which exercised a formative influence on O'Flaherty's work.

CHAPTER 1

THE ARAN ISLANDS: EARLY BACKGROUND

The three Iles of Aran half barony, extending in length from west to east, have the barony of Moycullin, Galway, on the north, the county of Clare, on the east, and the Cape of Kerryhead, far off in sight stretched out in the sea, on the south.

They are fenced on the south side with very high clifts, some three score, some four score and five score fathoms deep, against the Western Ocean's approach. The soile is almost paved over with stones, soe as, in some places nothing is to be seen but large stones with wide openings between them, where cattle break their legs. Scarce any other stones there but limestones and marble fit for tombstones, chymney mantle trees, and high crosses. Among these stones is very sweet pastures, so that beefe, veal, mutton are better and earlyer in season here, than elsewhere . . . In some places the plow goes . . .

From the Isles of Aran and the west continent often appears visible that inchanted island called O'Brasil, and in Irish Beg-ara, or the Lesser Aran, set down in cards of navigation. Whether it be reall and firm land, kept hidden by speciall ordinance of God, as the terrestial paradise, or else some illusion of airy clouds appearing on the surface of the sea, or the craft of evill spirits, is more than our judgements can sound out.

Roderick O'Flaherty, 1684.[4]

Liam O'Flaherty was born in the village of Gort na gCapall ('The Field of the Horses'), Inishmore, on 28 August 1896, the second son of a large family. His father, Michael O'Flaherty, describes himself under the 'Rank or Profession' column of the Birth Register as 'Landholder'. Like the vast majority of Aran men, he eked out a scanty living as a small farmer and fisherman and 'Landholder' hardly describes the reality. The family farm was the usual peasant holding or *cannogarra* of fifteen acres of rocky ground designed, ' . . . on the supposition that it could feed a cow with its calf, a horse and some sheep for their wool and give sufficient potatoes to feed one family.' The quotation is taken from the sociological section of an ethnographical study of the Aran Islands undertaken by Trinity College some three years prior to O'Flaherty's birth.[5] This study, by Professors Haddon and Browne, together with a large body of press reports in both the national and provincial newspapers from 1890 to 1920 provide the most accurate delineation of the social and cultural context within which Liam O'Flaherty spent his early years. J.M. Synge's *The Aran Islands,* written at intervals between 1898 and 1901, 'a direct account inventing nothing',[6] while always interesting and stimulating, has certainly omitted a great deal. Such accounts as those of Liam O'Flaherty's elder brother Tom, in *Aranmen-All*[7] and Pat Mullen's two volumes, *Man of Aran* (London, 1934), and *Hero Breed* (London, 1936), while useful, contain inaccuracies in detail and are largely prejudiced in their presentation of island life.

O'Flaherty was to remember his early years in Gort na gCapall as a time of extreme poverty and insecurity. His birthplace was, in fact, a rural slum. The village consisted of some thirty ramshackle, thatched cottages built on the crags to the south-west of Inishmore. A few hundred yards to the west the Atlantic breaks against vertical cliffs and sends grey plumes of spray drifting over the houses. At irregular intervals, when the seas run very high, the waves mount the 200 — 300 foot high cliffs and flood this, the narrowest part of Inishmore. An image of apocalypse, the island sinking beneath high seas, is a recurring motif in the village's folklore. To the north-east the crags descend in a series of terraces to a

crescent of relatively good land around the shore of Port-
murvey. For generations the men of Gort na gCapall have
hauled sand from this seashore, mixed it with seaweed and
silt from the lanes to turn bare rock into tillage land. The
fertile fields belonged to the local landlord, O'Flaherty
Johnston, who drove the peasantry to the crags lest their
cottages would take up any of his precious acres. His 'Big
House' with its belt of ragged, diminutive trees still shelters
under the last stony terrace. Over all, dominating the landscape from every point, stands the cyclopian fortress of Dun
Aenghus atop a 300 foot high cliff. By a trick of perspective,
when viewed from the lanes of Gort na gCapall, it seems to
tower directly above the village, mysterious and threatening.

The threats to existence in O'Flaherty's youth were of a
more tangible order. He was born in a hamlet such as that
described by a parish priest of Aran as 'the most poverty
stricken hamlets in the kingdom, probably in the world'.[8]
Poverty, famine and death were the everyday facts of life.
The *cannogarra* or fifteen acres did not always feed a cow
with its calf and the villagers lived for long years under threat
of eviction from the absentee landlords, the Digbys of
Kildare and Herefordshire, who drew a yearly rental of
£2,700 from these barren rocks. One such eviction campaign
in April/May 1894 brought to the islands a number of
'Special Commissioners' from the National newspapers who
filed extensive reports on island life. The following description
of Killeany village has to be darkened if we are to understand
conditions in Gort na gCapall. O'Flaherty's village was more
remote, more subject to famine, disease and eviction:

> I intend, now, to endeavour to give a picture of the
> conditions of life in a portion of the island where the
> evictor has not yet been, and to show that even without
> eviction existence here is carried on under the most
> appalling difficulties.
> I take as a typical instance the village of Killeany, in
> Arranmore. I visited it last evening, and most certainly
> say that the sights which I saw were shocking and revolt-
> ing in the extreme. No language could adequately des-
> cribe them. They should be witnessed in order to be

fully understood. In the village there are close on eighty families, all poor, wretchedly clad, with hunger stamped in every face. Despair seems to have seized on the people. The cabins reek with filth. They are almost entirely devoid of furniture. In short, all the surroundings suggest the deepest depths of misery and destitution. I went into several of the houses and talked with the poor people. They are all most courteous, even in their despair, and freely tell of their needs and conditions. One poor man told me a pitiable tale. His wife has been dead for some time, and he has three little children, whose appearances are enough to frighten one, and his little family have had to go to bed supperless on many a night this time back. In fact, at the very moment I was speaking to him he had not an ounce of food for his children, who were crouching beside a sickly fire. I asked to see the room in which the family slept, and was taken to it. I must say that I effected my escape from the door as soon as I could. It is a small dirty hole, with a few squalid rags in a corner which serve as bedclothes, and which are spread over some straw on the damp earthen floor at night. In almost every house which we visited in the village the same heart-rendering scenes are to be witnessed.

One fact that struck me most forcibly was the large number of widows and orphans in the village. The fishery industry has mainly helped to support it, and while pursuing their calling, which is of course a very dangerous one in bad weather, many fathers have been engulphed in the raging ocean, and have left behind them large families to mourn their loss. How these poor widows and orphans manage to live in Killeany is a perfect mystery to me. One and all are suffering extreme destitution, and bad as their position is, what is the prospect before them if something is not immediately done. When returning from this village I met a number of little children on their way to it. They had bundles of nettles with them and I asked for what purpose they had procured them. Imagine my astonishment when I was told that they were to be boiled for supper in their respective homes. This picture of Killeany is a picture of real life in these islands. It is not highly coloured or exaggerated in any sense. In fact, I must admit that it does not convey anything like the real truth, but if I have succeeded in conveying my idea of the condition of life in this ill-starred village, then I am satisfied. It is not an exceptional instance of acute distress; it is a typical case of what prevails all round. Go to any of the numerous hamlets and you will find a similar condition of things.[9]

Other witnesses, from the visiting M.P. for Northamptonshire East to the Chief Secretary agree with this very un-Synge-like presentation of island life.[10] Conditions were slow to change. As late as 1913 the *Coisde Gnotha* of the Gaelic League, which included Edward Martyn, published their survey of village life on the islands of South Connemara. Unlike the Chief Secretary they were ' . . . able to hear from the islander's own lips, as told in their own melodious Irish the sad story of their sufferings, privations and cheerless existence.'[11] Again, the details are not such as those who have mis-read Synge would have us believe. O'Flaherty too has suffered by being read through the eyes of Synge, the frequent brutality of his descriptions being put down as gratuitous insults to 'Holy Aran' rather than as accurate delineations of island life. The *Coisde Gnotha* report continues:

Most of the houses on the islands are very bad. A great many are one-roomed built of rough stones. With a hole in the roof for a chimney, and no window. To see the interior we had to strike matches. The floors are dirty and soft. The smoke of the turf fire sometimes goes through the hole intended for it, but more often it fills the room with a blinding blue fog and makes its way slowly through the door. This stagnant cloud of smoke covers roof and walls and furniture with a sticky, slime layer of soot. The furniture, indeed, is of the scantiest. We saw but one bedstead — a wooden one — which had neither mattress nor bedclothing. These had been burned by the sanitary authority five or six weeks previously, and had not been replaced.

In these wretched cabins the people sleep on the floor in their day-clothes, those who are fortunate enough to possess them being accompanied by the cow and the pig. In the cold winter both men and animals feel the better of the mutual warmth. To get an idea of the conditions of life of these islanders one must picture one of these wretched hovels with its smoke-reeking atmosphere, and six or eight human beings with a pig, or cow, or both stretched asleep on its filth-sodden floor. One must picture that family, after such a night, awaking with nothing to eat but potatoes and boiled tea, and nothing before them for the day but hard work, delving among barren rocks, or carrying on their backs seaweed which they must wade breast high to gather. Picture a human being condemned to this routine from day to day, from year's end to year's end, from the cradle to the grave, and one gets some idea of the kind of life these poor people lead. No pen can describe the dull, hapless misery of it. The reality that we saw is far worse than any pen picture of it that has yet appeared. And this is true.[12]

O'Flaherty's family was one of the poorest of the poor. Even today, after seventy years, during which the homes of Gort na gCapall have been altered and rebuilt, what was once the O'Flaherty homestead is one of the least flourishing. Poor as it was in the 1890s, it was still the object of the 'Agent's' attention. Tom O'Flaherty vividly describes the quenching of the fire on the O'Flaherty hearth in the course of one such eviction, and the abiding bitterness that remained.[13] In the peasant cottages of Aran the fire was never allowed to go out and the quenching signified a break in the continuity of family life. Liam's father's name, in Irish, was another symbol of that continuity. It ran *Micheal Mhicil Phadraic Mhicil Bartley Mhicil Bartholomew.* In island folklore the last named Bartholomew was credited with the founding of Gort na gCapall:

Bartholomew built his house upon a rock, not for

reasons of security or because he considered the rock symbolical of continuity, but because he did not want to waste a piece of good pasture or tillage land under a house.[14]

The mainstay of the family living in these conditions was, as so often in Irish life, the mother. She was a descendant of a family of Plymouth Brethern who came to the islands from Antrim in the early years of the century to build lighthouses. George Petrie, the rediscoverer of the Aran Islands in the 1820s noted with chagrin:

> The introduction, a few years since, of a number of persons into Aranmore for the purpose of erecting a lighthouse has had an injurious effect on the character of the native inhabitants of the island. Their unsuspicious confidence and ready hospitality were frequently taken advantage of and abused, and their interesting qualities have consequently been in some degree diminished. Till that time robbery of any kind was wholly unknown in the island.[15]

Micheal Mhicil Phadraic O'Flaherty bettered the lesson and abducted his future wife the very night a suitor from the mainland was asking for her hand. The runaway match is treated by O'Flaherty, in *Shame the Devil*, as a piece of high romance unusual in a fiercely conservative community.[16] It is one of many curious lapses where he shows himself ignorant of or willing to disregard island folk tradition in favour of more conventional explanations. It is precisely because of the conservative nature of their community that his parents got married in this way. William Carleton, in his autobiography, describes the popular method:

> There is not a country in Europe where so many rash and unreflecting marriages are made as in Ireland; the habit has been the curse of the country. The youngsters manage their 'runaways' in the following manner; they first determine upon 'running away' which is only another phrase for getting married: the lover selects the

house of some relation or friend of his own, and after having given notice to that friend or relation of his intention, and having gained his assent, he informs the friend of the night when he and his sweetheart will come to their house as a 'running away couple'; and in order that they may not be without the means of celebrating the event with a due convivial spirit, he generally places a gallon of unchristened whisky in their hands. The night of their arrival at the house of that friend or relation is of course a jolly one. On the next morning the friend or relation goes to their respective families and discusses the fact of their 'runaway'. The girl is then brought home to her family and remains there until the marriage takes place.[17]

On 20 February 1872 Michael Flaherty, aged twenty-six years, landholder of Gort na gCapall, married Margaret Ganly, sixteen-and-a-half years of age, from the village of Manister. He signed the Marriage Register in a clear flowing hand. His wife, along with the two witnesses, both Dirranes, appended 'her mark'. Carleton's warning about rash and unreflecting marriages was borne out: 'Her fairy-tale ended with her marriage. After that her life was a tale of hardship and misery, an endless struggle to find food for her many children.'[18]

Famine — or the official euphemism used by Government and newspapers 'Distress' — occurred so frequently in the Aran Islands and the western seaboard right up to the first two decades of the twentieth century as to be almost endemic. The euphemism blunted public response to the reality. People actually died of hunger in conditions as bad as those obtaining in the years of the Great Famine. The exactitude of Liam O'Flaherty's historical novel *Famine* has sometimes been wondered at. What requires an effort of the historical imagination for others was for him a living reality. Heavy rain in July and August frequently damaged the potato crop which was still the staple diet of most of the people. Conversely, a good season for the country generally meant a bad season for Aran. This was due to the peculiar nature of the soil on the islands. Frequently man-made, it lay to a depth of only a few inches on the solid limestone base. A spell of fine weather completely parched and burned it up, together with whatever crops were growing in it. Not only did the failure of the potato crop deprive the people of their staple food but it deprived them of the seed for the following year as well. Fine weather precipitated the 'distress' of 1894, '95, '97, '98, 1905 and 1906 on Inishmore. The casual visitor to the island, who found primroses blossoming in January and Alpine gentians in April, returned with a firm conviction that the islanders, when they talked of famine, spoke with a *beal bocht* ('A hungry mouth' implying lies and dishonesty). Galway's Board of Guardians, in whose care the islands were placed, consistently refused to recognize the hardship endured by the islanders. Incredibly, the Local Government Board appointed as their Inspector on the island a Major Fair who was bailiff to the landlords, the Misses Digby. There are cases on record of Major Fair evicting destitute families in his capacity as bailiff to the evictors and paying the same people a weekly allowance in his capacity of Local Government Board Inspector. No wonder then, that the euphemism 'distress' in the records of the Board of Guardians is always preceded by the qualification 'alleged'. A miserable and degrading system of 'relief' or 'allowance' was all that was done towards alleviating the lot of the islanders. The system and the temper of the times is brought into sharp focus by a letter written by a near neighbour of the O'Flaherty's called John O'Brien. He lived about half a mile from Gort na gCapall and there is every reason to think that the situation he describes was similar to that obtaining in the O'Flaherty household. The relevant minutes for 4 June 1895 of the Galway Board of Guardians reads as follows:

The following is a copy of a letter sent to the Local Government Board by a man named John O'Brien, a native of Aran, and forwarded by them to the Galway Board of Guardians for their consideration.

Oatquarter, Aran, Galway.
25th May, 1895.

The Right Hon. John Morley,
Sir — In my letter of the 10th instant I laid a small part

*of my miserable condition before you, but for all I
know it seems to have no effect. At least it has brought
me no increase of relief. I still receive the same allowance, 1s.6d. per week, as I did before I informed you,
sir, of my sad condition and my large family. My wife
and children are mere skeletons, having only something
less than one half-penny per day for the support of each.
We have to live principally on limpets, and a kind of seaweed called 'slowcawn' and consequently every one of
us have the diarrhoea. My wife went to Kilronan yesterday (a distance of about six Irish miles to and from) for
our weekly allowance, 1s.6d. to the relieving officer,
and she was barely able to come home with weakness . . .*

*Major Fair passed my house yesterday morning in a
car. I am sorry I did not see him until he had passed,
that I might show him the condition of my family. I
watched the whole day for his return, but when the car
returned it did not bring Major Fair, he having gone by
canoe to Connemara. If you, sir, do not do something to
save us immediately, we shall soon be beyond all human
help — I remain, sir, with the greatest respect, your
humble servant,*

John O'Brien.
*Mr. Kearns (A Galway Guardian) — I am sure Mr. Morley
will come to Aran to see him. That man is too smart
entirely. I did not think there were such clever writers
in Aran.*

Liam O'Flaherty does not treat of island life at any length
in his autobiographies, partly no doubt for reasons of family
pride. We are dealing, then, with a nearly anonymous peasantry and it is from stray documents such as this and the
memories of older inhabitants of the island that our picture
must be constructed.

If food was not forthcoming from the land there was
always the sea. Again the popular image of the islanders as
noble savages living on the wealth of the sea needs severe
correction. In 1891 there was not a single registered fishing
boat to be found on Inishmore. The fishermen used ' . . . the
frail canoe or currach — an utterly unreliable unseaworthy

and unsafe boat, from which to carry on fishing operations.'[19] The quotation is taken from a letter addressed by the parish priest of Aran to the national and local papers and it was destined to change the course of events. It was written out of a sense of outrage at the number of drownings that had occurred the previous year. A subscription was raised to buy boats for the islanders and the newly established Congested Districts Board was requested to take over. The request brought to the western seaboard one of the strangest and most effective figures in its troubled history — the Rev. W.S. Green and his yacht *Fingall*. It is worth recounting in some detail the way in which he established the fishing industry on Aran as it brought about a cultural change which became a leading theme of O'Flaherty's fiction. For the first time 'civilization' impinged with force on the 'natural' life of the islands. The learned Member of Parliament for Galway, Stephen Gwynn, remembering his Matthew Arnold, spoke of the Congested Districts Board and the Rev. Mr Green as bearers of 'sweetness and light' to the wild seaboard.[20] In 1892 the Rev. Mr Green ' . . . was solicited by the Government, nathless his clerical calling, to become one of her Majesty's Inspectors of Fisheries.'[21] He was asked to establish a fishing trade on the Aran Islands and he replied by demanding *carte blanche* from the Government. A telegraph wire was laid to Inishmore to connect it with the markets and a steamer supplied to maintain intercourse regularly between Aran and Galway. The islands were being drawn into the orbit of the 'civilized' world. In 1893 he brought to Aran seven crews of Arklow fishermen, with their boats, literally to teach the Aranmen how to fish. The islanders refused to accept his proposition that mackerel might be caught in April and May as well as in the traditional month of August. He stood firm by his convictions, ordered his small fleet to sea night after night until one morning in April they returned laden with mackerel. So great was the catch that a special train had to be ordered from Dublin and the fish fetched the highest prices. In two months fishing the seven crews earned what today would amount to about £8000 a piece. The islanders had been taught a lesson. By 1897 there were fourteen boats on Inishmore, all supplied and equipped by the

Congested Districts Board. Huge catches of fish were taken, up to 10,000 boxes of mackerel being caught in one week. So well organized was the industry that fish caught during the night were on sale the following morning in Manchester. This sudden increase in wealth had important social consequences which were seen by O'Flaherty as the rankest corruption. Odd as it may seem, the boats were supplied by the Board to the shopkeepers on the island rather than to the fishermen proper. The reason was that the shopkeepers offered better security for the boats. Thus the fishermen, who were already almost entirely in the hands of the shopkeepers, were tied to them even further. A new division arose in the previously homogeneous islands in the shape of a mean-spirited middle-class. The rise of this class and the results of the more extensive contact with the mainland figure largely in the fiction O'Flaherty was to write on his birthplace. His embittered attitude to these, apart from the larger social considerations with which he was intimately concerned, is sharpened by the fact that his family does not seem to have shared in the growing prosperity. Most of the children who survived early youth emigrated to America and had to make their way in the world by less traditional means. Michael Mhicil Phadraic, despite his eldest son's encomium of him as the strong man of the village and of his family, and as the best fisherman on Aran, died alone and in poverty, 'a babbling dotard, furious with insane fancies, kept alive only by some savage courage that resisted death.'[22] For his artist son he was to grow into an image of what he himself might become, and he recoiled in horror. Such scant references as there are to his father in the autobiographical volumes point to a nature very different from the gentle, emotional mother. He speaks of him as one: ' . . . whose stern nature had always seemed to be immune from influence by any emotion either of pain or of joy.'[23] Local tradition remembers him as a man who paid a great deal more attention to community affairs than to the well-being of his own family. An inveterate rebel, he had been a Fenian and later, as chief of the local branch of the Land League, had driven a landgrabber's cattle over the three hundred foot high cliff of Dun Aenghus. He had been imprisoned briefly on suspicion of shooting at a bailiff, (the shot was fired by a brother-in-law) and came under police surveillance. In common with his neighbours he had attempted to defend the island against fifty men of the Royal Irish Constabulary who had landed near Gort na gCapall to collect the 'cess'. Folkloristic retellings of the invasion and battle have given it heroic proportions and even in the report of the local, hostile press there is a certain primitive grandeur in the attempt to defeat the forces of the Crown:

> The police escort which accompanied the Aran barony constable, numbering about 50 men, returned here on Saturday. While escorting the collector they were met by a hostile mob of the islanders, who had taken up a position on the hills on each side of a valley through which the police were marching, and from their elevated site they commenced pelting stones, with the result that several of the men were struck. Remonstrance was of no avail, and so fierce had the stone throwing become, that the police were ordered to charge with their batons. At first the islanders showed a bold front, and endeavoured to prevent the police ascending the hills by pushing large boulders down on them, but the latter eventually succeeded in gaining the summit, where they were met by showers of stones from all directions. As a means of saving themselves they were compelled to use their batons, and there followed a regular battle which, however, resulted in the islanders beating a hasty retreat, leaving a large number of their friends behind, who had received wounds in the affray and were unable to make good their escape . . .[24]

Fiercely nationalistic, O'Flaherty senior passed his rebel nature to his sons. The elder, Tom, became prominent in social revolutionary circles in Boston and joined the Communist Party. Liam, styling himself 'Commander-in-Chief', with a handful of dockers, ran up the red flag over the Rotunda in Dublin and declared an Irish Soviet Republic. The rebel character which the father bequeathed to his sons seems, on the whole, to have been a legacy unwillingly accepted. Tom wrote: ' . . . I liked the emotional, soft, witty, story-telling

Ganlys (his mother's people) better than the harsh quarrel-some, haughty, "ferocious O'Flaherties" . . .'[25] Stray remarks of Liam have a similar import.

One of the recurring motifs in Liam's autobiographies, which give the volumes a precarious unity, is his ambiguous relation to the world of action and his espousal of various causes. He throws himself headlong into everything from Irish Republicanism to Soviet Bolshevism and as quickly and wholeheartedly retreats into a private world of fantasy to 'take refuge in the delicately fashioned world of my imagination'. To psychoanalyse is tempting but dangerous. The most one can say, on the scanty evidence available and without professional competence in the field, is that to a marked degree O'Flaherty failed to internalize or harmonize the conflicting attitudes to life represented by his parents. The resulting tension was personally debilitating, though artistically fruitful. Dissatisfaction, failure, and the impoverished circumstances of life in Gort na gCapall were exacerbated by the memory of an heroic past. O'Flaherty was to write: 'The only princely thing I possess is my name'[26] and constantly he would counterpoint the heroic past with the sordid present.

There were other views of the princely name and nature of the O'Flaherty clan than the one expressed above. Across the bay from Aran, the city of Galway had, in the sixteenth century, an inscription over the West Gate which read: 'From the ferocious O'Flaherties, good Lord deliver us.' The West Gate opened on the wilds of Iarchonnacht where the O'Flaherties held undisputed lordship for centuries. They earned the adjective 'ferocious' because of the barbarity of their internal feuding and a general hostility to strangers. As late as 1798, Monsieur Latocnaye, a Breton nobleman who visited Galway for his *Rambles through Ireland* was solemnly warned that he took his life in his hands if he ventured more than eight miles from the city. He would be ' . . . either shot as a land-grabber, drowned as a process-server, burnt as a witch or turned by spells into a dog because he was a Protestant.'[27]

The O'Flaherties of Iarchonnacht claimed descent from the mythical King Milesius of Spain and consequently laid claim to 'Milesian' secret knowledge and magical powers,

among which the changing of humans into animals was something of a speciality of theirs. Their subsequent history from
Milesius forward is a long and tortuous one with many
lacunae. Little of it concerns us here except those points to
which O'Flaherty directs a half-proud, half-ironic glance. Cut
off from the rest of the country by the wild terrain they
occupied, the great events of history passed them by. Their
activities, mostly horrific, are chronicled in the folklore of
Connaught rather than in formal history. Indeed the first
folktale published by the Irish Folklore Institute was a tale
of bloody fratricide among four O'Flaherty brother-
chieftains.[28]

The O'Flaherty involvement with the Aran Islands did not
begin until the late fifteenth century. They expelled the
O'Briens who had been lords of Aran, 'time out of man's
memory', as they put it in a pathetic appeal to the English
Queen. The new occupiers were not left in peace for long. In
1587, by letters patent of Queen Elizabeth, to whom the
O'Briens had appealed against the O'Flaherties, the Islands
were granted to one John Rawson of Athlone ' . . . gentleman,
on condition of retaining there twenty foot soldiers of the
English nation . . . .'[29] 'Gentleman . . . English nation': the
words spelled an end to the formal power of the hereditary
chiefs. Like many of their kind they sank into the peasantry
where they continued to exercise an informal chieftainship
over their people. Over two hundred years later, in 1823,
George Petrie wrote in glowing terms of the power and
respect still paid to a direct descendant of the chiefs of
Iarchonnacht, 'a gentleman, more by title of ancient lineage
than by property'.

> Mr. O'Flaherty may be justly denominated the *pater
> patriae* of the Araners. He is the reconciler in all differ-
> ences, the judge in all disputes, the adviser in all enter-
> prises and the friend in all things. A sound understand-
> ing and the kindest of hearts make him competent to be
> all those; and his decisions are never murmured against
> or his affection met by ingratitude.[30]

The vicissitudes of history were sharply portrayed when Petrie was startled to discover two portraits, the work of a court painter, in one of the rooms of O'Flaherty's humble thatched cottage. The gentleman's portrait was that of an uncle who had married into the English nobility, the other that of his lady, a daughter of Sir Henry Englefield, 'a respectable English Catholic'.

Mr O'Flaherty, who had been Petrie's host, was still alive thirty five years later when Petrie returned to Aran, in triumph, with some seventy members of the British Association to show them what he had found there. The party held their society's annual dinner within the ancient fortress of Dun Aenghus, on the cliff top of Inishmore. William Stokes, who attended with all the great men of Irish letters and scholarship of the day — Sir William Wilde, Sir Samuel Ferguson, Petrie, Whitley Stokes, Professor O'Curry and Dr O'Donovan — noted that 'The scene was indeed a strange one, and spoke of altered times and new modes of thought.' The crowd of visitors, dining in so odd a place, attracted the peasantry from all over the island and they crowded to the broken ramparts of the fort. The Provost of Trinity College presided at the meal and the first toast was proposed by Petrie. It was the health of Mr O'Flaherty, now resident magistrate of the island, ' . . . still the guardian and adviser of a pious, brave and simple people, who looked to him as to a chieftain and to a father and who loved him with all the force of Irish hearts.'[31]

More significant, perhaps, than the toast to the ageing chief were the speeches of Professor O'Curry and Dr O'Donovan to the curious peasantry on the walls above. Amazingly, both for the time and the Provost's presence, they spoke in the Irish language and exhorted their listeners to preserve their ancient heritage: 'To these addresses, one of the peasantry responded in Irish at considerable length, enforcing upon his hearers, by additional arguments, the exhortation of the last speaker.'[32]

The 'altered times' which William Stokes spoke of had brought the Provost and Fellows of Trinity and the chief of the O'Flaherties with his peasant followers together, amicably, on the same ground. A cynic might comment that the

same ground was a pagan fortress atop a high, crumbling cliff
and not much could be expected from so tenuous and
exposed a relation. The class represented by the Provost,
Protestant Anglo-Irish ascendancy, supplanted the native
chief in the next generation when O'Flaherty's land, but little
of his prestige, passed to one of its members. A Mr Johnston,
gentleman-farmer from the mainland, married O'Flaherty's
daughter and became his successor in what was now grand-
iosely called 'Kilmurvey House'. Mr Johnston seems to have
been unfortunate in numerous ways, not least in the fact that
in the mind of a boy from the next village, who vigorously
poached his estate, he would grow to be an image of the last
decadent remains of the Anglo-Irish aristocracy. Johnston
devoted more time to drinking than to the good management
of his lands or the proper placing of his numerous daughters
and entered literature as the jolly 'Mr Blake' of the poachers'
first novel and the pathetic 'Mr Athy' of *Skerrett.*

Liam O'Flaherty was to draw on the 'heroic' past of his
'family' but in ambiguous ways. At one point the past would
act as a foil to the actions of puny politicians, at another
became the source of the false posturing and empty rhetoric
which vitiated political debate on 'Inverrara', the island of
the novels. And 'Inverrara' or 'Nara' (Aran spelt backwards)
was shorthand for Ireland. The ambiguity is further complicated by the fact that he would project himself into his early
works as the dispossessed leader of an ancient clan to whom
the peasantry remain loyal. This, in spite of the fact that his
family were not directly related to *The* O'Flaherty. (Tom, in
his book *Aranmen-All* calls 'Kilmurvey House' the family
seat.) However, all of the approximately eighty families who
then bore the surname on Aran could claim some kinship and
bask in the glory of the 'princely name'. The islanders, living
in a closely knit, self-sufficient community, tolerated a great
deal of intermarriage so that everybody was more or less
related to everybody else. On the Middle Island (Inishmaan)
alone, there were, in 1893, only ten family names among the
400 inhabitants. Such clan and family connections complicated the social and political scene. Liam O'Flaherty would
see himself, not against a social context of class and property,

CHAPTER 2

THE SOCIAL AND CULTURAL CONTEXT

Socially, the Aran of O'Flaherty's youth revealed, depending on one's viewpoint, either a very thin or thickly-woven texture. Basically there were two, often opposing, social structures. The first, and by far the largest, was the informal social structure based on family loyalty and hereditary authority. Within this peasant group there were few gradations. Synge divides them into 'the prosperous, the struggling and the quite poor and thriftless'.[33] There were no class barriers as such. The formal structure was composed of a mere handful — the parish priest, curate, schoolmaster, one or two government officials, a few recluses from 'civilization', and the unfortunate Mr Johnston. With some qualifications to be made later, Haddon and Browne's summary is accurate (italics mine):

> The bulk of the men on the North Island may be described as small farmers who do a little fishing. There are besides two or three weavers, tailors and curragh builders; this about exhausts the occupation or trades so far as the *natives* are concerned. The butcher, baker and other allied tradesmen are mainly related to the small population, which may fairly be termed *foreign,* such as the representatives of the Government and the spiritual and secular instructors. There are two or three small shops on Aranmore where a few imported goods, hardware, crockery, clothing and the like can be obtained

and there are about as many houses licensed to sell
alcoholic liquor. The kelp (chemical substance obtained
from burning seaweed) is usually sold to a native who is
the accredited agent of the wholesale buyer.[34]

Liam O'Flaherty was to employ what we may call a topo-
graphical shorthand to represent the two groups. Kilronan,
the principal village and port of Inishmore was the residence
of the 'foreigners' and the source of all the island's ills. Here
were the rising middle class, the gombeen men who went to
Mass every Sunday and more often if expediency demanded
it. Westward to Gort na gCapall and Bungowla lived the
peasantry, threatened in their old ways and beliefs, who
turned to the dark god of Dun Aenghus. O'Flaherty's imaginative topography had a large basis in fact. Quite recently, in
1962, a close observer of Aran life, P. A. O Siochain, wrote
that the islanders beyond O'Flaherty's native village, ' . . .
look upon Kilronan and its inhabitants as a place and people
apart.'[35] In the regional novels, Kilronan and its people
became a symbol of all that O'Flaherty detested in Irish life,
particularly the 'urbanized peasants'. The action of his first
novel, *Thy Neighbour's Wife* begins there amid the corruption of clergy and laity alike and ends with the protagonist
seeking regeneration in the wild seas off Bungowla. *Skerrett*
has a similar direction, away from 'civilized' Kilronan to the
natural crags and seas of the north. *The Black Soul,* the novel
where he wished 'to storm the highest heavens'[36] by the
intensity of its evocation of life, is set, completely, in the
remote, 'pagan' village of Bungowla. In all this one notes the
poverty, in terms of the traditional concerns of the novel, of
the material available to an aspiring novelist. Social conditions
limited to a few minor officials and an anonymous peasantry
impoverished the range any realistic fiction could take.
O'Flaherty's work turns, perforce, to romance and folklore.
    The social situation on Aran had a cultural dimension
which is of importance for the direction of this study. The
line of argument has, of necessity, to be circuitous in order to
embrace the fragmentary and contradictory nature of the
evidence.
    The American folklorist, Professor Richard M. Dorson, in

an article, 'The Identification of Folklore in American Literature' establishes a method of demonstrating the relationship of a given body of work to folk tradition. Schematized it reads:

> Three principal kinds of evidence can be afforded.
> I An author may be shown through biographical evidence to have enjoyed direct contact with oral lore.
> II A second technique available to the folk critic proceeds from internal evidence in the literary composition itself, that indicates direct familiarity of the author with folklore. This evidence includes the alleged folktales, folksongs, folk sayings or folk customs imbedded in literature, as well as their setting.
> III (The critic) must prove that the saying, tale, song or custom inside the literary work possesses an independent traditional life. In other words, our critic must provide corroborative evidence to supplement his proof from biographical and internal evidence.[37]

It is with the first and to a lesser extent, the last of these three points that the present chapter is concerned. First, however, it is necessary to show in what way the culture of the Aran Islands was and is a folk culture as anthropologists define the term and to point out its peculiar qualities. In an 'anthropological critique' of the islands undertaken by John C. Messenger of the Folklore Institute, Indiana University, it is stated:

> The Aran islanders qualify as folk people in almost every respect, according to anthropological definition: the population has maintained its stability for at least 200 years; there is a strong bond between the peasants and their land, and agriculture provides them with the major source of their livelihood; production is mainly for subsistence and is carried on with a simple technology which includes as primary implements the digging stick, spade, and scythe; the island folk participate in a money

economy, but barter still persists on a small scale; a low standard of living prevails, and the birth rate is high; the family is of central importance, and marriage figures prominently as a provision of economic welfare; the islands are integrated into the county and national governments and are subject to their laws; the people have long been exposed to urban influences, have borrowed cultural elements from other rural areas on the mainland, and have integrated them into a relatively stable system; and, finally, the experience of living under foreign rule for over three centuries has created in the islanders an attitude of dependence on, yet hostility toward, government which continues to this day. The only conditions in Aran which run counter to those in most other peasant communities are low death and illiteracy rates and bilateral rather than unilateral descent (although inheritance is patrilineal).

The Aran cultural forms which are most publicized and attract the most tourist attention are the traditional garb of the islanders, their skill in rowing the famed canoe, or curagh, the manner in which they manufacture soils and grow in them a variety of crops, and their Gaelic speech which is thought by many to be the "purest" in Ireland. The indigenous costume for women is the ankle-length red or blue woollen 'petticoat' and heavy red, black, multi-coloured, or Paisley shawl; for men it is the blue woollen shirt, the brown or gray homespun vest and trousers, cowhide footwear, called 'pampooties', and the brightly coloured and intricately designed woven belt, or crios.[38]

Messenger's study was published in 1966 and refers to Aran life of the previous decade. Important qualifications need to be made to account for the folk culture of the previous fifty years.

The integration of the islanders with the rest of the country was only just beginning at the end of the last century. As we have seen, a regular steamship service to Aran, a telegraph cable and a fleet of trawlers were first introduced to Inishmore in 1892. In anthropological terms Aran was at the state of 'acculturation'. It is important to realize the degree to which the islands were isolated from the mainland and in particular from such urban centres as Galway, only thirty miles away. An interesting sidelight on the distance which separated the life on Aran and Connemara from that of Galway City up to 1910 is cast by a report in the local newspaper, the *Galway Express:*

> Three Irish plays were acted on Sunday on a stage on the lawn in front of the Connacht College, Spiddal. On Wednesday two young lady students, who had been in the plays, dressed in the characteristic peasant costume of Connemara — viz., red petticoats, shawl, &c., donned the costume again, and cycled into Galway to meet a friend at the station. The unwonted sight of bare-footed and bare-headed cyclists clad in red petticoats and shawls caused a sensation in the streets of Galway, and the cyclists, having gone into a shop, the street was soon blocked by a large crowd which gathered to see them. Many surmises were made as to who they were. Some thought they were Spanish travellers. Others thought they belonged to the circus, and at last some one suggested that they were students from Spiddal College. Finally several policemen had to come to make a passage for the cyclists through the interested crowd.[39]

The mainland was known as 'The Continent' rather as if Ireland was as strange and distant as the rest of Europe. Visitors to the islands had a similar sensation of their remoteness. Arthur Symons, who visited Aran with W.B. Yeats, noted in a book of world travel that here he had been: 'So far from civilization, so much further out of the world than I have ever been before.'[40] and again: ' . . . we seemed also to be venturing among an unknown people, who, even if they spoke our own language, were further away from us, more foreign than people who spoke an unknown language and lived beyond other seas.'[41] Synge, two years later, also felt himself to be moving away from civilization as he was rowed to Inishmaan where ' . . . life is perhaps the most primitive that is left in Europe.'[42] Ben Kiely's remark that, so far as

Ireland was concerned, Liam O'Flaherty always remained a
tourist from his native rock, has a certain point to it.[43] The
peasantry, as Synge noted, felt the distinctiveness of their
island. Part of what that distinction consisted in is well
brought out in O'Flaherty's brief account of his birthplace. It
occurs in an essay where he wishes to point to the difference
between himself and other novelists, notably Joseph Conrad.
He poses as the hard man from the North Island:

> *I was born on a stormswept rock and hate the soft
> growth of sun-baked lands where there is no frost in
> men's bones. Swift thought and the swift flight of
> ravenous birds and the squeal of terror of hunted animals
> are to me a reality. I have seen the leaping salmon fly
> before the salmon whale, and I have seen the sated buck
> horn his mate and the wanderer leave his wife in search
> of fresh bosoms with the fire of joy in his eye.*[44]

The rest of Ireland, in the distorted romantic vision of the
islander, could qualify as a 'sun-baked land'. There were more
factual distinctions. The islands, in common with other
remote areas along the western seaboard had preserved the
way of life, the language, rituals, and folk customs of earlier
times. It was these, and not the frost in the bone, which
shaped O'Flaherty's fiction in a direction different from that
of his English contemporaries.

The 'acculturation' process is hardly remarked on by
Synge in *The Aran Islands* but the statistics provided by
Haddon and Browne bear witness to it. On the one hand
there was the waning folk culture of the farmer and fisher
folk and on the other the rising middle class of Kilronan. The
peasantry, to list the words frequently applied to them, were
'Pagan, native, Gaelic speaking, primitive, colourful in dress
and speech, vital, honest sensitive, close to nature.' All the
others were 'civilized, foreigners, meanly Catholic and commercial, dull in dress and speech, dishonest and had lost their
vital contact with nature.' A number of these opposing terms
call for particular comment as they are directly relevant to
O'Flaherty's work. These are, in order of importance, the
distinction made between 'native' or 'primitive' and 'civilized'.

not just against the elements but against the nature of the
very ground the islanders trod on.[45] This struggle forms a
major theme of O'Flaherty's fiction. Man gained his true
stature, not by involving himself in the concerns of society
but by turning aside to face the forces of nature, at once the
preserver and destroyer of human vitality. In O'Flaherty's
vision, as indeed in that of other writers who had come into
contact with Darwinian notions of evolution, Aran appears as
an active agent in the evolutionary process. Only the strong
could survive the rigours of life there and the mere face of
survival cast an heroic aura round their lives. O'Flaherty
would intensify the struggle for life for his own artistic purposes and like his namesake Robert Flaherty, in the famous
documentary film *Man of Aran*, set his characters afloat on
seas the islanders would never dare to venture on in reality.
However he distorted the cultural reality of their lives, the
peasantry remained the centre of value in all his fiction.
Every artist selects certain aspects of the raw material that is
life. O'Flaherty, in his treatment of the peasantry, emphasises
their struggle against nature, the concord that existed between them and their surroundings which Synge had called
'the supreme interest of these islands' and, finally, the
'mediaeval quality' of their lives. This latter was a point of
great importance to the novelist concerned with the evils of
capitalism. Among the 'natives' there was no division of
labour. 'Every man possessed a wide variety of skills and
much of the work on the islands was done in common and
regarded as a festive occasion.' Haddon and Browne's account
quoted earlier does little justice to the variety of occupations
common on Aran. Each man was a skilled fisherman and
could manage a curragh. He could farm, make his own fields
and the materials for the clothes he wore, cut out pampooties,
build and thatch a house, mend nets and make everything
from a 'cradle to a coffin'. O'Flaherty was to flirt briefly
with what he called 'the worship of the machine' in reaction
to the organic life of the island community. The new world
of mechanized industry he found in America so fascinated
him that he wrote: 'When we drop our old gods and worship
the machine willingly without reservation, it will free us from
bondage to the earth and from making bond slaves of the

majority of our fellows.'[46]

As with so much else in *Two Years* this was in interim report. The old gods that tied men to the earth reasserted their hold over him as he became more closely acquainted with capitalist industrial society. The repugnance with which he had greeted the early incursions of the modern world returned with full force to impart a tone of savage indignation to his later work.

The 'foreign' influences on Aran began in the last decade of the nineteenth century and were largely the work of the Congested Districts Board founded in 1891. Great cultural changes resulted, few of which found their way into formal accounts of Aran life. Synge, in a revealing letter to Stephen MacKenna wrote:

> There are sides of all that western life, the groggy-patriot-publican-general-shop-man who is married to the priest's half-sister and is second cousin once-removed of the dispensary doctor, that are horrible and awful. This is the type that is running the present United Irish League anti-grazier campaign, while they're swindling the people themselves in a dozen ways and then buying out their holdings and packing off whole families to America. The subject is too big to go into here, but at best it's beastly. All that side of the matter of course I left untouched in my stuff. I sometimes wish to God I hadn't a soul and then I could give myself up to putting those lads on the stage. God, wouldn't they hop! In a way it is all heartrending, in one place the people are starving but wonderfully attractive and charming, and in another place where things are going well, one has a rampant, double-chinned vulgarity I haven't seen the like of.[47]

In another letter to MacKenna he put the matter more briefly and forcefully:

> As you know I have the wildest admiration for the Irish peasants, and for Irish men of known or unknown genius — do you bow? — but between the two there's an

ungodly ruck of fat-faced, sweaty-headed swine.[48]

O'Flaherty, in common with Synge, Yeats and Lady Gregory shared the 'dream of the noble and the beggar man'. The effects of commercialism forced itself more powerfully on his imagination than on theirs, however, as he experienced them from within, as harsh realities. One of his greatest creations was one of the 'fat-faced sweaty-headed swine', Ramon Mor of *The House of Gold* based on the rise to affluence of the MacDonagh family in Galway.

The history of the MacDonagh family offered him a paradigm of what was happening, on a smaller scale, among the more prosperous peasantry through the country. The founding father was Reamonn Mor who, legend has it, farmed the tiny island of Croppagh off Lettermullen. His eldest son became a priest, the first step on the road to affluence and importance. The second son Thomas moved to the even more desolate island of Garumna but soon became conscious of his retrograde step. He seems to have been a vivacious character and many stories of his activities have entered the folklore of the area. One of the stories goes that he became discontented with life on Garumna and downed tools. His wife, an Aran Islander, entered on a long altercation with him, the abusive terms of which are still recounted some hundred years after the event. The wrangle ended with Thomas' declaration that, 'a good plan is better than all the land in Garumna'. The plan was to move to Galway and there set up a shop to supply the peasantry of the islands and seaboard with all they might need. Family connections and clan loyalty ensured success. Thomas and family set up business on Galway Docks. He was very fortunate in many ways, not least of which was the fact that his son Mairtin Mhor (in folklore a 'big lump of a man') turned out to be something of a business genius. Mairtin Mhor was the model for O'Flaherty's 'Ramon Mor' of the *House of Gold* in which he telescoped the careers of Tommy and his son. By the turn of the century the McDonaghs virtually owned the port of Galway and much of the centre of the city. Most local industry, commercial activity and transport were in their hands. They had sent sons and relatives into the local professions and clergy, reminding one of

Synge's bitter comments on the network of 'groggy-patriot-publican-general-shop-man who is married to the priest's half sister and is second cousin once removed of the dispensary doctor'.

Since the MacDonaghs held a virtual monopoly of trade and commerce in Iarchonnacht they tended to stifle local initiative and could, to a great extent, dictate policy for the region. Reaction to their activities varied. If one wished to escape from the drudgery of rural life the paternal firm could place a man or advance the fare to America, provided of course, that he professed the right political beliefs. Many would think of Mairtin Mhor as a kindly, generous man, 'a great manager': 'He was a large employer and a good employer, a man of the type that builds nations. His name became synonymous with industry in Galway; he was the central figure in all the city's industrial concerns.'[49]

To the artist and social theorist, however, the power of McDonagh and Sons Ltd., Trader and Importer, would seem as monstrous as that of the Kulaks who betrayed the Russian Revolution. The novel where Liam O'Flaherty deliberately set out to portray a similar turn of events in Ireland is informed with a corrosive bitterness which at times upsets the balance of the work. Revolution in Ireland had been made in the name of the common people. In the dull aftermath 'urbanized peasants' — to use Sean O'Faolain's phrase — and entrepreneurs had risen to power and affluence. It seemed to O'Flaherty that the peasantry had merely exchanged one set of masters for another. The new men were more insidious because less obviously hostile to the people's aspirations. One knew them, on Aran, by their mode of dress, half peasant homespuns, half city jackets and hard hats. They spoke condescendingly among themselves in bad English of the 'natives' but traded with them in Irish. Synge had carefully kept such people in the background of his study of Aran life. His hasty withdrawal, however, from Inishmore to Inishmaan and his continuing to visit the middle island rather than the north was dictated by their presence. O'Flaherty, on the other hand, brought the new men into the foreground of his portrayal of island life. George Russell (A.E.), in a scathing indictment of the gombeen system in Connemara, added his testimony. He began by stating that the Connemara small farmer, for every article bought, pays twice its value and continued, laying the blame on the gombeen men:

> All the local appointments are in their gift, and hence you get drunken doctors, drunken rate collectors, drunken J.P.'s, drunken inspectors, — in fact, round the gombeen system reels the whole drunken congested world, and underneath this revelry and jobbery the unfortunate peasant labours and gets no return for his labour. Another enters and takes his cattle, his eggs, his oats, his potatoes, his pigs, and gives what he will for them, and the peasant toils on from year to year, being doled out Indian meal, flour, tea, and sugar, enough to keep him alive. He is a slave almost as much as if he were an indentured native and had been sold in the slave market.[50]

The contact then, between the 'natives' and the 'civilized' was not a happy one. The old culture was encroached on by the worst of the new, dully materialistic and self-seeking. O'Flaherty grew up in a broken world, the two halves of which hardly belonged to the same time or place. Yeats provides a convenient summary of their disparity. He had been to the village of Killeenan a few miles from Galway in the summer of 1903 to do honour to the memory of the Gaelic poet Raftery with the 'shawled and freize-coated people'. In the 1906 issue of *Samhain* he recalled:

> A few days after, I was in the town of Galway, and saw there, as I had often seen in other country towns, some young men marching down the middle of a street singing an already outworn London music-hall song, that filled the memory, long after they had gone by, with a rhythm as pronounced and as impersonal as the noise of a machine. In the shop-windows there were, I knew, the signs of a life very unlike that I had seen at Killeenan: halfpenny comic papers and story papers, sixpenny reprints of popular novels, and, with the exception of a dusty Dumas or Scott strayed thither, one knew not

how, and one or two little books of Irish ballads, nothing that one calls literature, nothing that would interest the few thousands who alone out of many millions have what we call culture. A few miles had divided the sixteenth century, with its equality of culture, of good taste, from the twentieth, where if a man has fine taste he has either been born to leisure and opportunity or has in him an energy that is genius. One saw the difference in the clothes of the people of the town and of the village, for, as the Emerald Tablet says, outward and inner things answer to one another. The village men wore their bawneens, their white flannel jackets; they had clothes that had a little memory of clothes that had once been adapted to their calling by centuries of continual slight changes. They were sometimes well dressed, for they suggested nothing but themselves and wore little that had suited another better. But in the town nobody was well dressed; for in modern life, only a few people — some few thousands — set the fashion, and set it to please themselves and to fit their lives; and as for the rest, they must go shabby — the ploughman in clothes cut for a life of leisure, but made of shoddy, and the tramp in the ploughman's cast-off clothes, and the scarecrow in the tramp's battered coat and broken hat . . .[51]

The distinciton between 'native' and the 'civilized' emerged most forcefully in matters of language. Up to 1850, the Aran Islands, in common with other remote areas were, to a great extent, Irish speaking. The 1852 Census of Population was the first in which information on language was included and such information continued to be included in each decennial census up to 1911. The figures show a hasty decline in usage — up to 50 per cent in some decades. More detailed statistics are available on Aran, traditionally regarded as the last bastion of Gaeldom. In 1891, 88.47 per cent of the population of the islands were returned as speaking Irish, of whom only 25 per cent spoke Irish exclusively. Thus over 70 per cent were bilingual and of these 44.20 per cent were illiterate. Haddon and Browne noted that the proportion speaking Irish only was least on Inishmore.

Statistics need to be augmented with concrete instances. Again we have to deal with hostile, contradictory attitudes. On the one hand, Irish was regarded as a mark of inferiority, the peasant patois of a defeated people. On the other hand it was the symbol of Irish identity cherished for its ancient usage and literature and the possibility of its becoming the national language. Synge reported the two extremes. He asked an islander what he thought about the future of the language on the islands:

> 'It can never die out,' said he, 'because there's no family in the place can live without a bit of a field for potatoes and they have only the Irish words for all that they do in the fields. They sail their new boats — their hookers — in English but they sail a curragh oftener in Irish, and in the fields they have Irish alone. It can never die out and when the people begin to see it fallen very low, it will rise up again like a phoenix from its own ashes.'[52]

Others were less optimistic. Synge was surprised by the abundance and fluency of the foreign tongue at Kilronan. He noted that it was falling out of use among the younger people and in this they had the support of their elders:

> In the older generation they did not come under the influence of the recent language movement, I do not see any particular affection for Gaelic. Whenever they are able, they speak English to their children, to render them more capable of making their way in life.[53]

The situation described by Synge is directly relevant to O'Flaherty's upbringing. In an irate reply to Padraic Colum who had upbraided him with not writing in his native language, he wrote: ' ... English was the first language I spoke. My father forbade us speaking IRISH. At the age of seven I revolted against father and forced everybody in the house to speak Irish.'[54]

The young boy's enthusiasm for his native tongue derived directly from the instruction and encouragement of the village schoolmaster, Mr David O'Callaghan. He had a strong influence on the young O'Flaherty and provoked his first imaginative efforts. The debt was handsomely repaid when as 'David Skerrett' of the novel *Skerrett,* O'Callaghan grew to heroic proportions, summing up in his person all the tragic conflicts of island life. He had tried, as headmaster of Oatquarter National School to reverse the policy of the national school system which, since its inception in 1831 had aimed to produce good, law-abiding British subjects. He took the courageous step of teaching his pupils to read and write Irish and as a result came into bitter conflict with the parish priest and the central educational authority. His quarrels with the 'foreigners' and slow absorption into the peasantry form the substance of *Skerrett.* Mr O'Callaghan's progress was all the more remarkable in that, as another pupil of his, Liam's brother, Tom, recalls, he was himself a foreigner to the islands:—

> . . . he had no word of Irish when he came to Aran. He learned the old tongue and after he had mastered it he impressed upon the islanders the importance of preserving it and taught them to pride themselves on its possession.
>
> In those days the island were being rapidly Anglicised. Policemen, tax collectors and the native shopkeeping shoneens were at work hammering a sense of inferiority into the people. "English is the language that'll stand by you when you go to America", was the maxim. Children were reared for export to the American market.
>
> Mr. O'Callaghan did great work. He was no cheap jingo nationalist of the type who froths at the mouth at the mention of an Englishman; but he hated British imperialism with all its works and pomps.[55]

His activities included the organization of Gaelic League branches on the islands and collecting folklore. Haddon and Browne's survey includes a short section, remarkable for its time, on the folklore of Inishmore, part of which was contributed by 'Master' O'Callaghan. Reading through it one wonders if Yeats was solely responsible, as he claimed, for sending Synge to Aran. The authors call attention to the importance of folklore and remind their readers that 'the lore is fast disappearing from the folk and that no time should be lost in recording the vanishing customs and beliefs of old times'.[56]

The language question was not simply a matter of utility. Indeed the Gaelic speech of the peasantry was the bearer of an oral tradition unique in Western Europe for its continuity and variety. The remoteness of the islands ensured the preservation into this century of what had been elsewhere destroyed a century before. The vitality of the oral tradition, even in recent times, is attested to by the fact that a number of the people already mentioned in this study — Mairtin Mhor MacDonagh, David O'Callaghan — have been incorporated into the folklore of the areas where they lived and worked. The MacDonaghs, in particular, figure in Lady Gregory's collection of folklore, *Visions and Beliefs in the West of Ireland* which was put together in the years 1898 — 1920.[57] It is generally agreed, too, among folklorists, that the seaboard of Galway had more unrecorded folktales in 1935 (when the Irish Folklore Commission replaced the more amateur Irish Folklore Institute) than had all the rest of Western Europe.

A distinction needs to be made at this point between orally preserved social-historical tradition and the folktale *(marchen)* proper. The social-historical tradition of rural Ireland, or 'seanchas' as it is called, was related by seanchai, a name ' . . . applied as a rule to a person, man or woman who makes a speciality of local tales, family sagas or genealogies . . . and recount many tales of a short realistic type about fairies, ghosts and other supernatural beings.'[58] Liam O'Flaherty's mother was one such person. He recalls, in *Shame the Devil:* 'Even when there was no food in the house, she would gather us about her at the empty hearth and weave fantastic stories about giants and fairies, or more often the comic adventures of our neighbours . . . '[59]

More rare and more highly regarded in the folk society were those who could relate the sean-sgeal *(marchen)* or oral versions of late mediaeval romances. Professor J.H. Delargy, the doyen of Irish folklore studies, in a famous lecture on the Gaelic story-telling spoke of 'the heroic age which survived until a generation ago in the islands of the Atlantic' and the story-tellers who entertained the folk on winter nights.

> The nearest European counterpart of the tradition —
> bearers and reciters of Gaelic heroic literature and inter-
> national *marchen* are the bylini singers and story tellers
> of Russia. Nowhere else today between Ireland the the
> Slav countries is there any living and appreciable
> remnant of the hero-tale and the wonder-tale; certainly
> nothing in any degree comparable to the tales which are
> now being collected in Ireland.[60]

'These stories derived from written romances composed or revised after 1300 A.D. for the entertainment of the native Irish aristocracy. After the fall of the aristocratic classes in the terrible years which opened the seventeenth century they found their way down to the 'hidden Ireland' of the peasantry and were orally transmitted from one generation to the next. The tales were organized into four broad cycles — the Myth-ological, Ulster, Fenian and King Cycles — of which the stories grouped round the mythical warrior band of the Fianna were by far the most popular. The world of the tales told round the firesides was in every way a contrast to the lives of the auditors, yet something of the heroic values por-trayed carried over into their lives. Delargy speaks of an 'heroic age' and the term is accurate insofar as it points to the values that were upheld — strength, courage, steadfastness, hard drinking and great boasting. These 'heroic' values or their degenerate offspring — strength and courage were mostly at the service of faction fighting — inform all the writ-ings that have come out of the Gaeltacht areas. One has only to think of the 'novels' of Seamus O Grianna or the literature of the Blasket Islands, notably Thomas O Criomhthain's *An tOileanach* to realize that the values portrayed are not those of modern society but go back to sterner times. Similarly, in the work of Liam O'Flaherty the thin realistic surface is corrugated by the subterranean convulsions of an heroic past.

Stylistic and other allied matters will be treated in the next section, for the present it is sufficient to note O'Flaherty's direct contact with oral lore and his use of it in later works.

He drew his material largely from the 'seanchas' or socio-
historical matter, all of which possessed an independent
traditional life on the islands. One has only to glance at, for
example, the Cuala Press book *Stranger in Aran* to find folk
variants of some of the stories used by O'Flaherty in his
novels.[61] An important sub-division of 'seanchas' was the
fairy story and animal tale. One of these *The Fairy Goose*
found its way, almost unchanged, into what many consider
O'Flaherty's best short story. His concentration, in the short
story form and sketch, on stories of wild animals and birds is
not surprising in view of the frequency with which animal
tales occur in the folklore of the region. A glance at the first
section of *The Types of the Irish Folktale*[62] reveals the
variety and number of such tales which have been collected
from the Galway area.

This brief discussion of the folklore of the region leads on
directly to our final set of contradictions which observers
have found in island life — the distinction made between
'pagan' and 'Christian'. Consideration of this topic usually
begins with the fact that the islands, for their size, contain
the greatest concentration of pagan and Christian remains in
Europe. On the one hand there are the massive Cyclopean
forts which dominate the skyline, on the other the broken
remains of monastic and church settlements which earned
for Aran the beautiful title: *Ara Sanctorum: magna est illa
insula et est terra sanctorum.* The old gods still haunted the
pagan forts and the peasantry feared and propitiated them in
due season. Westward of the islands the mythical island of
Hy-Brasil — the pagan underworld — rose out of the sea every
seven years, and some few of the islanders would claim to
have visited it. (The manuscript collection of the Royal Irish
Academy contained a manuscript book supposed to have
been bought from Hy-Brasil by an islander!) Fairies, ghosts
and spirits who rose out of the sea were part of the ordinary
hazards of life. Certain families possessed magical powers of
healing and there was a wide-spread belief, strong to this day,
in the efficacy of the Evil Eye. The menfolk wore bits of iron
about their persons to ward off malign spirits, and certain
days of the week were marked off as good or bad for different
kinds of work. Strange rituals, the detritus of pagan practice,

were performed to protect children and farm animals from the fairies who offered a constant threat to the human inhabitants. Women were particularly vulnerable to the machinations of the otherworld. Synge thought to find 'a possible link between the wild mythology that is accepted on the islands and the strange beauty of the women.'[63]

Prospective husbands had to be careful that the fairies did not substitute a 'changeling' for their future brides. On May Day and St John's Eve fires were lighted all over Aran, ostensibly in honour of the saints, but as every man who drove his cattle through the smoke or leaped the flames realized, the appeal was to the pagan god Crom Dubh and the more immediate concerns of fertility.

Little or no distinction was made between the natural and supernatural world of witches, banshees, fairies, and the ghosts of the dead. Ghost ships sailed the bay to the peril of fishermen and the farmer might find his crops fail if he disturbed a fairy path. Christian beliefs and practices were assimilated to the older pagan lore and vice versa. Thus there was a Catholic theory of the fairies recorded by Synge and others, and the 'Holy Wells' of the old monasteries were hung about with items of personal apparel to bring good luck to the owners. Haddon and Browne provide a convenient, if scattered, account of some of the syncretized pagan and catholic beliefs:

> Women pray at St. Enny's well, by the Angels' Walk when they desire children, and the men pray at the ragwell by the Church of the Four Comely Ones at Onaght.
>
> On the night before going to America the people will sleep in the open, beside one of the Holy Wells, in order that they may have good fortune. When any member of the family falls sick, another member makes a promise that if the sick one recovers, the person promising will sleep, one, two or three nights in one of the saints' beds. One bed at the Seven Churches is said to be occupied pretty regularly.
>
> Suspended priests are considered capable of working cures by touch of the hand.[64]

Further pagan retentions were numerous taboos, divinations through the seeking of omens, magical charms and an emphasis on 'natural' foods and folk medicines. One of the most fascinating accounts of Aran's 'relics of barbarism' is contained in a book written by the District Nurse for the islands in the last years of the nineteenth century and the early years of the present. Nurse Hedderman recounts her effort to replace the islander's reliance on witches and 'cures' with modern medical practice and incidentally fills her book with the islands' folklore and superstition. It reads like the account of a mission to darkest Africa:

> Directly an infant is ushered into the world, the first person entering the lying-in chamber must spit upon the new-born, then on the mother, and finally on the nurse, doctor, or attendant who happens to be present. This is not done with a view to expelling either a cocci or bacilli family, but as a life-long preservative for the child and its parents. Remonstrance or disapproval of this repulsive habit is not effective — the people will protest against interference and extol its virtue as a potent charm.
>
> At no time is superstition encouraged so readily as when acute disease sets in. I have seen lives ruined and lost that might have been saved, if only means could be found to dispel this black ignorance when sudden illness attacks the young and healthy. The first resort is the saliva cure, and should the person accused of casting the spell resent the insinuation and not be friendly disposed in that special direction, the patient's progress and relief from suffering are supposed to be hindered until he enters the sick-room and saturates the bed-clothes with this filthy secretion.[65]

Many of these beliefs and practices found their way into O'Flaherty's first novel *Thy Neighbour's Wife* and to a lesser extent in the novels thereafter. The 'pagan' peasantry were to afford him an important thematic contrast to the 'Christians'. Their retention of the old beliefs seemed to speak of a harmony with nature and a spontaneity denied to those less fortunate beings whose minds had been exercized, and incidentally poisoned, by the casuistry of the Church. Their mythology in which the land figures as both hostile to man's endeavours (the fairies) and the source of vitality and fecundity (the worship of Crom Dubh) added a further dimension to the central theme of man's necessary but unavailing struggle with nature.

It seems preposterous to state, after the foregoing, that the island folk were devoutly Catholic. Irish life, as had frequently been remarked, is nothing if not a series of contradictions. Despite the old ways, devotion to the Catholic Church was, generally speaking, unequivocal. Devotion might fail, as in the Dirrane affair, but always the Church remained the Church Triumphant. This was made possible by the many syncretisms of pagan and Christian beliefs. Thus frequent reception of the Eucharist was good for the soul but might also relieve rheumatic fever or bring good luck. It is the present writer's conviction that the power of the parish clergy over rural communities derived, not from any real appreciation of the mysteries of which they were the ministers, but rather in the simple fact that there *were* mysteries. The priest with his sacred powers (and the peasantry credited him with others not so sacred) was the closest figure in contemporary life to the figures of folktale. Cursings from the altar were not infrequent and the secrecy which surrounded the powers of exorcism added an appropriate feeling of dread. Priests had, in fact, become the heroes, more often the victims, of numerous folk-tales. *The Types of the Irish Folktale* lists numerous stories of this type from the Galway region. What is important to note here is that there were folk conceptions of Irish character which reflected prevailing types and the folk tradition contributed its concepts of character to the works of many of the Anglo-Irish writers. O'Flaherty in particular drew on such stereotypes — the priest, the patriot, the politician, the wild peasant — and raised them to a pitch of intensity not found in their folkloristic origins. He reshaped the characters but in a more important sense, as we shall see, they shaped his fiction to their own lineaments.

The parish priest, apart from his prominence as a religious

leader, was also important as the link between the formal and informal political systems, the 'natives' and the 'foreigners'. He came originally from the peasantry and unlike them he had been educated in the ways of the civilized world. Indeed the only way a peasant boy could hope to receive a formal education was by putting himself forward for the priesthood. His family deprived themselves to provide the necessary money and hoped for a fair return when, as curate or parish priest, their protege rose to importance in the community. By origin a peasant, by education a gentleman, the priest found himself in ambiguous relation to both classes. He acted as mediator between them but was never entirely trusted.

In the past, the Catholic clergy exercised extensive control over their flock. Every aspect of life was subject to their scrutiny and they did their best to eradicate those 'remote or proximate occasions of sin' — courting, drinking and dancing. All the evidence from historical and contemporary sources indicates that the clergy instilled in their people a sexual morality as puritanical as any found among the societies of the world, past or present. All observers of Aran life agree on the extreme puritanism that moulded island life, and on an almost total lack of romantic love. Liam O'Flaherty deviates greatly from cultural reality when he depicts sensuality as a prominent trait of the islanders. *There is no courting or love-making, nor do the young people ever walk together. The marriages are arranged for; as a rule the lad has his father's consent and may be accompanied by him when he goes to ask for the girl . . . . . Sometimes a young man may suddenly, a day or two before the beginning of Lent, decide upon marrying, and, after seeing what his father will do for him, he goes to the house where there is a suitable girl and asks her to marry him. If she refuses he might go straight on to another; and a man has been known to ask a third girl in the same evening before he was accepted. The marriage might take place immediately and the couple would live happy ever after.*[66] Love and marriage, then, were connected more with economic consideration than with sentiment. Clerical influence was further strengthened by the fact that the parish priest appointed and rigidly supervised the headmaster of the local school who, in turn, presided over social events and

acted as adviser to the islanders in many matters. In Liam
O'Flaherty's youth the two centres of local power were
respectively Father Faragher ('Father O'Reilly' of *Thy Neigh-
bours's Wife,* 'Father Moclair' of *'Skerrett'* and partly 'Father
Considine' of *The House of Gold*) and Master O'Callaghan
('David Skerrett').

One final consideration is relevant to O'Flaherty's bitter
treatment of clerical life and power in his novels. It is that
the Archdiocese of Tuam, of which the Aran Islands form
part, were probably the worst administered in Ireland and a
scandal to the Church. Dr MacEvilly, the Archbishop, was

> . . . put down among the few ecclesiastics who deserved
> and received the title of 'Castle Bishop' and his want of
> sympathy with the masses of the people was emphasised.
> Even his diocesan administration was made the subject
> of attack and the curates whom he so often changed
> from one parish to another were described as migratory
> curates who were arbitrarily shifted about from Aran
> and Achill to the Twelve Pins.[67]

Aran was a 'punishment station' for curates and most
ecclesiastical offenders were sent there at some stage. The
above quotation is taken from the official history of the
Archdiocese of Tuam, normally a reticent, even subservient
document. The pages where the author, the Right Rev. Monsignor D'Alton, narrates the twenty-year reign of Dr MacEvilly
are, however, informed with a barely concealed indignation
and disgust at his venality and tyranny. He concludes his
account of the 'Castle Bishop' with a piece of fine irony:

> Strong and sturdily built, and always careful of his
> health, he had outlived almost all his contemporaries;
> nor was it until the new century had come that he
> showed any symptoms of failing bodily powers. Men-
> tally, he was as alert at eighty-two as he had been at the
> age of thirty, though he had acquired to the full the
> garrulity of old age. And while he told the same old
> stories in the same old way, the priests at table were
> bound to be attentive and interested, or pretend to be.

For the Archbishop had become not only garrulous but impatient and irritable, and if any priest, and especially any young priest, broke in on his well-worn narrative, he was met with a withering glance of disapproval from the Archbishop. Even old priests were often treated with great asperity, their failings and defects shown up, their past services to the Church and to the Archbishop entirely forgotten.

To his own relatives the Archbishop was often partial, and rarely unkind. His nephew was promoted to a parish after a few years of curate life, while others, much older, were still left in obscure positions. Nor were other relatives overlooked though their advancement was not so rapid as that of the Archbishop's nephew. Such a course of action was not calculated to win the approval of the priests, and the Archbishop, who had never been popular, became more unpopular than ever in extreme old age. Nor was it unusual to have some priest express surprise that so many old men, like Bismarck and Gladstone, had passed away, but that their example had not been followed in the Archdiocese of Tuam. It was not, they avowed, that they wished the Archbishop's death, but they were anxious to see the Archbishop promoted to heaven. Dr. McEvilly seemed to appreciate the peculiar estimation in which he was held; and when his health was proposed at public functions his thanks were perfunctory, and he always added, as if to console his audience, that he was feeling well, and believed he would live for many years. Nature, however, could not be cheated of her due, and in the last days of 1902 the Archbishop got suddenly and seriously ill, and after a few days' illness breathed his last. And thus Tuam was left without an Archbishop with the passing of the dying year.[68]

This, then, was the world of O'Flaherty's youth, a world of explosive contradictions. The folk culture was beginning to disintegrate and the shaping forces within the society were incapable of establishing an alternative. Provincial rootedness was everywhere giving way before a rising, ruthless middle class. The broken world and its broken traditions scarred the boy and young man who was sufficiently at home with the locals to absorb their unspoken assumptions and aspirations. Yet he would remember the islands as a lost Eden to which, repeatedly, he would try to return. Things a great deal less tangible than the social and cultural forces we have outlined would draw him back. There was the extraordinary beauty and ferocity of nature and natural life which surrounded his youth. It so imposed itself on his mind and imagination that in London, New York or Paris he could write delicate, evocative sketches, minute in their detail, of a wave or seagull or the terror of a hunted rabbit. Nature, red in tooth and claw, one species preying on another, the hunter and the hunted, supplied him with an image of the human condition which survived all the complexities that Marxism, Nihilism and all the other -isms he was to espouse, introduced into his thinking.

CHAPTER 3

EDUCATION AND EARLY WRITING

Liam O'Flaherty's first attempt at fiction was made, according to himself, at the age of seven when Mr O'Callaghan set his pupils to write a short story. The story described the murder of a peasant woman by her husband:

> The wife brought him cold tea for dinner to the field. He murdered her with a spade and then tried to bury her in the fosse, or furrow, between two ridges. The point of the story, I remember, was the man's difficulty in getting the woman, who was very large, to fit into the fosse. The schoolmaster was horrified and thrashed me.[69]

In another version of the story he describes how he related the contents of the essay to his mother. This time he appended the names of a neighbouring labourer called McDonagh and his wife to add a note of realism — first instance of an unfortunate habit which was to land the writer into a great deal of trouble later on. The description of mayhem among the McDonaghs was so vivid ('her body was so fat that the murderer had to dance on it in order to make it fit into the furrow') that Mrs O'Flaherty rushed out to tell the neighbours only to find the murdered woman knitting at her doorstep. Returning in tears, she insisted that her son pray to God to cure his mind of such morbid fantasies. O'Flaherty claimed that this childhood experience taught him to hide his private world and left him with a dual personality: *And from that day I hid my dreams. I became a dual personality. The one wept with my mother and felt ashamed of his secret mind . . . and began to dream of greatness. And as my mind grew strong and defiant, I became timid and sensitive in my relationship with the people about me. I became prone to dreaming, quick at my schooling, ashamed of vulgar profanity and rowdy conduct.*[70] It is perhaps a mistake to read too much into juvenilia, but it is worth pointing out that the elements of O'Flaherty's first story remained to the last. There is first the violence of action and gesture:

> . . . how he struck with his spade on the head many times, blaspheming joyously at each stroke, how she sank into a furrow, where she bled so profusely that the ensuing blows made her gore splash into her murderous husband's face, . . .[71]

and secondly the realism of presentation combined with a wild extravagance of subject matter. Both qualities are pre-eminently those of the folktales which were popular on the islands. The story itself is close in form to the more famous one of the man who killed his da with a blow of a slane. That he should have fastened the story to a local labourer epitomizes a recurring problem of his later work — how to bring an imagination formed on folktales and given to wild imaginings into contact with some immediate reality? The naive solution arrived at in early youth — add a local reference — was not greatly improved on in later work.

We hear of one more attempt at fiction writing at the age of eleven, this time a novel, in co-operation with his elder brother Tom who had received a copy of the first Gaelic novel *Seadna* (1904) from Sir Roger Casement. 'Novel' is too large a term for *Seadna,* which is essentially a retelling in novel form of the folktale of the man who sold his soul to the devil. This book, with two others, A.M. Sullivan's *The Story of Ireland* and the Gaelic version of *Fairies at Work* by William P. Ryan, are the only books we hear of in the O'Flaherty household. Wind and tide permitting, the local weekly newspaper the *Galway Vindicator* was delivered to Gort na gCapall. One of Liam's fondest memories is of his father declaiming to the villagers the speeches contained in the House of Commons' Report.

Both brothers seem to have been exceptionally bright at school. The books mentioned above were presented to Tom by Casement when he visited Master O'Callaghan's school and were intended as an encouragement to the young scholar. Sir Roger planned to send him to Summerhill College, Sligo, where an uncle of the O'Flaherties taught, but the project fell through. Master O'Callaghan was even less fortunate in the way of introductions for the betterment of his pupils when he drew the attention of a visiting priest to Liam's zeal for scholarship. The priest, a member of the Holy Ghost Order, suggested that the boy become a postulant for his order. One of the more immediate benefits of such a step would be that his further education would be practically free. At the time, as has been pointed out, this was one of the few ways a peasant boy could hope to rise in the world. Twenty-four years after the event O'Flaherty claimed that he had accepted the offer for the sake of a free education and that at the time he despised the priesthood. We may doubt the retrospective evaluation of the man who had become the most renowned anti-clerical writer of the day. More likely he had listened to 'The Call of the Wild', as a piece of Holy Ghost Father propaganda styled a vocation: 'The sublime call has for us Irish boys a greater significance than for any other race in the world. May we not well believe that our destiny is to Christianise the world? It was so ordained when Patrick, answering to the Call of the Spirit of the Wilds, came across to our island and snatched our forefathers from the abysmal pit of druidical darkness . . . St. Columbanus . . . St. Findolin . . . Hosts of other noble men, Irish to the core.'[72]

At the age of thirteen, to the joy of his relatives, who had collected the small sum of money required, he became a postulant at Rockwell College, County Tipperary, ' . . . to be trained as a priest for the conversion of African negroes to the Roman Catholic Religion.'[73] Rockwell was one of the largest and most famous mission centres of Ireland and aspired to be 'a seat of Catholic moral and missionary culture'. It aimed, in common with other branches of the Church Militant, to 'convert the world in the present generation'. The College was a curious mixture of an English public school, a French *lycee*, and a monastery, all held together by reverence for Newman's ideal of the Catholic gentleman. It had been founded by a Frenchman. In its early years, French and German were spoken at supper and it was a rare privilege to be allowed to speak English instead of French during recreation time. On the other hand, cricket and rugby were the College's strong points as far as games were concerned. Teams from the military garrisons at Cahir and Tipperary were welcome guests and during the cricket season the South Irish Horse came in flannels. The President of Rockwell, Father Nicholas Brennan, continued a minor, eccentric public school tradition by translating four cantos of Byron's *Childe Harold* into Latin and thence into Greek verse. Everybody rose at 5 a.m. for Mass and much of the day's discipline was similar to that of a monastery.

For years Rockwell had led all the schools and colleges of Ireland in the number of distinctions, medals, and exhibitions won at the Intermediate Examination. In 1911 the school was, once more, first in Ireland with 34 Exhibitions, 25 Prizes and (from a total of 15 candidates) 15 University Entrance Scholarships. Essentially the teaching method was one of cramming the students with the prescribed texts to the exclusion of everything else. In view of O'Flaherty's later work it is interesting to have a look at the range of the English Literature course studied by the students of Rockwell over four years:

Preparatory:	Kingsley's *Heroes:* Macaulay's *Lays of Ancient Rome*
Junior:	Scott's *Lady of the Lake:* Selections from the *Spectator*
Middle:	Scott's *Talisman:* Poetry-Selections
Senior:	Selected Chapters of Coleridge's *Biographia Literaria:* Selections from Wordsworth.[74]

A commentator on the English course for Intermediate schools remarked: 'In English, students could do the whole five years of the Secondary School course without ever having read a line of Shakespeare, with absolutely no knowledge of the vast majority of English poets or prose writers, with nothing, in fine, save a pretty detailed knowledge of one or two (never more) short works of three or four English authors.'[75]

Rockwell College was and is a middle-class establishment and the boy from Aran did not integrate very well with the other students. He compensated for his isolation by working very hard with the singular effect, for a seminarian, of becoming, as he says, 'a complete agnostic'.[76] His studies had more positive results in other directions however. He competed for a gold medal offered by an American society for an essay in Gaelic. Here at least he was on home ground. With an essay on emigration he won the medal and a free day for the students of Rockwell. The medal would later be pawned to raise the price of a revolver when he joined the Republican Army. A contemporary at Rockwell remembered Liam O'Flaherty as a shy, pious boy who was a brilliant Classical Scholar. After four years in the scholasticate a postulant was called on to take the soutane, the first major step on the way to ordination. This O'Flaherty refused to do, probably for reasons of conscience, and he transferred to Blackrock College, county Dublin, in 1913. He was placed among the ordinary boarders instead of in the scholasticate with the result that he had more freedom of action. The way in which he used his freedom is instructive — he organized a corps of Republican Volunteers among the schoolboys with the encouragement of Professor Eoin MacNeill, then in command of the Volunteers. He continued to work hard for the Board of Intermediate Education examination which he sat in 1914 at the age of eighteen. In the Senior Grade he won a first class exhibition (Irish and Latin) and an entrance scholarship (Classics, 1st Class) to University College, Dublin.[77] Once more he turned his eyes toward the priesthood and was accepted by the Dublin Diocesan Seminary at Clonliffe. Since 1881 the students of the College had been taking the examinations of the Royal University and with the change, in 1907, to the National University they continued to attend what was now University College, Dublin. O'Flaherty, in common with his fellow First Arts students, walked to and from Clonliffe in a bowler hat, rolled umbrella, and clerical black. He attended lectures in Classics and Philosophy during the Michaelmas term of 1914. Fr Peadar MacSuibhne, St Patrick's College, Carlow, recalls, in a letter dated 5 January 1971:

> I remember Liam O'Flaherty during the term Oct – Dec 1914. I think he did not return after Christmas. I remember walking with him during vacation after tea on the short corridor near the College Chapel . . . . He was rather tall and well built . . . . I formed a favourable opinion of him. That is, he gave me no reason for forming an unfavourable opinion of him. I can't recall my fellow students discussing why Liam had not come back or ever referring to him at all . . . .

Liam, in *Shame the Devil,* gave a reason for his departure that might surprise Father MacSuibhne:

> I detested the other students and the priests in charge, who were soon outraged by the violence of my opinions. After a few weeks, I danced on my soutane, kicked my silk hat to pieces, spat on my religious books, made a fig at the whole rigmarole of Christianity and left that crazy den of superstitious ignorance.[78]

O'Flaherty either over-reacted or, more likely, touched up the event to harmonize with the demonic pose ('spat on my religious books') of *Shame the Devil.* Other evidence points to a loss of religious faith at a later date.

After leaving the seminary at Clonliffe, O'Flaherty returned to University College, Dublin, and attended lectures there for a further few months. An account of his life at this time which, on the whole, seems to have been rather mean and sordid, entered the first part of *The Black Soul.* The ex-cleric, in an unfamiliar city, tries to come to terms with his own nature and the world about him. His personal difficulties were exacerbated by the restless, excited nature of the times. Germany and England were on the brink of war and in Dublin the Republicans were arming and preparing for a rebellion. War, of one kind or another, was in the air. O'Flaherty continued his membership of the Volunteers while studying at U.C.D. but there he learned of a different ideology which was to claim a more lasting allegiance from him. In his first volume of autobiography, *Two Years,* he says that while he was a university student he read the works of Karl Marx, Friedrich Engels, Ferdinand Lascalle, Ferdinand Bebel, James Connolly, Pierre Proudhon and Jeremy Bentham. The reading list is an impressive one and one might arrive at the conclusion that U.C.D. was a liberal institution for its time and place. In fact, despite its official character as 'non-denominational' in religious matters, the College was overwhelmingly Catholic. The Department of Philosophy, in which O'Flaherty studied, was staffed by priests who taught Thomistic Philosophy. Other systems might be introduced but only to highlight some point of Thomism or be refuted by the perennial philosophy. A lecture on value by the Jesuit priest Fr Finlay, in which Marxism was mentioned *en passant* sparked off O'Flaherty's interest in the subject. The interest remained largely dormant for a few years and did not blaze up again until he came in contact with members of the 'Industrial Workers of the World' in America.

What is of interest in the foregoing is the establishment of a pattern that will recur. The seminarian destined for the priesthood becomes, for a time, an agnostic. The student of Thomistic Philosophy, which ultimately rests on Thomistic theology, turns to Marxism. The physical law that to every action there is an equal and opposite reaction seems to have a psychic counterpart in the case of O'Flaherty except that in him the reaction is seldom equal, rather excessive. Two other points are worth noting: firstly the quality of the education he received up to and including his twenty-first year. Yeats, in an extract quoted earlier, spoke of an 'energy that is genius' necessary for a peasant to break loose and acquire the ways and taste of the cultivated world. From remote Gort na gCapall to Rockwell, Blackrock, Clonliffe and University College was, in the early years of the century, something of a grand tour of the best that Irish Catholic education had to offer. These colleges maintained high standards of instruction along with a rigorous formation of their students in the general direction of John Henry Newman's ideal of the Christian gentleman, liberally educated. Had O'Flaherty been the son of wealthy parents, he could not have hoped for better in the way of schooling. One notes the erratic progress. Four different colleges in as many years is not exactly a recommendation, but the unsettling factor was, as so often in such cases, the problem of a religious vocation. This is our second point. O'Flaherty was now, on Aran, and points east and north, a 'spoiled priest'. It requires, in more ecumenical days, an effort of the historical imagination to recapture the indignation and scorn which was visited on such a person in the rural Ireland of sixty years ago. Rather than adduce social evidence it is sufficient to point to the literary embodiment of the social fact. The figure of the 'spoiled priest' is perhaps the most enduring creation of all those writers and dramatists who rose from the peasantry from William Carleton forward and who saw in him an image of the alienated, persecuted artist. The theme became something of a *cliche* of Abbey plays and regional novels. The tired situation is repeated again and again of the loving mother who prays that her son be called to the priesthood, works herself to the bone to realize her ambition (cynical commentators have noted that it is Irish mothers and not their sons who have priestly vocations) only to find her son return on a summer's evening in lay clothes. The play *Maurice Hearte* and Brinsley McNamara's *The Valley of the Squinting Windows* are the best products of what is almost a *genre* of Irish writing. In the first, the protagonist is driven insane, in the second, he is driven to drink by social pressures and the failure to realize parental ambitions. Most did not return home in the summer evening from Maynooth or Clonliffe but emigrated to places where reverence for the clergy did not have the corollary of hatred for those who tried and failed to reach such exalted heights.

Alienation is a major theme of O'Flaherty's fiction and one that he experienced more completely than most. In a sense, any education other than in the traditional skills of farming and fishing could only set him at a remove from his own people. The priesthood was a traditionally sanctioned

CHAPTER 4

FIRST WORLD WAR AND WORLD WANDERING

In the casuistry of the Church one is warned that, having committed one mortal sin, the sinner is very likely to compound his guilt by committing another and worse. Abandoning St Thomas for Karl Marx was followed in O'Flaherty's case by the abandonment of the Republican Volunteers for the British Army. He left University College, Dublin, joined the Irish Guards under his mother's name (Bill Ganly) and was sent to Caterham barracks for training. This was sin indeed, though in the retrospect of twenty years it would become a liberating experience:

> This was a far greater blow to my relatives than my refusal to become a priest, and it was the event in my life most responsible for the outcast position in which I now find myself. May the devil be praised! No matter how we may curse the war, my generation was fortunate in being given this wonderful lesson in the defects of the European system of civilization. Had it not been for my participation in the war, I might still be a petty Irish nationalist, with a carped outlook on life, one of those snivelling patriots who would prefer an Irish dunghill to an English flower garden in full bloom. Be that as it may, when I came home from the war in 1918, I was regarded as a pariah and a fool and a renegade.[79]

He tried on various occasions to rationalize what seemed to

many a betrayal of everything his 'princely' name stood for. (His family and relatives seem not to have known of the portrait Petrie spotted in *The* O'Flaherty cottage). Absurdly it was really to desert to the Germans and indirectly fight the Republican cause. From the welter of contradictory statements he made on the matter one seems most likely in the context of the whole life. It was, he says, ' . . . What an adventurous youth felt impelled to do, not through idealism, but with the selfish desire to take part in a world drama'.[80] If not idealism, then romanticism. In fact, going to war was the first of the picaresque adventures that occupied a large part of his life. In the context of the times his decision was not so strange or exceptional as he would afterwards want it to appear. There was, first, the need to escape the 'spoiled priest' syndrome and secondly, many of his contemporaries at University College joined the ranks. Indeed, it was the thing to do. On the Role of Honour of the College between 1914 and 1918 only the names of those students who had died fighting for England appear, those who fell in the Easter Rebellion and later, such as Kevin Barry, were not recorded.

O'Flaherty's experience while training at Caterham barracks marked a decisive change in his life. Heretofore he regarded himself as an intellectual, a worshipper of the mind, one who had bruised the body to pleasure soul. Now he was brought into forceful contact with the body, his own and others, and it seemed like a descent into hell: 'I passed that night numb with horror of the future; horrified by the coarse beings who had joined the same day as myself as much as by the inhuman rigidity and ferocious language of those already trained as soldiers'.[81]

Slowly he came to terms with his fellow soldiers. In a phrase redolent of his seminary days he speaks of the vinegar of life turning into wine. Henceforward he would value the body more than the mind, and the uneasy alliance established between the two would plague his life and works. He discovered too the joy of anonymity, of sinking his own rebellious individuality and personality in the mass of similarly dressed and disciplined soldiers, thinking their thoughts, acting like them. In many ways it was a return to the kind of life on Aran: the primitive simplicity of life in the lower ranks. After

his training O'Flaherty was sent to France as a replacement in
the front lines. Instead of the romantic adventure he had
hoped for he found himself trapped in the sordid reality of
mud, boredom, death and vermin. He noted with irony how
exciting it was to read a thrilling newspaper account of some
dull engagement in which he had taken part.[82] (In *The
Return of the Brute,* his novel about the trench warfare of
World War 1, O'Flaherty made direct use of his terrible
experiences at the front — too direct — the experiences are
raw and unassimilated and the novel must be one of the
worst ever published). At Langemarch in September 1917 he
was caught in a shell bombardment and seriously wounded.
He lay for lengthy periods in various hospitals in a state of
coma and was eventually discharged from the King George V
hospital in Dublin. His physical wounds had healed and he
had a war pension to boot but his discharge certificate had an
ominous note: he was described as a severe case of *melancholia acuta. Melancholia acuta* is a major psychological fact
both of the man and his work. Speaking of himself he wrote:
'You have to go through life with that shell bursting in your
head.'[83] The statement might equally well be directed at all
his major fictional characters. They go through his imagined
worlds in a state of acute depression and fear of an impend-
ing calamity. The calamity they fear, and the recurring fear
of the autobiographies, is that of final descent into madness.
O'Flaherty wrote his fiction in an attempt to exorcize that
fear or at least temporarily to assuage it. The novels are on
one level a kind of therapy. His fear of insanity was, however,
an important stimulus to artistic activity. In later life he grew
to be more stable: gentleness replaced violence and with it
came an end to his creative work.

The ambiguous effect of his war experience, at once harmful and beneficial, led to a corresponding ambiguity in his
attitude to war. At one point he would declare 'I loathe war'
and everything the soldier stood for. At another he would see
it as a means of liberation and insight. His early training as a
soldier became emblematic of the training the artist must
undergo. In both, the raw recruit must become disciplined
and serve an ideal greater than himself. More, the experience
of war seemed a necessary preparation for human greatness:

'Socrates got the prize for valour at Potidaea. Sophocles served as a hoplite. Tolstoy was at the siege of Sebastopol. Those who shine out most brightly as apostles of peace and human brotherhood in their writings are those who kept their rendezvous with death and were respited. Cervantes also fought and lived to sing of laughter.'[84] The list is impressive but the reader is disquieted by the hint that he is to add ... 'And O'Flaherty was at Langemarck'. His World War 1 experience nevertheless remains central to an understanding of the work. It occupies something of the importance of the War of Independence and Civil War in the lives of Frank O'Connor and Sean O'Faolain. They learned the lesson of disillusionment in the grey years that followed the Revolution's promise and it entered into the fabric of their work. O'Flaherty's reaction to the World War was typically different and more extreme. He espoused a form of nihilism where good and evil ceased to matter and human activity was purposeless. Repeatedly he would try to rise above such a minimal position but nihilism remained his most enduring view of the human condition. 'View' is used advisedly. O'Flaherty is no philosopher, his predilection for chaos derives more from *melancholia acuta* than from any careful intellection.

The end of his active service seemed, in retrospect, to be the conclusion of the first act of the drama of O'Flaherty's life. He himself frequently employs the dramatic metaphor and this first act came to an end with an even greater drama in the background. In London the young actor is saddened by the end of World War 1:

An end is always sad. It is a little proof that nothing lasts, whether good or evil. I wandered about all day and night. The intoxication of the vast multitude increased until it seemed that the city was given over to loot; the most astonishing spectacle I have ever seen. There was no dignity in this rejoicing. It was bestial as the war had been. Here was no enthusiasm over the triumph of an idea, no hosannas to some glorious star risen in the firmament of human heroism. It was merely the riot of a mob in celebration of the victory of a mob over another mob, equally senseless. That barren and inglorious war, whose record is mud and noise, and obscure poison, ended in a common debauch of drunkenness, gluttony and fornication.

I watched it most of the night and then towards dawn I travelled eastwards, making for the docks to find a ship and the sea.[85]

The months between O'Flaherty's discharge from hospital and departure for South America were spent in London where he worked in turn as a labourer, porter, and office clerk. It is worth dwelling briefly on his account of this time contained in the opening chapters of *Two Years*. They reveal the spirit in which he set out to, as he says, 'conquer the world'. No less an ambition would satisfy the Romantic soul, impatient of limits. This was to be the great adventure of his life. World conquest received a dubious definition as 'the expression of the personality to a satisfactory degree ... since the world only contains what we desire from it.'[86] His sojourn in London reveals a little of what O'Flaherty desired from the world. It was necessary for him to feel that his life was surrounded by a bright penumbra while he himself dwelt in the shadows. London provided the appropriate background. The city fascinated him, its size and the variety of human life to be found there met all his imaginative requirements. He felt himself to be at the centre of the civilized world, yet his account hardly touches on the civilized aspects of life. Rather is there the familiar obsessive identification with the oppressed and the outlawed. Socially, the city seemed to be Aran writ larger: 'London had the appearance of a well-ordered feudal mansion, its centre being the dwelling of the lord and his family, its poor quarters the dwellings of the menials.'[87] He would use the 'absolute independence of all other human beings' which his pension conferred on him, to live among the menials. Those he encounters he turns, in *Two Years*, into emblematic figures of the corruption of modern civilization — the half-drunken workers skimming the foam from the brewery cauldron, 'the withered prettiness of the manageress (representing) the soul of the hotel.' His emblems are partly figures of what he feared he too might become were he to give his complete allegiance to the menials. Bourgeois life, characterized by the figure of the clerk with his ideals of order, obedience, bodily cleanliness, and mass-consciousness, offered no real alternative to the young man who believed that all good came from unrest and dissatisfaction. He found himself suspended between two worlds and incapable of deriving solace or satisfaction from either. Finally he encountered a man and a style of life which seemed to offer a way out of the dilemma. This was an Australian soldier who had deserted his unit and who seemed to have fled all the nets cast out to catch the growing soul. The terms of O'Flaherty's assessment of his worth are significant:

> All those except the Australian were the same as myself fundamentally, with the same conceptions of right and wrong, of honour and dishonour, the same superstitious fears, the same cowardly adherence to the principles that are born of our crowded society and our gloomy climate. Each of us groaned at his fate, and yet was bound to it. The Australian alone, although the only palpably dishonourable man there, was the only man of courage, because his dishonourable act meant nothing to him. He was of different stuff, born under a different sun, with a consciousness of vast and uninhabited spaces, an individual whose personality was but slightly bound with the personalities of others. The accidents of his life were his laws, and he accepted the chances of fate with calm.
>
> I saw this man coming thousands of miles from wild backwoods to Europe and the war, and looking contemptuously through half-closed eyes at puny men crawling about in sunless places, cripples, slaves and degenerates, and becoming so proud of his strength and health that these two qualities made him almost a god among his kind.
>
> Then away to swallow lungfuls of wild air untainted by human breath and there to recover the balance that the war had overturned. I swore that I would go at once.

Where? Anywhere. Away from Europe, somewhere that
had never been desecrated by crucifixes and churches
and schools and shops and all the shoddy armanent of
civilisation, which produced nothing better than cripples
screaming at their fate, wishing they were whole in
order that they might join the whole men who were
crippled in thousands on the battlefields.[88]

The basic impulse is to flee life in society and the value-
system inherent in European civilization. He will define himself not by reference to social norms but by opposing and
standing over against them. In this mood of romantic
rebellion he began the two years of wandering in search of
'vast and uninhabited spaces' which was to bring him back to
the closest approximation he could even find to them — the
Aran Islands.

Late in 1918 O'Flaherty went to sea as a tirmmer in the
stokehold of a tramp steamer bound for Rio de Janeiro. His
irrepressible romantic nature, rising above the disillusionment
with war and with London reached out 'towards a romantic
tropic land, still believing that the unknown contained fairy-
lands as wonderful as my childhood's dreams had fashioned
them'.[89] He left his ship at Rio de Janeiro and lived for some
time as a beach hobo. The city proved yet another disillusionment. Once more he identified himself with the outcasts
of society, the starving beachcombers that haunted the water-
front. It is almost as if a filter interposed between O'Flaherty
and the world about him. Things which possess grace and
beauty are blotted out and what is diseased and horrible
comes gaping to the surface. He compares himself at this
point to a surgeon taking joy from mangled limbs and
gaping skull wounds. With this too came the realization that
however far he might travel he would never find anything
more wonderful than his own village.[90]

After an excursion inland he returned to the city to read in
a morning newspaper: *Republica Declarata na Irlanda*. It
seemed that his homeland might now provide the adventure
he craved and which was so sadly lacking in far-away places.
He took ship for Liverpool with the intention of seeing the
revolution consequent on the declaration of an Irish Republic.

Arriving in Liverpool, the events across the water seemed dull and commonplace, and O'Flaherty signed on a ship bound for the Mediterranean. These facts are at variance with the popular image of O'Flaherty as a Republican soldier and writer, a sort of Dan Breen of the imagination. The Rebellion of 1916 had made no impresssion on him and in 1918 'more important matters occupied my attention.' While guerrilla warfare ravaged the country, O'Flaherty, now a deck-hand, spun fantastic stories to the ship's captain to get out of work. When the ship put in at the Turkish port of Smyrna he got involved in a mysterious gun-running transaction. This provided the money for a wild drinking bout which left the picaresque hero and half the crew with *delirium tremens*. His ship turned about and after a stop at Gibraltar, sailed for Montreal.

In Canada he supported himself on his travels by working as a farm labourer for French-Canadian peasants, as a factory hand in a condensed milk plant and as a railroad worker. His life ran between the usual extremities. The peasantry seemed brutish, the most uncivilized people he had so far encountered. Their work had, in his estimation, no dignity. Proximity to the clay had moulded them to its substance:

> The earth serf is a boor, uncivilized, a hater of all beauty, the lowest of slaves, the enemy of all Gods who are not in his own brute likeness. Truly, the chief aim of civilization is the destruction of the peasant, or rather his liberation from servitude to the earth.[91]

There is a strange atavistic sense in his descriptions of the rural landscapes at this point, as of some brute monster bent on destruction.

The civilization which he had brief hopes might liberate the peasantry from their servitude was present in the form of a condensed milk plant. In his first enthusiasm he saw the automation of the factory as more beautiful and worthwhile than the organic life of the plains about it. The 'Machine God', as he termed the new civilization, had replaced all other gods. American man stood, as a result, in the vanguard of human progress. O'Flaherty, always eager to attach himself to the vanguard, became a worshipper. But not for long. With the grandiose claim that, like Karl Marx, he was too lazy to work, he left the factory. He journeyed to Toronto and from there decided to strike out into the forest and plains to the north. In Northern Ontario he worked with a lumber gang and there met a strange character named John Joseph Peterson. From him O'Flaherty claimed that he gained his 'interest in human psychology'. Peterson was a member of the Industrial Workers of the World and converted O'Flaherty to that organization's programme of social revolution. They were sacked from the lumber camp because of their propaganda for the I.W.W., and moved to Port Arthur. There O'Flaherty at length grew tired of his aimless existence and began a slow return to a more social way of living. He had come to realize the hazards of pursuing a purely individual, solitary existence, ' . . . man, when sane, vigorous, and in full possession of his faculties, needs to be in a crowd or near a crowd.' He decided to cross the border into the United States and head for Boston where his brother and sister lived. Tom was by now a prominent member of the socialist movement in the city and he introduced his younger brother into social revolutionary circles. The immediate effect of the new environment was a quickening of his intellectual life which had lain dormant for years. Tom urged him to be a writer. Liam, preferring the life of action, made a half-hearted attempt at writing short stories, and was unsuccessful. There followed various jobs — Western Union messenger, printer's assistant, factory hand in a pastry factory and, finally, construction navvy. He was nothing if not mobile. His restlessness was contagious and he persuaded Tom to join him in order to learn more about society. The brothers moved from job to job until Liam ended up alone in New York, an employee of Du Pont Explosives and a habitue of Greenwich Village. More to the point, he came across a translation of Maupassant's complete works and tried his hand at writing in the manner of the master, but only succeeded in convincing himself that the art of writing was incomprehensible. Finally, in a mood of disillusion, he took ship for home. His account of himself at this time betrays strong regressive tendencies.

Unable to unite his diverse experience into a coherent whole he retreated from the world into his imagination and sought some place to nurse his isolation:

> Where? What place could be more remote than the place
> of my nativity? A rock forgotten by the world. On its
> bleak rocks I would make my soul dance and rock my
> songs on the cradle of the great ocean winds that blow
> against its cliffs, and then set forth into the world armed
> with a wiser weapon than my hands could wield.[92]

Like Fergus O'Connor of *The Black Soul* who had returned
to 'Nara' from similar adventures, a broken man, O'Flaherty
hoped for renewal and a return of vitality. That he was, in
many ways, a sick man is demonstrated by the recollection of
an acquaintance, Pat Gill of Killeany. He remembers walking
with Liam on several occasions when ship horns sounded in
the bay. Liam would go to pieces and duck for cover under
the nearest stone wall, the wailing of the horns bringing back
his experience of the First World War.

We next hear of him as active in the 'troubles' in Dublin.
These activities, mostly journalistic, earned him an unmerited
reputation as being *au fait* with the inner circles of various
secret organizations. In January 1922, he made a dramatic
gesture at revolution in his own right. Shortly after the
establishment of the Irish Free State Government, O'Flaherty,
with a handful of unemployed dockers, seized the Rotunda
and raised a red flag over it. A journalist on the staff of the
Freeman's Journal, Gerald Griffin, recalled the incident. The
casual tone of his account captures something of the casual
violence of the times and the absurdity of O'Flaherty's
gesture:

> Although 18 January 1922 was my fortnightly day off,
> or rather night off, on the Freeman's Journal, I took a
> busman's holiday and dropped into the office just to
> hear the latest news.
>
> At the entrance to the Freeman I ran into Michael
> Conway, one of our reporting staff.
>
> 'Liam O'Flaherty has seized the Rotunda,' he said
> breathlessly. 'He has run up a red flag from the roof of
> the building. Some say that it is a challenge to the

Government — others that he has declared an Irish Soviet. My belief, however, is that he just wants to draw the attention of the Government to attend to the desperate plight of the Dublin poor. Well, I'm off to see the fun.'

'Are you covering it for the papers?'

'No. Another chap is on the job. Mere curiosity on my part. So long.'

'Wait. I'll come with you, Michael,' I said, as anxious as himself not to miss the promised *entertainment.*

When we arrived at the Rotunda we saw a large red flag floating from one of the windows. An enormous crowd had assembled in the streets converging on the building. We approached a sentry who was posted outside the main entrance.

'The Commander-in-Chief says that nobody is to be admitted without authority,' he replied curtly.

'Who is the Commander-in-Chief?' asked Conway.

'Mr. Liam O'Flaherty.'

'Let's beat it,' said Conway to me. 'We're both off duty and we'll read about it in the papers to-morrow.'

The information in the papers next morning was rather vague, but we gleaned that Liam O'Flaherty's official title was "Chairman of the Council of the Unemployed." Liam and his followers held the building for three days, during the course of which the crowds massing in Cavendish Row and Rutland Square (now Parnell Square) became larger and larger, and were getting more and more excitable, although there was no display of violence. Eventually bodies of Dublin Metropolitan Police, representing the regime that had passed, and of the I.R.A. embodying the new order of things, combined to force the crowds back into O'Connell Street.

At nightfall on 21 January Liam O'Flaherty was notified that if he did not withdraw the unemployed from the Rotunda by midnight he would be forcibly ejected. And in order to avoid futile shedding of blood, he gave orders to his followers to evacuate the building. He fled to Cork with two companions.[93]

The Irish Soviet Republic fell in three days without a shot being fired and left its would-be Lenin with a permanent chip on his shoulders: 'Ever since then I have remained in the eyes of the vast majority of the Irish people a Communist, an atheist, a scoundrel of the worst type, a man whom thousands would burn at the stake if they had the courage.'[94] O'Flaherty greatly exaggerates the concern of the Irish people with his welfare, good or ill, but the event did lodge him in the popular imagination as a dastardly Communist.

On the outbreak of the Civil War he joined the Republicans against the Free State. From the scanty evidence available he does not seem to have been very active. He did, however, turn the atmosphere of the times and the characters he met to good account in the psychological thrillers which deal directly or indirectly with the Civil War period. His farewell to arms and to Ireland are best described by himself:

> It was O'Connell Street in Dublin during the capture of the Republican headquarters by the Free State troops in June 1922. I was standing on the south side of the bridge with a comrade. We had been disbanded on the previous day, and we were now watching the destruction of the hotels where headquarters were still holding out. The Free State soldiers were throwing incendiary bombs from across the street into the hotels. . . . Then I heard an old woman in a group behind me say:
>
> 'Did ye hear that bloody murderer, Liam O'Flaherty, is killed, thanks be to God?'
>
> 'Who?' said another old woman.
>
> 'Liam O'Flaherty,' said the first. 'The man that locked the unemployed up in the Rotunda, and shot them unless they spat on the holy crucifix. The man that tried to sell Dublin to the Bolsheviks.'
>
> 'Is he dead?' said a man.
>
> 'Shot through the heart this morning in Capel Street,' said the old woman. 'The Lord be praised for ridding the country of that cut-throath. . . .'
>
> The old woman cheered the soldiers who were now running across the street to take the headquarters by storm. . . . A great cheer came from the watching

people. I nudged my comrade and we walked away together.

'I'm going,' I said, 'There's nothing more to be done.'

'Where?' he said.

'To England.'

'Surely to God, ye're not quittin'.' he said. 'It's only startin' yet. . . .'

'No,' I said. 'That old woman was right. I'm dead.'[95]

CHAPTER 5

LONDON AND DUBLIN: LITERARY BEGINNINGS

Dead to Catholicism, Republicanism and Communism, O'Flaherty began his literary career. At twenty-six years of age he thought it time to adopt a profession of some sort. An old friend provided the opportunity. This was Mrs Casey, a small London shopkeeper who befriended Republicans on the run and had read some of O'Flaherty's articles in revolutionary papers. She invited him to stay with her and her only daughter. Miss Casey, confident of the young man's talent, urged him to be a writer. In September 1922 he definitely began to write and in a few months produced a novel and a few short stories. The 'thrashy' novel as O'Flaherty describes it was full of mayhem and slaughter and was returned by Allen and Unwin. The short stories fared no better. He resolved not to write anymore and intended returning to America but was restrained by Miss Casey who had fallen in love with him. A further rejection slip with some sarcastic verses attached on the *gaucherie* of his portrayal of London life determined him to seek out a new subject matter. His thoughts turned to the Aran Islands, to the beauty of nature there and the simplicity of their people. These were borne in on him all the more forcefully as he grew more acquainted with the artificiality and ugliness of his surroundings: *It seemed as if a dam had burst somewhere in my soul, for the words poured forth in a torrent.*[96] He began to write what was to become his first published work, *Thy Neighbour's Wife,* and felt the old joy that story-telling had brought him on Aran. He wrote furiously for a fortnight and, though the spate of words dried up, he eventually finished the novel. It was accepted by Jonathan Cape on the recommendation of their reader, Edward Garnett. Garnett knew the novel would not sell but he recognized in it the work of a promising young writer. In the joy of the novel's acceptance O'Flaherty rushed back to Miss Casey and proposed marriage, a proposal he revoked in a fortnight. In the meantime he had met Edward Garnett and begun the most important and fruitful friendship of his life:—

> In fact, I owe Edward Garnett all I know about the craft and a great deal of all I know about the art of writing. To his kindness, his help, his marvellous critical faculty to his loving friendship I owe whatever success I have had subsequently in creating my work. We practically wrote *The Black Soul* together. I remember his burning about 30,000 words of manuscript upon which I had spent a whole month. I could have shot him.[97]

Garnett changed the whole course of O'Flaherty's life and work. The older man not only directed his talents but became the father-figure O'Flaherty had been seeking. Garnett's influence was wholly to the good of the young author:

> Like a father he took me under his protection, handling me with the delicacy with which one handles a high-strung young colt. ... It was the first time I had come in close contact with a cultured English gentleman. The calmness of his judgement, the subtlety of his intellect and the extraordinary nobility of his character were a glorious revelation to me ... Artistic beauty being the only thing of real importance in life to him, I became a fervent disciple of that religion.[97]

He had found a creed to which, more than any other, he gave lifelong allegiance. It is necessary to say a little about so influential a master.

Edward Garnett (1869-1937) belonged to one of the great

English literary families. His father Richard Garnett (1835-1906), a writer and bibliographer, was keeper of printed books at the British Museum Library and noted for his encyclopaedic knowledge. He wrote studies of English and Italian literature and translated Dante and Petrarch. His modern fables, *The Twilight of the Gods,* (1888) caused a sensation in its day. His son Edward was of a more critical bent. After being privately educated he became successively literary adviser to the publishers Fisher Unwin, Heinemann, and Jonathan Cape. In the course of his long career he exerted considerable influence and did much to help the success of John Galsworthy, Joseph Conrad, Edward Thomas, and D.H. Lawrence. Even more influential on the literary scene was his wife Constance (1861-1946) who translated the great Russian authors into English. Their son David was being lionized in London for his novel *Lady into Fox* (London 1922) at the time of O'Flaherty's visits to the family.

H.E. Bates was another writer who had cause to be grateful to Garnett. In the affectionate portrait which he wrote of him the old man emerges as a sort of London A.E., pontificating to the rising young writers from his *chaise longue* at Pond Place.[98]

Bates includes in his volume a letter which Garnett wrote to him about his draft novel *The Voyagers.* The criticism it contained gives an insight into what he required from a novelist. Everywhere there is an insistence on firm outlines and exact details. He demands realistic painting of daily actualities and cuts out romantic passages. Bates is berated for simply describing and not realizing his characters in action:

> '. . . you've written it in the facile, flowing, over-expressive, half-faked style, gliding over the difficulties, not facing the real labour of realistic painting. All that I've condemned in your bad sketches — the generalities, the vague cynicism, the washy repetitions and the lack of firm outlines and exact touches . . .
>
> . . . All that is Hardy and water. Hardy at his worst romantic side . . . .
>
> For what is disconcerting is that you've written it in that hollow-sounding, repetitive style — like a muffled

echo of Conrad, with a lot of cliches. It's not artistically written, written in the sense of every sentence being clear and exact. It's written in a semi-poetic, semi-journalistic way. I don't say there aren't good things in it — good phrases, images and impressions, scattered here and there; but it's full of those sounding generalities of those long-winded reflections. You keep commenting and explaining and repeating things.'[99]

We may be sure that O'Flaherty got the same criticism ('We practically wrote the *Black Soul* together'). Certainly his wild imagination could do with some such ballast.

Bates's book includes a brief account of one of O'Flaherty's visits to Garnett and the latter's handling of him:

New gods were appearing after Conrad, Thomas, Laurence and Davies and to one of these supper evenings came Liam O'Flaherty, a virile and impassioned Irishman who, rather like me, had a facile demon in him. Together, over supper, we put our signatures as witnesses to Garnett's will, and some weeks later O'Flaherty rushed excitedly into Cape's office with the unconfirmed report that *The Two Sisters* had won the Hawthornden Prize, a rumour for which there was evidently no foundation at all, though it continued to dog me for some years afterwards. O'Flaherty, true Irish, could talk a donkey's hind leg off and with fierce, blue unstable eyes would stand up in the middle of the room and begin reciting flowing nonsense from some as yet unwritten book, about "women pressin' their thoighs into the warm flanks of the horses", until he codded you that it had really happened and was really true. O'Flaherty had arrived in London with a firebrand swagger, a fine talent and a headful of rebellious fury about the English and had sat down to write pieces of episodic violence about London, which he hardly knew at all. Garnett promptly and rightly sent him back to Ireland to write about seagulls and congers, a peasant's cow and the flight of a blackbird, and he at once produced sketches of the most delicate feeling and visual brilliance that few, even among the Irish, have equalled.

It was the end of the golden age of Irish literature.
Yeats in poetry, O'Casey and Shaw in drama, Joyce and
Moore and O'Flaherty in fiction, were giving to Irish
literature — through, let it be noted, the language of the
despised English — the last of the shining glory it has
never regained.[100]

The return to Ireland was metaphoric rather than actual.
O'Flaherty left his London garrett and moved to a farmhouse
in Oxfordshire where Bates was also living. He began work on
The Black Soul and as he reveals, submitted it to Garnett
page by page for approval.

The Black Soul was finished early in 1924 and O'Flaherty
returned to Dublin hoping to take the city by storm. He
rented a cottage near the Hell Fire Club in the Dublin
mountains and used the ruined, eighteenth-century club, as
his address. He felt the address to be an appropriate one for
the demonic author of *The Black Soul,* and hoped that
people would say of him that 'the priests soon put their
curse on him.' The satanic pose was only one of many he
adopted through his life. Alternatively he could pose to
Garnett as an 'ancient Gaelic warrior' holding out in his
mountain fastness.

When he did descend from the mountains he was taken up
by George Russell. He attended his Sunday evening 'At
Homes' and it would seem from the letters to Garnett that he
deliberately cultivated A.E. for his own ends. He considered
himself superior to the people who attended the gatherings
and his remarks on them are patronizing. Dublin's literati
did not measure up to their London counterparts. London
had schooled him, not the 'At Homes' of A.E., W.B. Yeats or
James Stephens. It is hardly surprising then, that his most
important contact at these gatherings was not with the
established writers but with a budding authoress, the wife of
Professor Curtis of Trinity College. She was, as photographs
reveal, a very beautiful woman and at their first meeting
surprised O'Flaherty by making 'violent eyes' at him. He was
not greatly impressed at first but soon they began living
together and later, despite great opposition, they got married.

He wrote to Garnett that of all the women he had known she alone combined 'sex appeal and the mind' and added, revealingly, 'All the women I have ever lived with were a curse.'

The mind which he admired in Mrs Curtis was no doubt her talent as a writer of sketches which she published under the pen name of Margaret Barrington. These, with his own work, were sent to Garnett for his *imprimatur*. Mrs Curtis seems to have been one of those women of whom John Keats wrote: 'I have met with women whom I really think would like to be married to a poem and be given away by a novel.' O'Flaherty wrote later: 'She fell in love with me . . . in order to attach herself to my power of expression.'

If our surmise is correct, the novel which gave Mrs Curtis away was *The Black Soul*. Publication had been delayed and he wrote: 'I have the population of Dublin in a white heat of excitement about it and if it is delayed much longer the dam thing will fizzle out and they will say "Oh that chap O'Flaherty is a bore".' Shortly after this outburst the book was published and reviewed by A.E. in the *Irish Statesman*. His praise was fulsome. It was: . . . *the most elemental thing in modern Irish literature, written with amazing energy from the first page to the last . . . Nothing like* The Black Soul *has been written by any Irish writer . . . The book reminds us of Dostoyevsky . . . O'Flaherty's name may be great in Irish literature.*[101] The tribute went to O'Flaherty's head. He felt that he had established his place in Irish letters and wrote vindictively to Garnett: 'I pat myself on the back. I licked all these swine into a cocked hat. When I came here nobody would speak to me. Everybody hated me. I wound them all round my fingers. I got A.E. to give me a thundering review. I got all the old women to praise me. Now that I have fooled them I am telling these damned intellectuals what I think of them in choice scurrilous language.'[102]

It, was, however, only a local success. The English critics came out solidly against it and Garnett wrote that they had killed the book for ten years. O'Flaherty was wounded to the core. Obviously, literary success meant for him the acclaim of London, not Dublin. In despair, like a petulant child, 'I got on the train for the Aran Islands, swearing that I would never leave it again.'

The account of his brief return given in *Shame the Devil*
and corroborated by the letters to Garnett is a miniature
picture of the alienated artist. He felt an alien among the
people who stood on the pier at Kilronan. He had been afflicted with 'the madness of prophecy' and he saw a mute fear in
the eyes of those who greeted him. Aran was as lovely as ever
and tugged at his heart strings but the people were more
hostile than the critics who had denounced his book. In Gort
na gCapall his home was falling into ruins and his father had
sunk into senile decay. He failed to recognize his erring son
except for brief intervals of lucidity. His wife had died the
year before and only a young daughter remained to tend his
old age. Everything O'Flaherty saw was like a wound to him
and after three days he fled back to Dublin. There, at least,
there was work to be done.

The details of O'Flaherty's life in Dublin over the next few
years are meagre and confused. It is possible, however, to
construct a general picture from the literary works of the
period 1924 to 1927. His main concern during these years is
clear enough — it was the replacement of the literary establishment with one of his own choosing. He formed a loosely
knit Radical Club which included Cecil Salkeld, Francis
Stuart, Austin Clarke, F.R. Higgins, Brinsley MacNamara and
his fellow Galwayman, Padraig O Conaire. The main point of
the group was to oppose the 'old fogies' as O'Flaherty called
Yeats, Gogarty and A.E. in a letter to Garnett. Sean O'Casey
in his autobiographical volume *Inishfallen Fare Thee Well*
casts an interesting light on the new literary clique. It was
directed against Yeats in particular.
    '. . . A group of young writers disliked his booming
opinions on literature and insubstantial things without any
local habitation or name.'
    Instead they would '. . . nourish the thoughts and ambit-
ions of the young writers, in opposition to the elderly and
wild speculation of Yeats and the adulatory groups that
trailed longingly after him.'[103]
    O'Flaherty thought that O'Casey would be a likely recruit,
and a valuable one, to the new group. He had met him in
March 1924, 'sweeping out a hall where workmen gamble at

night', and had liked him – 'He is an artist, unlike the other bastard writers I met here.'

Sean O'Casey takes up the story and, incidentally, places O'Flaherty perfectly:

> Some of these wanted to hook in Sean so that his newer influence might be useful in putting Yeats in his improper place. As a preliminary, O'Flaherty brought Edward Garnett to the tenement where he lived, and coaxed Sean to tell Garnett a good deal about the play he was then trying to write, for foolish innocent Sean had told O'Flaherty something about it. Garnett said he was delighted with the description given, and O'Flaherty bravely simulated the happiness of his companion. On the strength of this praise, O'Flaherty built a hope that Sean would do anything he wished; and so for long, and continuously, he argued against the influence of Yeats on literary thought in Ireland and elsewhere, saying Yeats was too damned arrogant, too assured of the superiority of his own work over that of all the others. Sean however, had no bubbling desire to be O'Flaherty's gillie, so he countered the arguments used, for he saw clear enough that O'Flaherty, in a way of arrogance and sense of being a superior being, was worse than Yeats, without the elder man's grace and goodwill; while the cloak worn by the story-teller wasn't near so fine or colourful as the fine, silken mantle of poetry draping the shoulders of the poet.[104]

Events proved O'Casey right. When *The Plough and the Stars* ended its stormy run at the Abbey Theatre the young radicals – or 'fame-flees' as he called them – ganged up on him. O'Flaherty, Higgins and Clarke all wrote to the *Irish Statesman* condemning the play. O'Flaherty went so far as to call its sponsor and defender, W.B. Yeats, a 'pompous fool' and Austin Clarke called the play a 'crude exploitation of our poorer people in an Anglo-Irish tradition that is now moribund'. Ironically, O'Flaherty had become the hunter rather than the hunted.

We have moved forward in time to follow O'Casey's

relationship with what Austin Clarke identified, in a letter to
the *Irish Statesman*, as the 'New Irish School of Writers'. It is
necessary to go back to August 1924 when the opening salvos
were fired against the established literary figures. In that
month appeared the first and penultimate issue of *To-
Morrow*, a new monthly sponsored by O'Flaherty. Francis
Stuart, a young poet, and Cecil Salkeld were the editors and
it was designed to act as a platform for the group. Or so they
thought. O'Flaherty in an ominous note to Garnett wrote:
'Of course I use it merely as a platform for myself' Subterfuge
cloaked subterfuge. The list of contributors included the
names of Yeats and Lennox Robinson — the very people
To-Morrow was supposed to undermine. A coincidence of
mutual need brought about the publication of one of the
great poems of the century, 'Leda and the Swan' in its first
issue. The editors of *To-Morrow* needed the prestige of an
established figure to sell the paper and Yeats needed a place
to publish a poem which had been refused by the *Irish
Statesman*. The violence and apocalyptic overtones of the
poem were oddly consonent with the ideals of the group. The
most coherent statement of these occur in the editorial of the
first issue written by Francis Stuart and Cecil Salkeld and in
two letters written to the *Irish Statesman,* the first by
O'Flaherty, the second by Austin Clarke and F.R. Higgins,
shortly after *To-Morrow* had ceased publication. The editorial is addressed 'To all Artists and Writers':

> We are Catholics, but of the school of Pope Julius the
> Second and of the Medician Popes, who ordered
> Michaelangelo and Raphael to paint upon the walls of
> the Vatican, and upon the ceiling of the Sistine Chapel,
> the doctrine of the Platonic Academy of Florence, the
> reconciliation of Galilee and Parnassus. We proclaim
> Michaelangelo the most orthodox of men, because he
> set upon the tomb of the Medici 'Dawn' and 'Night',
> vast forms shadowing the strength of antideluvian Patri-
> archs and the lust of the goat, the whole handiwork of
> God, even the abounding horn.
>   We proclaim that we can forgive the sinner, but abhor
> the atheist, and that we count among atheists bad writers

and Bishops of all denominations. 'The Holy Spirit is an intellectual fountain', and did the Bishops believe that Holy Spirit would show itself in decoration and architecture, in daily manners and written style. What devout man can read the Pastorals of our Hierarchy without horror at a style rancid, coarse and vague, like that of the daily papers? We condemn the art and literature of modern Europe. No man can create, as did Shakespeare, Homer, Sophocles, who does not believe, with all his blood and nerve, that man's soul is immortal, for the evidence lies plain to all men that where that belief has declined, men have turned from creation to photography. We condemn, though not without sympathy, those who would escape from banal mechanism through technical investigation and experiment. We proclaim that these bring no escape, for new form comes from new subject matter, and new subject matter must flow from the human soul restored to all its courage, to all its audacity. We dismiss all demagogues and call back the soul to its ancient sovereignty, and declare that it can do whatever it please, being made, as antiquity affirmed, from the imperishable substance of the stars.[105]

The letter by Liam O'Flaherty is doubly interesting in that it contains a statement of what he conceived to be the relationship between Art and Life. It was provoked by a review of Romain Rolland's biography of Mahatma Gandhi. The reviewer, A.E., had praised Indian passive resistance as against Irish violence. O'Flaherty wrote:

... the human race has not advanced from savagery to culture on the feeble crutches of philosophy. What epics have there been written about the disputations of scholars? Did Homer write of philosophy or of the hunting of wild boars and the savage wars waged around stone-walled cities? Did Shakespeare live in the days of twenty per cent interest on oil stocks and the loathsome mouthings of Ramsay MacDonalds at Geneva about Leagues of Nations that are based on fraud, corruption, and the usury of slim-fingered, cultured bankers? Did he not live in the days when piratical adventurers carried the standards of Britain across the ocean and the continents? Did he not live in the days when his race was emerging, with bloodshot eyes, lean, hungry, virile, savage, from the savagery of feudalism into the struggle for Empire?

In Ireland, to my mind, we have reached that point in the progress of our race, the point which marked the appearance of Shakespeare in English literature. Let us not be ashamed that gunshots are heard in our streets. Let us rather be glad. For force is, after all, the opposite of sluggishness. It is an intensity of movement, of motion. And motion is the opposite of death. India is cultured. It is an age-long culture. It is a culture of sweet, beautiful words and of slim fingers, slim, long, aristocratic fingers that are effete and on their death-bed. It is a ghostly culture, the culture of dead men walking the earth, crying out in a wilderness peopled with ghosts. Beauty and peace, sweet, melancholy peace.

But ours is the wild tumult of the unchained storm, the tumult of the army on the march, clashing its cymbals, rioting with excess of energy, Need we be ashamed of it?[106]

The second letter, a joint statement by Clarke and Higgins supported O'Flaherty's position in much the same terms. The 'passionate events' of the previous decade had changed the mind and a new movement in Irish letters must take cognisance of 'the primal emotion of our time'. They were unashamed of their modern unrest and admired more 'the intoxication of Cathal Buidhe' than his repentance:

We agree with Liam that vehemence and even excessive energy are needed in prose — and we may add, also in verse. It is necessary to be objective, elemental, to rejoice in primary colour and in the hard sun. Is not this intensity a reverberation of the present world emotion? . . . Having still an anvil, why should we like Americans linger over the little teacups of Japan? But since the Elizabethans are recalled — was not their strength, as in Jonson, known by its sweetness?[107]

They concluded the letter with a curt acknowledgement of the technique which they had inherited from the older school. The acknowledgement was further qualified by the insinuation that technical proficiency had led to preciousness and meaness of spirit. In short they were reacting against what they conceived to be the Alexandrianism of their elders. A.E. replied to both missives on behalf of the older generation. O'Flaherty's piece of invective was met with a measured dismissal. National energy had not decreased; it merely flowed in other channels. The clashing of cymbals and the beating of drums was one of the least attractive manifestations of human energy. 'It is rather like the unintelligent yell of the baby continued in mature years, and we at least find it impossible to exult over it.'[108]

His reply to Clarke and Higgins was more reasoned. He argued that every literary movement tended to develop its opposite. People were fascinated by O'Flaherty because of his temperamental difference to others: he was a novelty, and opposites attract. A.E. concluded with a challenge: 'We would like our correspondents to develop a little further the doctrine they enunciate at the close of their letter, which seems to be that the artist who uses words carefully must be mean in spirit. Our own belief is that it does not indicate a niggardly soul, but a passion for truth and beauty, and that the reverence for these is so great that the writer will not offer cliches, clumsy sentences, confused thinking on the altar where he worships.'[109] Clarke and Higgins replied by contrasting the ascetic verse that had resulted from a concentration on technique with the native Irish tradition which was 'rich and wild, colorful, lavish.'

It is, on the whole, difficult to understand just what O'Flaherty and his friends were rebelling against. Certainly, as John Zneimer suggest, they wished to establish themselves in the literary world away from the overpowering figures of Yeats and A.E. The impression remains, however, that O'Flaherty was not so much concerned with aesthetic differences as with personal antagonisms. His rebellious personality could not brook the authority of the established order. His

opposition to Yeats is even harder to understand when it is
considered that the poet was bettering the lesson of his
young contemporaries in both prose and verse. Indeed Yeats
was liberal in his praise of the young novelist and wrote
recommending *The Informer* and *Mr. Gilhooley* to Olivia
Shakespear. O'Flaherty never wrote a word in praise of
Yeats.

The years spent in these controversies were also years of
great literary activity. Between 1924 and 1927 O'Flaherty
published *Spring Sowing, The Informer, The Tent* and *Mr.
Gilhooley* as well as numerous sketches and short stories. In
1926 his play *An Dorchadas* was produced in the Abbey
Theatre and later published as *Darkness; A tragedy in Three
Acts.* The play represented an abortive attempt, undertaken
with Padraig O Conaire, to start a new literature in Irish, but
thirty years were to pass before O'Flaherty again used Irish as
his medium of expression. His creative activity gained him a
place with James Joyce and Sean O'Casey as a 'new realist' in
the current literary criticism. The triumvirate was repeatedly
invoked in reviews and articles to point up the reaction to the
'Celtic Twilight' writers. An article, 'Heredity in Literature',
from a regular contributor to the *Irish Statesman* ('Y.O') is
typical:

> Twenty-five years ago Anglo-Irish literature was
> romantic, idealist or mystic. But what a change in the
> writers who come after these! At what a remove from
> the *Wanderings of Usheen,* the *Land of Heart's Desire* or
> the *Shadowy Waters* is the *Portrait of the Artist as a
> Young Man* or *Ulysses!* In what a remote world are
> O'Grady's *Bardic History* and *Flight of the Eagle,* if we
> set them beside *The Informer* or *Mr. Gilhooley,* by Liam
> O'Flaherty. What has happened in the national being
> that a quarter of a century should have brought about
> such a change? From the most idealistic literature in
> Europe we have reacted so that with Joyce, O'Flaherty
> and O'Casey, the notabilities of the moment, we have
> explored the slums of our cities, the slums of the soul.[110]

The title of the essay 'Heredity in Literature' derived from the author's opinion, half-playfully entertained, that Newton's Third Law "To every action there is an equal and opposite reaction", might also hold good for literature. Every generation of writers created their opposites and literature progressed by a series of antitheses. Joyce was the antithesis of Yeats, O'Casey of Synge and O'Flaherty of Standish O'Grady — 'If *Cuchulain* had not been so noble, the *Informer* would not have been so ignoble.'

At any rate, O'Flaherty had established himself in the literary world and his name was now linked with writers more weighty than Cecil Salkeld or F. R. Higgins. Of the triumvirate — Joyce, O'Casey and O'Flaherty — only the last was to sink into relative obscurity. Despite his brief success and acclaim in these years there is a curious silence about his personal life. His letters reveal a growing sense of isolation and disgust with Ireland — a few phrases from them tell their own story: 'Everybody has turned against me — I have no money — Thanks for £10 — snowed down with depression — Simply at point of disintegration — I'm an outcast.'[111] He wrote a last letter to the *Irish Statesman*. The Irish people were 'too hopelessly sunk in intellectual barbarism to be capable of being saved by a single man.' He concluded with a renewed dedication to his art:

> I don't write for money. If I wanted to write for money I could be a rich man now. I am a good craftsman and I am cunning enough to understand the various follies of mankind and womankind. In fact, if I ever get so hard up that I'll loose my self respect, I'll start a religious paper in the Irish language and make a fortune on it.[112]

It is impossible to set realistic bounds to the different stages of a man's life. In so far as one can do this, the *Irish Statesman* letter marked the end, for over twenty years, of his direct association with Ireland and Irish life. Henceforward he would be an exile and in the chit-chat of literary conversation in Dublin somebody would be sure to pose the question, 'I wonder where is Liam O'Flaherty now?'

CHAPTER 6

EXILE

'I wonder where is Liam O'Flaherty now?' — the biographer is faced with a similar question. In the five years between 1927 and 1932 the only definite knowledge we have of his whereabouts for any length of time is that he was in Russia during the Spring and Summer of 1930. It appears from the memories of his acquaintance (he does not seem to have had many close friends) that O'Flaherty's life was spent mainly in England and America with occasional visits to Ireland. Then, in April 1930, he set out on a Soviet ship en route to Russia to collect material for a book on Bolshevism. *I Went to Russia*, which he published the following year, is a very strange account of his visit. There is very little of Russia in it, not to speak of Bolshevism, and much of O'Flaherty. It is a prolonged meditation on himself, society and art with the Soviet Republic acting as a stimulus to his thinking. This visit to Russia and the subsequent book were both undertaken, primarily to make money, but also with the idea of finding . . . *a new purpose in life, something to which I could attach myself, a community as vital and as worthy of great poetry as Elizabethan England. Why did I remain hostile?*[113]

The quest of his youth for something larger than himself to which he might give unreserved commitment continued into middle age. As the question mark which concludes the quotation shows, he was meeting with no better success. Communism continued to fascinate him all his life, but his visit to Russia taught him an important lesson. However much he might envy the 'Elizabethan' exuberance of Russian life, 'I must still remain suspect and in reality an alien, because a different religion and culture had become part of my being.' Parts of the book make unpleasant reading in view of later events. There is a prevailing anti-semitism in it and he shares the blindness of other visitors to Russia in the 1930s to Stalinist terror. He returned to London, confirmed in his disillusionment:

> ... when I reached London, a delicious sense of the futility of human effort drowned my melancholy. This city represented the culmination of an imperial effort greater than that of the Romans, if not in military conquest, at least by the diversity of its achievements. Yet it was now halted, stagnant, beginning to rot at the core and to wither at the extremities, using all its ancient skill to maintain its power. So does everything come to an end. So will the Leninist movement come to an end and give way to another. The star of human genius is not fixed.[114]

Our next point of contact with O'Flaherty is a letter to Edward Garnett in February, 1932. His news is the usual tale of misfortune tempered only with his hopes for a new novel, *Skerrett,* which he is writing. His personal life is in ruins but the resume of his life to date ends on a hopeful note:

> I have been through a lot during the last few years; so to speak, deliberately undergone a rather stupid cycle of experience to arrive at a clearer consciousness of what I want to do. Now, it's coats off and to do it.[115]

The autobiographical volume *Shame the Devil* which brings us up to 1934 belies these expectations. It is the record of yet another 'rather stupid cycle of experience', a long, often tiresome, account of his despair at even becoming a writer of real worth. He drinks to forget his past failures, contemplates suicide and even turns to religion as a possible solution to his problems. It is difficult not to come to the conclusion that for lengthy periods O'Flaherty was mentally sick. Finally, in a remote Breton island not unlike the Aran of his youth, he began to recover his delight in nature and find release in the return of creative power. Thereafter O'Flaherty went to America which, until 1949, became his principal place of residence. But the answer to 'Where is Liam O'Flaherty now?' at any time over the past forty years might just as easily be Paris, Rome or New York. The Aran Islander, unable to accept Irish life, became a cosmopolitan. Yet his imagination never left the Ireland of his youth which continued to supply him with material for his work. His last three novels *Famine* (1937), *Land* (1946) and *Insurrection* (1950) are an effort to place the Irish experience in an historical perspective, an effort undertaken with failing powers. In 1953 O'Flaherty took up once again a challenge he had abandoned in the 1920s — to create a modern literature in Irish. He collected, at the prompting of some Irish language enthusiasts in Dublin, a selection of his short stories in Irish from the pages of defunct Irish-Ireland magazines. They were published under the title *Duil (Desire)* and received a very hostile reception from the critics. O'Flaherty gave up writing completely. A novel in Irish, *Coirp agus Anim (Body and Soul)* remained unfinished. 'A man's life', says Keats, 'is a continual allegory — and very few eyes can see the mystery of his life — a life like the scriptures, figurative.' There is something extraordinarily figurative in this end to O'Flaherty's artistic career — a novel in Irish called *Body and Soul,* and unfinished! In a sense all the Anglo-Irish novelists were striving to write a novel with just that title. That it should have been attempted in Irish and remained unfinished is oddly consonant, not only with the whole tendency of O'Flaherty's artistic career, but with the broken culture from which he derived.

CHAPTER 7

ART, THE ARTIST AND IRELAND

The external detail and movement of O'Flaherty's life is important in itself but also in so far as it reveals the pattern of the inner life. The basic pattern of that inner life, as of the outer, is one of quest for the meaning of existence. Essentially his is a romantic character in search of a Holy Grail which forever eludes him. We may identify his romanticism in its initial phase as of the kind condemned by T.E. Hulme. It revolves round the central proposition that: '. . . man is by nature wonderful, of unlimited powers and if hitherto it has not appeared so, it is because of external obstacles and fetters, which it should be the main business of social politics to remove . . . . We may define Romantics then, as all those who do not believe in the Fall of Man.'[116]

O'Flaherty is obsessed alike by the vision of man's unlimited powers (his own in particular) and the hard, intractable reality which thwarts them. The first, with its wonder and wild idealism, is the source of his genius and the romantic strain which informs everything he did and wrote. The second, his violent confrontation with *'la realite rugueuse'*, earned him an unwarranted reputation as a realist and even a naturalist.[117]

There is a curious air of knight-errantry about his questing as of a Don Quixote innocently stumbling down the *iter fabulosa*. It is in this light that Sean O'Faolain assessed his character:

The recurrent theme of his life is travel. He is our
Waring. 'And where is Liam O'Flaherty now?' Movement; restlessness; explosion; the eternal search; a
creature of emotion, always up to something . . . . Essentially, I do believe O'Flaherty is like every known Irish
writer, an inverted romantic. That is, he sets out in the
most self-conscious and deliberate way to attack with
violence the things that hurt the inarticulate dream of
his romantic soul. For he has a romantic soul; he has the
inflated ego of the romantic, the dissatisfaction of the
romantic, the wild imagination, the response to the
magic of nature, the self-pity of the romantic, his
masochistic rage, the unbalance. And there are the claws
in which he takes reality and, like a gull with a shellfish,
he lifts it up to an enormous height and lets it fall with a
crash; while we are yet stunned by his gyring flight, and
the reverberation of the impact, he then swoops to see if
there is anything worth his respect in what he has
already destroyed and, screaming, he flies away,
unsatisfied.[118]

The image of the bird rising high into the sky is peculiarly
appropriate to O'Flaherty. It is an image he employs repeatedly to describe his own aspirations. One is reminded of
Joyce's bird-man, Dedalus, only to be made aware of the differences. Joyce's image is vibrant with mythological meanings.
O'Flaherty's comes straight from the natural world of his
childhood. Only once does he employ bird imagery with a
literary connotation. Down and out in Paris he is a 'sick
hawk' among 'sparrows from the gutter of a city slum'. One
is reminded of Keats's 'sick eagle looking at the sky'. More
often O'Flaherty sees himself as a swan among ugly ducklings
or grey geese. He counsels his soul: *Why be a goose? Let the
geese and ganders of the earth waddle in their muddy ponds,
plunging their beaks into the mire and excrement in search of
gold, or God, or the perfection of their ephemeral institu-
tions. Let them hiss and flap their shabby wings and, pick to
death their rivals, when they are beset by the base confusions
born of their ignorance. Fly high, my soul, and when the icy
hail has pierced the snow-white armour of your beauty, let*

subtle grace be your purse, full to overflowing with hypnotic rubies, to make soft your fall. But while you soar in sunlit splendour, the petty loves and hatreds of geese and ganders are no concern of yours. When he did descend to the earth, his Leda, it would be with some of the brute energy and apocalyptic violence of Yeats's poem.

However individual the images in which he tried to capture his fate, the conditions they embody were general ones. It is of the kind dissected by David Daiches in his *Poetry and the Modern World* and a hundred other studies before **and** since − isolation, alienation, the problems of the artist **in** an age without a stable background or an acceptable system of belief. The artist as rebel against convention and society is the dominant image and O'Flaherty is the Irish rebel *par excellence.* The autobiographies speak with many voices pleading, self-pitying, haughty, disdainful. But rising like a crescendo through these is the hectoring, defiant voice of rebellion: *Make a fig at whatever duty you owe society and your dependants. Only one thing is important to a living being, and that is life. Preserve it.*[120]

And again: *Recant? Crave forgiveness? Clip the wings of my fancies in order to win the favour of the mob? To have property and be esteemed? To attend banquets as a guest of honour? To kiss the Pope's toe and win a title? Ho! Devil! Rather the whore of London shining in her jewels, than such an unwashed nun canting her sombre superstitions. Better to be devoured by the darkness than to be hauled by dolts into an inferior light.*[121]

Life, as the first quotation reveals, is not capable of being defined in social terms. In the second he opts for the devil and the title of the book from which these extracts are taken, *Shame the Devil,* suggests that he will not make final peace even with *that* gentlemen. Rebelliousness, in fact, became an almost instinctive reaction with O'Flaherty. His conception of human happiness was a full-blooded, unrelenting struggle against the environment which would end in the individual achieving omniscience. Human motives are never simple and one senses behind the rationalizations of endless struggle and renewal an inner vacuity that occasionally comes to the surface in remarks such as the following: *It is always good for a writer to be ready to go anywhere, with anybody, at any time. It is especially good for a writer who is contemplating suicide. Monotony, boredom and staleness lead to suicide. To set forth, no matter how, where, or with whom, is the best antidote to these evils.*[122]

O'Flaherty's pursuit of an ideal is, in another perspective, a flight from reality. He was aware of the ambiguous nature of his progress and it produced some tormented soul-searching. In *Shame the Devil* there are three schizoid conversations, modelled on the debate between self and conscience in George Moore's *Confessions of a Young Man,* in which O'Flaherty's identity dissolves and reforms into two distinct and contending personae. In the first, O'Flaherty the artist is confronted by O'Flaherty the man at a race track where he (man or artist?) is betting wildly. His conscience upbraids him for neglecting his duties as a husband and father. The artist replies defiantly and quotes Shakespeare for his purposes. Conscience makes cowards of us all. He is ashamed of its nagging voice. Marriage and women mean nothing to him except as material for his art. Moral responsibility is the link between him and mediocrity. The desire to love and be loved is a weakness which he will stand against. That part of him which suffers and is afraid has been useful to the artist, in it he can study the frailty of human nature. Conscience leaves him with a parting shot. Perhaps he is insane. The hallucination disappears and, in O'Flaherty's analysis of it, he puts it down to the after-effects of shell shock sustained twenty years before. The claims of the world and the claims of art, 'perfection of the life or of the work', pull him apart once more as he watches a father bidding a fond farewell to his wife and child at a railway station. The child sets him to brooding on his own deserted offspring and the rootlessness of his life. The hallucination returns but the roles are reversed — O'Flaherty the artist comes to upbraid O'Flaherty the man who has grown sentimental over the departing family. The man yearns for the old verities — the blessings of love and tenderness. 'Why', he asks, 'must you dissect what is holy, the holiest thing in life?' The artist is unequivocal in his statement of his creed:

I'd cut off your hands and feet in order to write a
phrase. I'd have you annihilated for the sake of creating
something really perfect. What you call the holiest thing
in life is holy when it is the food of the imagination.
When it ceases to feed the imagination it ceases to be
holy. It ceases to exist and the wise man deserts the
empty store-room. . .[123]

The position is a romantic extreme: only those areas of life
amenable to the operation of the imagination truly exist.
Reality is merely grist to imagination's mill.

O'Flaherty, the man, goes on to protest that though he is
merely the artist's mask yet it is necessary for him to retain
his self respect. The artist will have none of this. Only
through disorderly conduct can he keep his distance from
social entanglements. To be orderly and civil is to court social
respectability. The artist must always be an outcast, 'an angel
of discontent' who must be as ruthless with himself as the
ancient hermits of the desert. Living dangerously is the sever-
est form of discipline. Blake and Nietzsche provide support-
ing texts. Thus, O'Flaherty, harkening to the voice that calls
on him to eschew delight and live laborious days, abandons
his family and breaks all ties of love. There remained a
further temptation. Rebelling against convention and social
respectability, might not the artist attach himself to a revolutionary movement and subsume his own identity in that of
the larger group? This was at bottom the appeal which
Communism and other social revolutionary programmes
exercised over O'Flaherty. He hoped that by giving his allegiance to the cause he might escape, with dignity, the intoler-
able isolation of the artist. Republicanism, Communism,
Socialism, were attractive, not so much for their theoretical
content, as the 'Elizabethan' energy they generated in their
followers. 'Elizabethan' is a favourite term of praise with
O'Flaherty. It connoted for him a sense of movement, of
great forces clashing, the colour and splendour of Shakespeare's history plays. Shakespeare was the last great artist
because he had lived in a society which met his imaginative
requirements and he could with justice be its poet. 'Nor
should I, as an Irishman, deplore the conquest of Ireland, if

that conquest helped to inspire the proud genius of Shakespeare.'[124] Ireland, he thought, was at an Elizabethan stage in its development: 'We have reached that point in the progress of our race the point which marked the appearance of Shakespeare in English literature.'[125] He had hoped to become the Shakespeare of the Celtic Renaissance. Failing that, Communist Russia held out hopes that there he might meet the embodiment of the century native to his mind. He found among some Russian sailors, 'the same force and enthusiasm one finds among the characters of an Elizabethan drama; the same violence of gesture, the same crazy sincerity, the same extravagance of emotion.'[126]

While meditating on Communism, towards the end of *Shame the Devil,* he once more becomes enamoured of social revolutions. The artist *persona* returns again to warn him that:

> If a writer makes himself the idol of the mob by voicing the ambitions of the mob, then he is reduced to the common level of the mob's intelligence. The mob will not allow him to rise above that level.[127]

The man is plunged into despair; he had thought to rehabilitate himself among human kind by entertaining humanitarian feelings. The artist is reassuring. He has now escaped but does not realize it. The thing he must fear is not the torture of mind, the 'continual vacillation between one enthusiasm and another, a rapid passage from despair to exaltation and from exaltation to despair', but rather the indifference born of self satisfaction. His artist *persona* bids him look into the face of nature — 'the earth, the sea and the air are man's substance and his sustenance.' By renewing his acquaintance with the earth he will regain peace and harmony.[128]

O'Flaherty's concern for the place of the artist in society is confused and confusing. When it does reach a focus he sees himself in the conventional romantic role of prophet, druid, or demon. His powers have set him apart from 'the herd' and as a result he is proud and arrogant. His duty is to observe, never to participate. He is 'a vessel into which life pours sweet wine or vinegar. I must accept and drink it to the dregs'.

Edward Garnett gave him a text which he invokes again and again and which might stand as a rubric to his work, 'To the artist, everything that exists justifies itself by the fact of its existence.'[129] It is a belief which leaves little room for humanitarian feeling.

What the superhuman observer sees is seen *sub specia aeternitatis* and is all the more depressing for that. Man's life, in this perspective, is nasty, brutish and short. The great fact is death and it reduces everything to motion without purpose. His recurring image of man is that of a creature grown pompous and ridiculous with intellect, inhabiting a dying planet. The evolutionary process brought man from the sea and it will carry him into those infinite spaces, the silence of which so terrified Pascal:

> Ten million years and they were tiny bladders floating in a warm pool, whence they climbed the cliff into the shape of monstrous elephants and whales and megalomaniac men begetting gods in their fantastic brains. Ten million years and all may pass once more into a savage wilderness of prowling stars.[130]

We have invented God to protect ourselves against the discovery that annihilation is inevitable. 'After such knowledge, what forgiveness?' ... The artist at any rate, cannot seek forgiveness. He must cry out his *Non Serviam* to any creed which obscures the vision of ultimate futility. It is here that O'Flaherty finds his ally in the natural world and why it should act as a catalyst to his creativity. The life of nature does not pursue a purpose, and it is indifferent to human fate. The 'otherness of nature' which pains and bewilders many of his generation is to him a joy and a consolation. Yeats's spiritual advisers gave him 'metaphors for poetry', O'Flaherty's natural environment gave him metaphors for life. One form of life preys on another, there is only the endless circularity of hunter and hunted. Caught in that vicious circle it is often difficult to discern if the boarhound pursues the boar or *vice versa*. The superhuman observer is only aware of motion and the fine energies displayed. Scattered references to the observer as a 'superior being' and

the collocation of animal imagery — hawk, stoat and field-
mouse, suggest that O'Flaherty's thinking derives in part
from a passage in one of Keats's letters:

> The greater part of Men make their way with the same
> instinctiveness, the same unwandering eye for their
> purposes, the same unwandering eye as the Hawk. The
> Hawk wants a Mate, so does the Man — look at them
> both they set about it and procure one in the same
> manner. They want both a nest and they both set about
> one in the same manner — they get their food in the
> same manner — The noble animal Man for his amuse-
> ment makes his pipe — the Hawk balances about the
> Clouds — that is the only difference of their leisure. This
> it is that makes the Amusements of Life — to a specul-
> ative Mind, I go among the Fields and catch a glimpse of
> a stoat or a fieldmouse peeping out of the withered grass
> — the creature hath a purpose and its eyes are bright
> with it. I go amongst the buildings of a city and I see a
> Man hurrying along — to what? the Creature has a
> purpose and his eyes are bright with it.

And later in the same letter:

> Though a quarrel in the Streets is a thing to be hated,
> the energies displayed in it are fine; the commonest Man
> shows a grace in his quarrel — By a superior being our
> reasonings may take the same tone — though erroneous
> they may be fine — That is the very thing in which
> consists poetry.[131]

The extracts quoted occur in a letter where Keats strives to
define his moral ideas of 'disinterestedness'. 'The Greater part
of men', whom he likens to the Hawk, have no such concern.
O'Flaherty would have said all men, and those who do enter-
tain such notions are reaching after the impossible. Brooding
over the collective struggle of the Russian people to realize
the ideal of equality he writes:

> ... human life is governed by the same ruthless com-

petition and brazen anarchy which governs the growth of nature. Plant wars with plant, insect with insect, animal with animal. The elements destroy life with the same power that generates and feeds life. All is in continual movement, ever-changing, blindly moving, being born, flowering, dying, from a miraculous beginning to an unexplainable end, beautiful only in movement, incomprehensible in purpose.

So are man's ambitious movements incomprehensible and without purpose when examined by reason. Each successive culture crumbles into ruin and desolation spreads over the sites of his proud cities. His gods are forgotten. His works of art become dust. His philosophies and religions become a gibberish, unintelligible to his descendants. His music becomes the moaning of the rough winds. Hordes of ants march over battlefields, where his armies, with their banners, passed to victory.

I saw the Bolshevik god as a wooden dummy like the rest, of no nobler quality than the fetishes which the Chinese and the Egyptians and the Assyrians and the Greeks and the Aztecs and the Romans carried into the strong places of their enemies. Born in the hungry bellies of the Bolshevik masses, he would die when those bellies were full to repletion, just as Odin and Thor died when the Norse conquerors were glutted with loot. Loot! Loot! Man appeared no whit more divine than the foraging ants, which gnaw their way across continents, leaving desolation in their trail.[132]

How must the artist conduct himself against such a panorama of desolation? He too is a beast of prey to whom nothing is sacred. O'Flaherty recalls in *Shame the Devil* a visit he made to his mother's grave while writing *The Puritan*. ' . . . drunk with creative enthusiasm', he smiled and looked about him, '*looting* the scene with *fierce, avaricious eyes* . . . '.[133] Those things which excite his emotions and imagination have a more immediate relevance as material for his art.

Holding such views on the nature of reality and of the artist it is scarcely surprising to find that O'Flaherty disregards the finer points of artistic technique. (We have earlier reviewed his impatience with the technical expertise of Yeats and the older generation). He specifically rejects any idea of cultivating a style. In a letter to Garnett (3 April 1924) he wrote: *There will be written on the tombstone of most of the young English writers of talent: 'there might have lain a genius were he not cut off in his youth by the mania of style'. Dammit man, I have no style. I don't want any style. I refuse to have a style. I have no time for a style. I think a style is artificial and vulgar. If a man is lucky enough to have a natural gift for saying somethings in a pretty manner, good luck to him. If he has not that natural gift, he's a fool to cultivate it.*

Art is the work of inspiration and genius. Once more, one is reminded of Keats's dictum that 'if Poetry comes not as naturally as the Leaves to a tree it had better not come at all.' Keats's poetry belies his statement, they are certainly the result of a sustained and deliberate effort at self education. O'Flaherty, on the other hand, waited for inspiration to well up in him. It is as if he needed an inner tumult to match the tumultuous world he perceived about him, and having achieved that he could write equally tumultuous prose. The grey times between 'when the fire is out' are periods of soul sickness. A Keats learns Italian or Greek to prepare himself for his next raid on the inarticulate. O'Flaherty languishes, giving half-hearted allegiance, now to one cause, now to another. When the fires burn again they consume cause and all. There is little evidence of a critical faculty at work while he creates, or even subsequent to creation. If utterance is inspired, then it is impious to meddle with it.

We have dealt with O'Flaherty's view of the relationship between the man who suffers and the artist who creates, his view of art, *per se* and the kind of universe within which it operates. There remains one final consideration, his assessment of the material with which he had to work and which called for all his best imaginative efforts — the Irish people. He has left an indirect statement of his views on Ireland in *A Tourist's Guide to Ireland* which in method and ideas is very closely related to the novels.[134] It is a gallery of types which find their way with greater individuality into his more creative work. Superficially, the *Guide* sets out to give to the tourist an understanding of the social conditions he will find in Ireland. Underneath the surface, however, O'Flaherty the novelist is everywhere at work to show how the appearances falsify the reality. His theme is the contradictions within Irish society. It is a bitter, unrelenting expose of all the social classes, creeds, or causes to which an Irishman might give his allegiance.

O'Flaherty begins by characterizing his reader as a helpless tourist who needs the advice and guidance of the honest author. The first group of people he must beware of are the clergy. Irish society is, in the tired phrase, 'priest-ridden'. Priests are the one constant in social history since men first set foot on the island, druids give way to parish priests and so on. Only the religion changes. Today and for the last two thousand years, Christianity is the approved religion and shows no signs as yet of a serious rival. Such people as A.E. and W.B. Yeats are to be avoided because of their interest in other manifestations of the religious spirit. Dublin's drawing-rooms and their fashionable liberalism can be disregarded. At any rate Dublin is not Ireland, the real Ireland is to be found in the rural districts. Here the priests are all powerful, though the tourist may disregard the curates. The parish priest is his own man and like all of O'Flaherty's fictional P.P.'s he is a type. He has a finger in every pie and is the only power in the district. The peasantry have a blind worship of him and he is master of their lives:

> When they are born they are brought before him and he baptizes them for a few shillings. When they begin to go to school they come under his supervision. He hires and sacks their teachers at his discretion, very often at his whim. He flogs them if they mitch from school or if they fail to learn their catechism. When they become striplings, he watches them carefully lest they make love clandestinely. When they reach marriageable age he marries them for a few pounds. If they don't get married he nags at them, eager for his fees. He abuses them from the altar unless they pay him what he considers sufficient money at Christmas and Easter.

> When they die he buries them, . . . From their first yell
> at birth until the sod falls on them in their grave their
> actions and thoughts are under his direction.[135]

This is, in summary, the kind of society depicted in the regional novels. Its presiding evil spirit, the parish priest, is able to wield such powers, partly because of a superstitious awe of his priesthood but also because he himself is of peasant extraction and so up to all their tricks. He has no great interest in religion, books or art. O'Flaherty imagines a conversation between the reader and a typical parish priest where all the salient points of his case against these community leaders emerge. The tourist is advised to mention Canon Sheehan *en passant* as the world's greatest novelist but otherwise to forego any mention of literature. El Greco's painting of St Francis is to be referred to as a 'Holy Picture'. On no account is education to be brought into the conversation. This is purely a matter for the clergy and any layman who professes an opinion on the matter is to be suspected of Free Masonry. Forms of amusement are another taboo subject, being a danger to faith and morals. Politics may be discussed but in an oblique manner — it is sufficient to agree with the parish priest in his demands for a strong government to halt the moral decay of youth, all-night dancing, and English Sunday newspapers. Thus the parish priest emerges as a man concerned only with consolidating his own power to which all ideas and culture pose a threat. In O'Flaherty's analysis, the basic reason for this is that the clergy owe allegiance, not to the state, but to Rome. They occupy the position and pose the same threat to the state as the Jews of the Diaspora were reputed to hold in other European countries. 'Like an army of black beetles on the march' they invade the seat of Government in Dublin. Unable to take a seat in parliament they control all local representative bodies and exclude anybody of 'revolutionary or unchaste sentiments'. Being themselves members of a secret society they abhor all others, from Fenians in the nineteenth century to today's Communists: 'For he (the Parish Priest) sees in all these societies and ideas a tendency towards strengthening the power of the state and robbing the confessional of some of its terrors.'[136] O'Flaherty modifies his condemnation a little by attempting to explain how such a state of affairs has come to pass. The clergy are the victims of a debilitating environment. Their's is the forgiveable tyranny of the big boy in the village school. Badly educated, trained in suppression, hemmed in by fetishes and dogmas, what can the tourist do but pity them? Whatever kindly emotion is to be reserved for these 'stupid, good-natured sort of village tyrants' the tourist is to hold no brief whatever for religious priests, Jesuits in particular. Unlike the rural parish clergy these men are educated and refined but all the more sinister for that. They are primarily responsible for the 'heavy, hairy garment of Puritanism (which) has fallen and enshrouded the whole of society.'[137] O'Flaherty contrasts the pleasures of an urban middle class society, music, theatre, the cafe, with the social life of Ireland where such things are lacking. There is only the 'secretive sousings in dirty public houses, where no female dare enter unless she be clothed in rags and bleary in the eye.'[138]

Since almost all post-primary education is in the hands of the religious clergy, it is they who are responsible for the formation of the middle class. They have given to it its peculiar tone of narrowness, fanaticism in religion and hostility to new ideas. The peasant has his close contact with natural environment to rid him of what few things he learns at school but no such opportunity is available to the middle classes. If the tourist really wants to get into contact with Irish intellectual life he will have to go to England, America or Paris 'where the author of *Ulysses* is living in exile.' In short, the amenities of cultural life are almost totally lacking. What little is to be had of it in Ireland will be found in occasional drawingrooms and city pubs. He concludes his ironic diatribe against the clergy by classifying them as the new landlords, engaged in a speedy accumulation of property. In this section of the *Guide* O'Flaherty uses the clergy as a stalking-horse to attack what most offends him in Irish life, its authoritarianism, puritanism, and a general anti-intellectual bias.

Next, O'Flaherty directs his ire at the politicians. After the priests they are the most important class in the Irish community. He typifies them as a race of sophists, expert in the

national pastime of endless conversation. Once a man finds
that he has an ability to talk at length on any subject he is
well on the way to being a politician. The system of pro-
motion into national politics is from peasant farm to huckster shop to public house and thence to Parliament. Such
'huckstering peasants' are the backbone of the political
parties. Leadership comes from the middle-classes, from
those in the legal profession in particular. And these have
been formed by clerical educators. The result is that they
more than any other section of the community suffer from
the 'national disease' which he diagnoses as *the attempt to
unite mysticism with reality*. Mysticism is all right, he argues,
when regulating the affairs of the Heavenly World. More
mundane qualities are called for when dealing with practical
matters. But Irish politicians, taking the lead from Irish
Catholicism, conceive of Ireland as a woman, Caitlin Ni
Houlihan, Roisin Dubh, or the Hag of Bere. They concern
themselves, that is, with the welfare of the mystical soul of
Ireland and neglect, in true puritan fashion, her bodily needs:
. . . *Holy Ireland is above such coarse ambitions as wealth,
culture, bathrooms, toothbrushes and machinery*.[139]

Party politics is a ridiculous affair and is typified at its
most ineffectual and absurd in the Civil War fought over the
wording of an oath. The kind of casuistry which brought an
assembly of bishops together to argue on the presence or
absence of souls in women is still active in Ireland. The tourist may enjoy the clowning but must not trouble himself to
see the misery behind the grinning faces. As he had earlier
imagined a meeting between his reader and a parish priest, so
now he confronts him with a typical politician. He must be
met with in Dublin 'for as the honey bee settles on the
honeyed flower, so does the politician settle near the money.'
It is best to pose as a foreign capitalist with money to invest
in the country. At this, a member of the Government is sure
to take him under his wing and give him an insight into our
national affairs. He will learn that the Government regards
the peasantry as a hopeless lot who can only be brought out
of their barbarism by appealing to their innate greed and
ignorance. Nationalist sentiment forces the Government to
continue its Irish language policy but this is a problem that

will solve itself when the last native speaker emigrates to America. In the meantime 'the Government have hired a few men in Dublin to manufacture Irish words according as they are needed.'[140] O'Flaherty's typical politician is portrayed as venal, eager to exploit his position for his own ends, a man who views the state as an institution to be exploited. Members of the opposition since they possess no power here recourse instead to 'the national characteristic virtue of Puritanism which fattens on empty pockets.'[141] Revolutionary groups within the state are little better, spending their time in conversation and vague schemes none of which are even put into operation. 'Yet there is no country in the world where a Cromwell or a Lenin is more needed.'[142] All political groupings, then, are condemned equally for their failure to remove the bonds, spiritual and temporal, which fetter Irish life. The section concludes with a vision of a society dying of ennui and torpor:

> The present government have pensioned a great number. The opposition, if they come in to power, are likely to pension as many more. Add to that the number of politicians who do no useful work. Add to that all the priests who do no useful work . . . . Add to that the police, the army and the civil services, who do not produce wealth. Add the shopkeepers who do not produce wealth but merely distribute it. There remains only the peasantry and Guinness's Brewery and a few industries that are rapidly dying out. The peasants are going to America as rapidly as they can. Those that remain are living on the old age pensions of their fathers and mothers and cursing the government for not providing them with sufficient doles.[143]

O'Flaherty concludes his *Guide* with a meditation on the peasantry. Priests, politicians and publicans live like parasites on these, ' . . . the only natural type of human being in this country that I consider an honour to the country and to mankind.'[144] Only with the peasant nation is there any hope, but O'Flaherty says little further in the way of praise. The peasant is stupid, frustrated, ignorant and superstitious, but

'I see in him the germs of future greatness.' O'Flaherty claims that the peasant stage of society is like the childhood stage in human life. Brute instincts dictate behaviour. Yet he discerns some likeable traits — simplicity, lack of vulgarity and the ease with which both children and peasants amuse themselves. Most of all, O'Flaherty has regard for the peasant's harmony with nature:

> He responds to the seasons like a bird or beast, clothing himself heavily or lightly, ploughing, reaping, sowing or hiding in his hut, according as the cold or heat of nature bids him. He reproduces his kind methodically, without any concept of romantic love and he dies practically without effort, since his imagination is not strong enough to torment him with visions.[145]

But if the peasant has the good qualities of a child, he is equally endowed with the bad ones. He is cruel, selfish and obstinate.

In O'Flaherty's view over ninety per cent of the citizens of Ireland are peasants. Unlike their equals in other countries, such as France, they are not an economic asset to the state. Many of them do not produce enough to feed themselves. All sections of the community (the word hardly applies to O'Flaherty's view of Irish society) are exploited by priest and politician but the peasants' special incubus is the gombeen man. Once a young couple get married they are almost invariably plunged into debt to the local shopkeeper. By a slow process of attrition they are either forced to emigrate, in which case the gombeen man takes possession of their land in return for the fare, or else they must live out their lives on credit. O'Flaherty relates a number of horrifying anecdotes to back up his point that the gombeen man has brutalized peasant life beyond belief. His tourist will see:

> ... these decent peasants, shiftless, dirty, hungry, without a concept of truth or high morality, subservient, fawning, grovelling, terrified of life and death, eager for revenge, envious of success, fickle in their allegiance, unstable in their resolutions, excitable in temperament;

for it is the decent human being who is most easily and surely broken by an overwhelming oppression of this description.[146]

His tract ends with an apocalyptic vision of the damned souls rising from their rural hell to establish a new social order.

The priests, politicians and peasants described in O'Flaherty's *Guide* reappear in the novels more as types than fictional characters proper. His fictional world is built from the society he experienced in his youth and from his own individual, spiritual life. The result is at times disjointed: the reader is aware of a disharmony between the two. His priests and politicians are burdened with the complexity of his own mind, even his own *melancholia acuta*. Typical figures think untypical thoughts and experience degrees of agony and nightmare that flat characterization can hardly contain. In the long gallery of portraits from Fr MacMahon of *Thy Neighbour's Wife* to Kilmartin of *Famine*, the costumes and gestures differ but the agonized faces are all more or less the same. Their prototype is the O'Flaherty of the autobiographies.

CHAPTER 8

LIAM O'FLAHERTY: THE CRITICAL HERITAGE

The history of critical response to Liam O'Flaherty's novels
from the 1920s to the early years of the 1970s presents a
curious picture. In the pages of the *Irish Statesman* he is hailed as a leader of the new realist school, often as the equal of
Joyce and O'Casey. In 1969, in *Hibernia*, a latter-day equivalent, he is applauded by John Broderick as 'Ireland's greatest
living writer' and the equal of such diverse novelists as
Mauriac, Gide, Evelyn Waugh, and Joyce Cary.[147] Between
these laudatory assessments there is the neglect of forty years
broken by the occasional article and review. Both the attention and the neglect seem excessive. Decidedly, O'Flaherty is
not the equal of any of the writers mentioned. Nor does he
deserve the disregard which has resulted in so few of his
novels being currently in print. Confusion as to the scale of
O'Flaherty's achievement is matched by a variety of contradictory critical appraisals. O'Flaherty is a writer of melodrama, he is a realist, a naturalist, a romantic, a symbolist,
most recently an existentialist. Our review of criticism will
indicate the various approaches that have been taken to his
novels in the last fifty years.

O'Flaherty got his first full-length reviews in the pages of
A.E.'s *Irish Statesman*. It is instructive to compare the
reviews of his first two novels, one written before, the other
after his acceptance by the literary establishment. They set
the tone for much future criticism. Aodh de Blacam's sober
review of *Thy Neighbour's Wife* is largely hostile. He links

O'Flaherty with Brinsley McNamara and the realist school. The theme of the novel is the 'conflict of the flesh with religious duty' but his style is too weak to do it any justice. O'Flaherty fails, too, in the creation of his chief character who should embody this conflict and here McNamara's influence is, perhaps, to blame. There is the 'suspicion of mere sensationalism'. Finally 'A. de B' warns the regional novelist against wounding local sensibility by identifying the scene of his fictions too readily.[148] The review of the second novel, *The Black Soul,* is very different and not entirely because it is a better or a different book. In a sense, if O'Flaherty had never been born, the Celtic renaissance would have had to create him — a peasant, Gaelic speaking novelist from the Aran Island who wrote works full of 'primitive' passion! It is in this fashion that A.E. himself greeted *The Black Soul,* '... the most elemental thing in modern Irish literature, written with amazing energy from the first page to the last, the sentences following each other like gusts of wind.... I call the book elemental because ... the primitive passions run free.'[149] (Compare, forty-five years later, Broderick's encomium.) 'The Black Soul ... is breath-taking in its force. Its characters are primitive but human; and its evocation of the island of Inverara in all seasons is both realistic and mythical, like the moors in *Wuthering Heights*.'[150] A.E. supplied both O'Flaherty and his critics with a few key descriptive words — 'energy', 'passion', 'elemental', 'primitive', 'power' and a supposed link with the composers of early Irish legend who asserted a similar sympathy between the spirit of man and of nature. Reaching after comparisons he finds not the dour realist McNamara but Fiona Macleod of the *Barbaric Tales,* and Dostoyevsky. 'The future development of Liam O'Flaherty will be watched with intense interest by many.'

The Informer, published in 1925, fixed O'Flaherty in the public and critical imagination as a fellow explorer with Joyce and O'Casey of 'the slime of the Dublin slums.' He is still regarded as 'an instinctive creator' and is warned that his 'fever of realism must not seduce him towards the monstrous.'[151] The works of the next two years, *Mr. Gilhooley* (1926) and *The Assassin* (1927), confirm critical reaction to *The Informer.* It is worth quoting at length from 'Y.O's'

review of *Mr. Gilhooley* in the *Statesman* as he seeks to place
O'Flaherty in a broader perspective than had yet been
attempted:

> Between Joyce and O'Casey and O'Flaherty we are
> amassing a library of books about the Irish underworld.
> They have turned up the subsoil of Irish life and shown
> us terrible and writhing creatures from which we shrink.
> Have we any right to shrink from *The Informer* or *Mr.
> Gilhooley* in literature? Is the realist as many think the
> enemy of our dream? The idealist imagines his Irish
> humanity and by depicting it he believes after generat-
> ions will fall into the mould and continue the tradition.
> Nearly all the writers of twenty years ago — Standish
> O'Grady, Yeats, Hyde, Colum — were idealists. Then,
> writer by writer, the pendulum swung to the other
> extreme. There seems a kind of inevitability in it.[152]

Taking these five novels, together with three slim volumes of
short stories as a basis for his assessment, the American critic
William Troy wrote the earliest, and in many ways the best,
extended treatment of O'Flaherty. For Troy, O'Flaherty at
thirty-two years of age is already a neglected figure, at least
in America (his bibliography includes only the American
edition of the novels). He isolates two reasons for this neglect
which he claims are inseparable from the value of his work —
his nationality and his use of melodrama. Within the Anglo-
Irish tradition, Troy places O'Flaherty with Synge and Joyce
as against Swift and Shaw but detects his deeper allegiance to
the writers of early Gaelic folk literature. All this is familiar
territory. The main interest of Troy's article however lies in
his second assertion: that the novels of O'Flaherty belong to
the category of melodrama:

> Melodrama . . . might be accepted as the elaboration of
> human motives on a grand scale, against immense back-
> ground, and to the accompaniment of enormous music.
> In terms of function, one might discover in this form
> the most appropriate medium for the working out of
> certain crises or highly intensified human situations, the

proper conditions for which depend on a hightening of the common laws of circumstance. ... It is part of O'Flaherty's distinction as a novelist that he has had the courage, through all his five novels, to adopt what is at once the most dangerous and the most unpopular of literary modes.[153]

Troy supplies two reasons why O'Flaherty should adhere to this mode. His themes demand firstly, the violent conflicts of melodrama and, secondly, the exceptional nature of his environment. Interestingly enough, for an Irish reader, he likens the Aran Islands to 'those western islands around which Odysseus sailed' and Dublin 'often takes on the colors of the Elizabethan version of the Italian cities of the Renaissance.'[154] He goes on to conduct his analysis of the novels in the light of these considerations: *The Informer* is a melodrama of the conscience, *The Assassin* of the intellect. His special praise is reserved for *The Black Soul* where he more or less adopts the same line as A.E., and the article loses much of its brief interest. Troy states, for the first time, what he believes to be the single underlying theme of all O'Flaherty's novels — the conflict between nature and the intellect. This and his examination of the melodramatic mode are of importance for later criticism. *The Bookman* in which this study appeared also published an article the following year, shortly after the appearance of *The House of Gold,* by a C. Henry Warren. There is much padding but the critic does pick out an important element in the whole of O'Flaherty's fiction: *All of O'Flaherty's best writing seems to have as its theme, in one shape or another, the hounding of man. In war and revolution, by the law: in civil life by poverty.*[155] The new novel, *The House of Gold,* is described as 'a kind of pure allegory.'

It is not an accident, one feels, that the most perspicacious criticism of O'Flaherty came frequently from American critics. After all melodrama, allegory, the theme of the hunted man and the conflict of intellect with nature were all leading features of their own novelistic tradition. In this sense O'Flaherty has been more 'visible' to American than to English critics.

The first extended attempt to relate the novels to the life

of the writer and to the Ireland of his day came from the pen of yet another foreign critic, L. Paul-Dubois, in the pages of the influential journal *Revue des Deux Mondes*.[156] It is a remarkable article, not least for the fact that M. Paul-Dubois, with his French sense of the niceties of literary distinctions, tries to grapple with the nature of O'Flaherty's 'realism'. Indeed his lengthy study is entitled *Un Romancier Realiste en Erin,* but he is forced to give realism a rather special meaning to fit the subject of his study.

For M. Paul-Dubois, O'Flaherty is first and foremost 'un rebelle. Le rebelle en soi', and later ' . . . loin de tout ecole et de tout tradition; un primitif, et un refractaire.' He is a realist in his art and the word is used with the special force it had gained in France of dealing with 'low' subjects. Dans les milieux ruraux qu'il a sous les yeux, il ne voit que le cote rustre et sordide, bestial et revolte, la luxure, l'argent, l'apre ambition, l'ioresse ou l'alienation mentale.

M. Paul-Dubois goes on to take up some of the points made by previous commentators and enlarges upon them — the dramatic quality of his writing, the supplanting of a generation of idealists by one of brute realists. He relates both to social rather than literary causes, especially the disillusionment following on the Civil War. At the conclusion of his study the critic makes his qualification on the writer's realism. He detects in him a 'late romantic' — *un romantique attarde* — and a vivid imagination. Beneath the 'hard man', beneath the tough realism of the books, is a sensitive poet: Nous trompons-nous en pensant qu'en ce sens son realisme lui tiens plus ou moins lieu de masque, et que sa 'ferocite' n'est la que pour recouvrir sa sensibilite?

We next turn our attention to the reaction to his novels on the part of O'Flaherty's younger contemporaries in Ireland — Sean O'Faolain, Benedict Kiely, and Vivian Mercier. One has the sense of a ritualistic breaking of the silence about a forbidden subject and, in the case of the first two writers, an act of piety and propitiation. For O'Faolain, O'Flaherty is an inverted romantic, the Don Quixote of Irish letters following an ideal Dulcinea. He blames Don Quixote O'Flaherty for vagueness in defining this ideal and he himself is no less vague in his rhapsodic, impressionistic account of 'my friend. . . '

Benedict Kiely subtitles his study 'A Story of Discontent' and goes on to write of O'Flaherty as a pure romantic forever at odds with the world:

> The dreamer grumbling with dissatisfaction at his own dreams is the funniest, most pitiable object on God's earth, because his own fancies oppress him with a weight heavier than all the woes of the world. He is as pitiable as Dark Daniel in O'Flaherty's one quaint stage-play *Darkness* when he says: 'I have no kinship with people. I'm an ungainly lout.'[157]

Kiely sees the Dark Daniel side of O'Flaherty's genius obtruding again and again in his works and spoiling them artistically. Only *Famine* is free of him, and it is his best work.

The first and only study devoted exclusively to O'Flaherty's novels was written by Vivian Mercier under the title *Man against Nature*. Mercier sees this as the central theme of the novels but a theme presented only in the very simplest terms. O'Flaherty's sympathies lie with the natural man: ' . . . in opposition to nature on the one hand and to civilization and the civilized 'unnatural' man on the other.'[158] Mercier pursues the permutations and combinations of these two forces through the novels. *Famine* he finds to be O'Flaherty's major achievement, which brings him to a question to which he provides an interesting answer:

> What happened to O'Flaherty after 1937, the publication date of *Famine?* Why did the creative drive that had produced twelve novels, three volumes of short stories, and four other full-length books in fourteen years culminate in a masterpiece and then peter out almost entirely after two further, inferior novels?[159]

He finds an explanation in the details of O'Flaherty's biography. His creative outpouring is a form of mental therapy. The *melancholia acuta* of his youth continued to threaten him with madness and he visited upon his deranged characters (his books are full of them) the fate which he feared for himself. With the passing of this fear and a growing kindness to himself and to others, O'Flaherty looses his vital need to create.

This concludes our review of what we might call the informal or occasional criticism of O'Flaherty's novels. It is prompted by either enthusiasm, a new novel, friendship, or the wish to bring a neglected author to the public eye. The academic criticism, with which we conclude, functions largely independently of these concerns.

Two dissertations on Liam O'Flaherty — by Vivian Mercier and Anthony Canedo — are pioneering documents. Mercier, in a dissertation entitled 'Realism in Anglo-Irish Fiction', (Dublin, 1943) treats of O'Flaherty's novels *en passant* as a member of a supposed school of Irish realist writers descended from Synge. His introductory chapters on *In Search of Realism, Daniel Corkery* and *Life and Literature in Modern Ireland* have a permanent interest.

Exactly twenty years after Mercier's work, Anthony Canedo presented a dissertation entitled 'Liam O'Flaherty, Introduction and Analysis' to the University of Washington. This began the present spate of theses on O'Flaherty. Mr Canedo treats the novels chronologically and groups them according to thematic patterns. He finds that all O'Flaherty's work is concerned with themes of alienation: 'His sense of alienation voices a sincere concern with the reality of the divisive forces of the modern world, especially with oppression, to which he was made sensitive by Ireland's long tragic history.'

Two formidable studies which centre around much the same area are J.N. Zneimar's *The Literary Vision of Liam O'Flaherty*[160] and Harold J. O'Brien's dissertation, 'The Representation of Religion in the Fiction of Liam O'Flaherty' (Dublin, 1967).

Zneimar's work is the most exhaustive study to date. It draws on all the material available at the time of writing to determine O'Flaherty's true subject and his characteristic artistic vision. The first part of the book deals with the man and artist, and sketches O'Flaherty's reaction to the Irish literary scene in the 1920s. He treats of the novels in terms of a broad division represented first by a 'black soul' group where O'Flaherty mirrors himself *(The Black Soul)*, and a second group where the writer tries to create characters other than himself *(The House of Gold)*.

Zneimar's study concludes that throughout O'Flaherty's writing the pattern of spiritual crisis is central. His spiritual concerns are essentially a-social. The individual is not so much a product of society or cultural forces but is seen, more radically, in relation to existence. Since this is so, O'Flaherty is not primarily an Irish writer but belongs to the western 'existentialist tradition'. The present work, with its stress on O'Flaherty's Irishness is, hopefully, complementary rather than hostile to Zneimar's.

Harold J. O'Brien's dissertation deals only in part with O'Flaherty's novels and short stories but it is nonetheless highly interesting and stimulating. He takes a sharp, narrow focus, his basic purpose being to ' . . . investigate the representation of religion in modern Irish fiction through an analysis of character and the relationship between character and events in the imagined worlds created by Liam O'Flaherty and Francis Stuart.' He finds that, unlike Stuart, O'Flaherty's imagination focuses on neurosis and hate. Religion, anarchy and neurosis form a nexus in his work. ' . . . Both writers deal with characters searching for the values of the ideal life and colliding with the values of a Juridicial, puritanical version of Roman Catholicism.' O'Brien's study is often highly technical, since his procedure is to analyse the literary devices through which the author reveals his character's response to religion.

CHAPTER 9

THE SPIRIT OF PLACE

Every people is polarized in some particular locality, which is home, the homeland. Different places on the face of the earth have different vital effluence, different vibration, different chemical exhalation, different polarity with different stars: call it what you like. But the spirit of place is a great reality.[1]

The Spirit of Place — a vague but nonetheless 'great reality' — is best rendered by the novel or romance-novel, which are, to a greater or lesser extent, bound up in the local, the immediate, the ordinary everyday world of human experience. The two great co-ordinates of both forms are time and place, the latter being the crossroads of circumstance, the 'local habitation' which gives a reality to character and event. Speaking of the importance of place in the novel, Eudora Welty states:

Place in fiction is the named, identified, concrete, exact and exacting, and therefore credible, gathering spot of all that has been felt, is about to be experienced, in the novel's progress. Location pertains to feeling; feeling profoundly pertains to place; place in history partakes of feeling, as feeling about history partakes of place . . . From the dawn of man's imagination, place has enshrined the spirit; as soon as man stopped wandering and stood still and looked about him, he found a God in that place; and from then on that was where the God abided and spoke from if ever he spoke.[2]

Regionalism in fiction is not a matter of 'local colour', which might be defined as the use of environmental details and characteristics with a picturesque intent. The truly regional work is not only nominally located in a given region but derives its actual substance from it. 'Local colour' will be reported — the natural background, the climate, topography, the flora and fauna even — but reported as these things affect human life in the region. More important, it will draw for its substance on the different patterns of culture and character which operate profoundly on the lives of its people. In a real sense, most works of literature are regional in some respects: we need more delicate instruments of discrimination if we are to mark off literature that has its whole *raison d'etre* in regionalism. Happily, a P.E.N. book by the novelist Phyllis Bentley on *The English Regional Novel* has gone a long way towards providing such instruments. She begins by defining the regional novel: it is the national novel carried to a further subdivision. It depicts the life of the region 'in such a way that the reader is conscious of the characteristics which are unique to that region and differentiate it from others in the common motherland.' She continues:

> To understand the characteristics of the regional novel we must ascertain how far the elements of the novel are affected by regionalism when it is present, how far and how deeply the local colour dyes. I shall define the elements of the novel as *character, plot, setting* and *narrative,* with the *theme* as the circumscribing factor. The theme is the aspect of life the writer wishes to illuminate; the plot is the chain of actions, linked by cause and effect, which exemplifies the theme. The characters are the imaginary but typical human beings who perform the actions; they do so against a background of time and place which constitutes the setting; the whole being related in words so arranged as to form a narrative in prose. Other elements might perhaps be proposed for the novel, other definitions of these supplied; I ask that those I have put forward be accepted in the present

discussion for convenience of reference.[3]

If we begin with a similar plea and apply Miss Bentley's five points to the works under discussion (with the exception of the special case of *The Wilderness*) we see that they readily emerge as regional fiction.

The scene, the setting, of all four is Galway county, more specifically Inishmore, the largest of the three Aran Islands, and the city of Galway. O'Flaherty creates an imaginary topography in interesting ways. There is, for instance, no mention of the two smaller islands, Inishmaan and Inisheer. By concentrating his fictions on the largest island he not only achieves a greater unity but also establishes a nice balance between the wild, primitive island life and the 'Big Town on the Mainland', which poses a constant threat to the islander's way of life. Within Inishmore itself — variously called 'Nara' and 'Inverara' he establishes a further division between the Anglicized inhabitants of the south and the Gaelic people to the west. It is interesting to note the shifts of interest that are reflected in the changing locales of O'Flaherty's romances. *Thy Neighbour's Wife* concentrates on the area round the village (town?) of Kilronan on Inishmore. He next moves to the near-deserted headland of Bungowla for his exploration of naked human passion in *The Black Soul*. Then, as if finding the island too constricting for his purposes he changes the scene in *The House of Gold* to the mainland and Galway City ('Bara'). His explicit purpose is to lay bare the forces at work in post-revolutionary Ireland and hence the need for a broader canvas. The islands figure here as a dim mystery athwart the horizon, a lost *Tir-na-nOg*. Finally, with increased power he returns to Aran, to Kilmurvey, midway between Kilronan and Bungowla and writes his greatest work — *Skerrett*. In all four works the setting is intensely regional; the actions of all take place either on the unmistakable rocky island or in the decayed city of Galway. Long, lyrical passages — especially *The Black Soul* — evoke the beauty and harshness of this highly individual part of the western seaboard. The single, instructive exception to the above is the unpublished short novel, *The Wilderness,* which was serialized in *The Humanist* during 1927. So far as one can judge from internal and external evidence it is set in a valley in the Dublin Mountains. Once again O'Flaherty embodies part of his theme in terms of fictitious topography — just beyond the 'wilderness', twinkle the lights of the corrupt city. The novel was never published because, according to O'Flaherty, it was never finished. One can see why. Despite the many fine lyrical passages there is an almost total failure of realization, it is lacking in precisely that quality, that sense of place, which gives strength and reality to the other works. Although O'Flaherty lives in the region of the Dublin mountains, he does not seem able (unlike Synge) to capture anything of their life. His characters are borrowed from Connemara and even his hero is quite explicitly a migrant from the west of Ireland. One has the sense, reading through *The Wilderness,* of an ever increasing tenuity. This work provides interesting insights in other directions also. Because it is so unencumbered with place, the ideas and metaphysical searchings which occupy O'Flaherty are starkly visible. The illustrator in *The Humanist* in his line drawing for the first episode depicts what might stand as an emblem of the O'Flaherty of the regional romances. A Christ-like figure, arms outspread, the suggestion of a halo round his head, stands almost naked in the middle of a stream. Two goats stand peacefully looking up at him in obvious admiration. Beyond the stream a group of horses, heads held high, are attracted to this charismatic figure. The whole takes place in a wooded valley ringed by high mountains. White pentecostal birds emerge from the trees above the figure and to the left, in the dusky air, black shapes of bat or crow suggest a contrary note of evil. Beneath is the legend: *Can all this beauty have no meaning?*

O'Flaherty's reporting of the outward scene is the result of close knowledge of the history, traditions and folklore of Aran and Connemara. Folklore — everything from belief in the evil eye to the secret worship of the pagan god *Crom Dubh* — is particularly evident in his first book and to a decreasing extent thereafter. Local, traditional character types are the dominant personages in all the romances and these O'Flaherty views most commonly with the sardonic eye of one who has inside information. Some are drawn from life and can be identified even at this distance in time. Many incidents and episodes in the four books, indeed the whole of *Skerrett* and *The House of Gold* are based directly on the recent history of Aran and Galway. This study attempts to demonstrate, particularly in relation to the last named works, the way in which O'Flaherty used this local material which has been independently preserved in the files of provincial newspapers, court records and not least in the folklore of the region. The works, when related to the time and place of their subject matter, gather an added resonance and interest which is lost by a purely aesthetic approach. Experience of life in Galway and Connemara shows that here there are certain situations, for instance the transfer of a schoolteacher or of a village post office — where the characters are as firmly established as the characters in a morality play and the plot as formalized as that of the Japanese Noh. Gombeen Men, Grabbers, Greed and Politics act out their accustomed roles. O'Flaherty is writing about such near-stylized incidents in the regional romances. We must seek to understand both the artist's and regional societies' principle of selection and emphasis.

Next we turn to consider the element of *plot.* Plot, we remember, in Phyllis Bentley's useful simplification, is the chain of actions, linked by cause and effect, which exemplify the theme. In all of the romances, to a greater or lesser degree, the episodes and incidents are intimately interwoven with the way of life of the Aran and Connemara people. As we follow the fortunes of Fr Hugh McMahon in *Thy Neighbour's Wife* we find ourselves involved in the various activities of the farmers and fishermen. When we ask why (as E.M. Forster has taught us to ask of plots) Fr McMahon abandons himself to the sea in the final episode we can only answer it by reference to the peculiarities of life on the island, in particular to the conflict of Christian and pagan values there. More immediately and exactly, he is impelled to his final choice by the legends, the very spirit of *Ara Sanctorum:*

It is told that in the monastery of Cregean standing on the site of what is now called the village of Rooruck, the holy monks had a singularly severe manner for doing penance for their sins. Each evening they set out to sea in an oarless coracle, and allowed themselves to be carried away by the tide. If any of them were in sin he was drowned and if they were in the state of grace, Divine Providence brought them back safely to land. I relate the story as a tradition, but it is firmly believed to this day in Inverara. . . (*TNW* p. 260)

To put our point more bluntly — the setting out of a young Catholic curate on heavy seas in an oarless boat from the North Wall, Dublin, would have vastly different connotations from the same gesture undertaken from Bungowla, Aran Islands ('Rooruck, Inverara'). Similarly, all the major events in this work are inextricably interwoven with the events of island life — the political meeting at the crossroads, Sunday Mass, the secret shebeens where poitin awakens in McMahon an ancient thirst, the Friday confessions where the confessor is himself in the state of sin, 'the sports' — races and currach competitions, and finally the fires that blaze like uncontrolled passions in honour of the pagan gods on St John's Eve.

In *The Black Soul* O'Flaherty brought regional causality to a new intensity. The action of the whole work springs directly from the interaction of the character known as 'The Stranger' and the wild Island of 'Nara'. True, there is another important character, the peasant woman Little Mary, but she is more an embodiment of the natural forces of the island than an individual human being.

The book is divided into four sections, named after the seasons of the year. As Nara moves hesitantly from Winter through Spring and Summer to a rich Autumn, so too does Nature heal the mental wounds of the war-shattered hero and he turns to the fulness of life. 'Ripeness is all.' Throughout there is a poetized version of the Aran landscape, each section beginning with a lyrical description of the island as it is affected by the seasons. The island, in its sheer physical aspect, is an essential part of the action, the story could not take place without it, rather as Egdon Heath is an essential part of *The Return of the Native*.

One of the tests of whether a plot is regional in character or not is to ask of it: does it depend on the region for its causality, could it have happened elsewhere? The plot of *The*

House of Gold turns on the rise and fall of a gombeen man, Ramon Mor, a figure modelled on the owner-manager of Galway's largest firm. Gombeenism is not a phenomenon confined to the west of Ireland but here it was and is particularly virulent. It was in the poverty-stricken area of the Congested Districts Board that the gombeen first flourished and gained his defining characteristics.

This system involved and degraded the whole of the Connemara region. The Minutes of Evidence of the Royal Commission on Congestion in Ireland, taken in counties Galway and Roscommon, reveal yet another quintessential Irish situation with its firmly established characters and formalized plot. The Rev. John Flatley who had served in 'nine parishes along the coast from Spiddal to Achill' and hence had 'an exceptionally extensive acquaintance with the conditions of the people all through that district' gave his evidence on gombeenism to the Commissioners in the following terms: the evidence constitutes a miniature picture of the social and political conditions which O'Flaherty imaginatively portrays in *The House of Gold:*

> 52371 In addition to the want of employment and the scarcity of land and the bad quality of the land there is another cause of poverty to which I wish to call the very serious attention of the Commission, and I believe that it is worse than all the other causes of poverty in the congested districts, and that is the habit which the people have acquired of living on credit and of paying exorbitant prices for the goods that are supplied to them. The consequences are not merely economic consequences, which are very bad, but there are also terrible consequences of another kind to the man who is in debt to the shopkeeper and who is his actual slave. Practically he must elect the shopkeeper or his nominee to the District Council or to the County Council, and every other position that is going, with the most frightful results to the district. Another very bad thing in Connemara, and one which is injurious, is that they have to a very large extent got a very low class of magistrates, who are not the right kind of men to appoint. There are

about 10 or 12 magistrates who are provision dealers. You have most of the District Councillors and County Councillors provision dealers. Without talking of the disadvantage of that to the general community who deal with them it is decidedly unfair to the provision dealers who are not magistrates or members of the Council, and causes a preference to be given to the men who are on the Council or who are magistrates; because the magistrates utilise their position on the bench for the purpose of promoting their business. It is quite a common thing to see magistrates back out their own customers in the face of evidence. They do not look upon it as a thing to be ashamed of, although it is a most flagrant injustice, but as an advertisement for their business. That is a very well recognised thing all over Connemara, and on account of this there is tremendous rivalry among shopkeepers, and intriguing and canvassing going on for years and years to try to get on the bench as a means of promoting their trade by the way in which they act unfairly in support of their own customers. And not only is this so, but it is a well known fact that magistrates go to the length of coaching witnesses as to the evidence they will give before the court, and an awful curse in this district, at all events before we got this present doctor, was to use influence with drunken doctors to give such evidence as would either bear heavily upon or tend to make light the charge against people in assault cases. So that it is not only economically but socially a large number of magistrates in the district are the greatest curse in it. I say that deliberately from a knowledge of the facts, and I am not alone in my opinion on that subject; and the wonder is that the country is so peaceable considering the injustice that is done very often in the courts. When people could not get justice in the courts they took justice into their own hands, and there is a great deal of that prevails in this part of the country. I have often been struck with what Hallom says in his History of the Middle Ages, that most of these disturbances arose from the fact that it was impossible to get justice in the courts.

52373 What you want to impress on the Commission is that one of the causes of poverty and one of the causes of perpetuating congestion and keeping the people from rising is an inflated and exaggerated credit system — is not that what it all comes to? — Yes.

52374 Is there anything in the nature of truck in the business of shopkeeper and people? — Yes, very extensive. The shopkeeper gets their cattle and their pigs and sometimes gets holdings of land. Within the last month I saw a specially endorsed writ issued for shop goods against a tenant so that his holding might be seized.

52375 If a customer wants to buy tea we will say, and to sell eggs, they are exchanged? — Yes. The eggs are sent to the shop and he gets tea and sugar in exchange for the eggs. And when a man is in debt to the shopkeeper the shopkeeper will watch his cattle at the fair, and he will buy the cattle, and you may be perfectly certain that the shopkeeper will not pay too much for them. Here is another way in which it works out. The origin of a good many shops in Connemara, Achill and County Mayo is that a man got a contract for a bridge or a road or some public work for the Government. Immediately he got the contract he started a shop just beside the work and paid the people, not in cash, but altogether in truck. That is a very common thing through the place. Several shops commenced in that way, and men who were very poor when they got their first contract are very well off to-day, and they are the graziers and the grabbers of the country.[4]

We have given Fr Flatley's evidence in some detail as it provides the immediate local background for *The House of Gold*. O'Flaherty traces the further development of gombeenism in this work and in the figure of Ramon Mor has given Anglo-Irish literature its finest portrayal of the gombeen type. Like *The House of Gold*, *Skerrett* is built around another classical situation from the Irish countryside — a dispute between the two powers of every parish, the National Schoolmaster and the parish priest. *Skerrett* is a fictional account of a series of events stretching over some fifteen years, that constituted a *cause celebre* in their day. We have pieced the evidence together from a variety of sources and the story that emerges is, in its surface details, substantially the same as the plot of this work. It is a sordid tale of political intrigue, pride, litigation and violence which took place on the Aran Islands at the turn of the century. Much of the story has entered local folklore, though it is one of the tales that people on the islands are very reluctant to tell. O'Flaherty's brief prophetic chapter which concludes the book has largely come true:

> Thirty years have now passed since Skerrett's death and already his name has become a glorious legend on that island, where his bones were not allowed to bleach and moulder into substance of rock, that was so like his spirit. His enemy Moclair, who left Nara two years after Skerrett to become bishop of the diocese, has also become a legend; but his legend grows less with the years, while that of the school-master grows greater. (*S* p. 274)

'Father Moclair' (Fr Faragher, later Canon Faragher) did not, in fact, become bishop of the diocese but achieved the next best thing, a canonry and the Parish of Athenry. He lies there in an unmarked grave and his successor is not even sure of its location. (Older residents of Athenry derive a certain grim satisfaction from the forgotten grave). Since the material available on both men and the events they precipitated is, comparatively speaking, quite extensive, our examination of *Skerrett* will provide a useful occasion on which to examine O'Flaherty's re-shaping of local events and character.

'The theme is the aspect of life the writer wishes to illuminate.' To speak broadly and generally the themes of these romances are: the struggle of man against nature, the corruption and alienation of the 'natural man' by civilization, the regenerative power of the natural world, spiritual and fleshly values in conflict, Pagan versus Christian. There is nothing specifically regional in these themes; rather are they of universal significance. Aran or Galway does not become the theme and overmastering interest as The Five Towns are the theme of Arnold Bennett's fiction. This then is our first qualification on O'Flaherty's regionalism — a qualification, incidentally which he shares with a much greater regional novelist, Thomas Hardy.

Two further elements remain — character and narrative. The first is easily disposed of, for we have only to list the 'imaginary but typical human beings' who perform the actions in these works to see them as truly regional in character. They cover the whole range of Galway inhabitants from the parish priest, curates and schoolmaster, through the shopkeepers, 'graziers', returned emigrants and 'spoiled priests' to the small farmers and fishermen who form the centre of value in all of these books. Miss Bentley, in her study of the regional novel elaborates, in relation to Thomas Hardy's characters a scale of value grounded on the character's closeness to the soil: the closer they are, the more vital they are.[5] We might do the same in regard to O'Flaherty's characters with some interesting results. The farmers and fishermen are completely alive, the shopkeepers and burgeoning middle class less so, the professional men are half dead. Oddly enough — and very unlike Hardy — another and perhaps less worthy consideration cuts across this scale. When O'Flaherty deals with the 'eternal triangle' of love relations it is always the lover of *higher* social rank whom he treats of as the superior human being. The Trinity-educated rebel and descendent of the chiefs of the O'Malley's is superior to the Catholic curate who in turn is preferred to the returned emigrant for the hand of Lily in *Thy Neighbour's Wife*. He prefers, in *The Black Soul,* the University College, Dublin-educated 'spoiled priest' to the fisherman Red John, and in *The House of Gold* a doctor and a disillusioned journalist-cum-rebel are the preferred mates for the enigmatic Nora. Quite unfairly, except on the level of allegory, he makes Nora's husband impotent. The issue is complicated here in that Ramon Mor, despite his peasant ways and origin is, socially, the more powerful man. O'Flaherty, however, exploits the device of impotence — rather as D.H. Lawrence exploited it in *Lady Chatterly's Lover* — to belittle the character he disfavours. This raises a large question about the morality of these works — in each of the three romances impotence is used in similar fashion. One could press the argument along the same lines as an argument about the

morality of *Lady Chatterly's Lover,* basing one's case not at
all on the explicit portrayal of sexuality but on the point that
the author simply fails to do justice to the opposing forces
and characters in his work. A virile gamekeeper or I.R.A.
gunman is not the equal, in sexual matters, of a crippled Lord
or Irish parliamentarian. Works where social classes and attitudes are typified in this way fail to hold together, in Yeats's
marvellous phrase, 'reality and justice'. The complicating
factor here is, once again, 'reality'. If one accepts the almost
Platonic notion of correspondences that the romance form
demands, that the good, for instance, are always the beautiful, then it is equally imperative that one should accept the
proposition that gombeen men are always impotent, (there is,
too, a traditional belief, held in Ireland and elsewhere, that
the avaricious are impotent). Ultimately one is forced into
making the perhaps abstruse point that O'Flaherty was cen-
sored by the Censorship Board and reviled by his neighbours
because of their failure to distinguish between the Romance
and Novel form! Sadly, we must admit that the case is not so
simple. O'Flaherty himself seems confused on this issue and
thought of publishing *The Black Soul* as a pornographic novel.
The problems raised by his methods of characterization will
be broached in a detailed examination of the relevant works.
It is sufficient to note, at this point, that the characters are,
at least, regional. One further minor point is worth mention-
ing, that the very titles of these works come — with one exception — from a mind haunted by phrases enshrined in the
doctine and the liturgy of Irish Catholicism. 'Sixth, thou
shalt not covet *thy neighbour's wife*' (the Ten Command-
ments), ' . . . Tower of Ivory, pray for us. *House of Gold,*
pray for us . . .' (the Litany of the Blessed Virgin Mary). *The
Black Soul* and *The Wilderness* are catch phrases of every
missioner's sermon. The exception — *Skerrett* — is the family
name of one of the Ten Tribes of Galway, 'City of the
Tribes'.

We come finally to the actual *words* of these romances. Do
the characters speak in a regional way, preserving the rhythm
and idiom of the spoken language? How largely does dialect
bulk in them? Ultimately our question becomes: how oral are
they?

There is an immediate objection to the authenticity of the
oral quality of O'Flaherty's works which has been most
lucidly stated by Vivian Mercier in an essay on 'The Irish
Short Story and Oral Tradition'. It is worth giving his case in
full as he raises several important points and account will
have to be taken of them:

> As for Liam O'Flaherty, he is a native speaker of Gaelic
> and therefore born into the oral tradition, but, paradox-
> ically, he is also the least oral in his approach to narrative
> of all five writers. I agree with Frank O'Connor's state-
> ment that O'Flaherty's English "lacks the distinction
> and beauty of his Gaelic", but — even in Gaelic
> O'Flaherty writes far more for the eye than he does for
> the ear or the speaking voice. Why is this? One's first
> answer must refer to individual temperament: O'Flaherty
> writes as naturally for the eye as the mature Joyce
> wrote for the ear; it is no accident that *The Informer*
> provided the outline for one of the most admired films
> ever made in Hollywood. I could point to thousands of
> passages in O'Flaherty's novels and short stories which
> are seen through the eye of a camera; two notable
> examples occur to me at once, the murder scene in *The
> Assassin* and the short story called 'The Laming', though
> every one of his animal stories is also conceived in cine-
> matic terms; O'Flaherty resembles no single writer so
> closely as he does the late great documentary film
> director Robert Flaherty, who filmed so many of his
> namesake's subjects in *Man of Aran*.
> I would suggest a second reason, connected with the
> revival of Gaelic, to explain why O'Flaherty is so
> exempt from the influence of the oral tradition: he is
> literate in Gaelic, and doubtless has been so since his
> earliest years in elementary school. In contrast, Carleton
> was completely illiterate in Gaelic until the day he died;
> some of the phonetic equivalents for Gaelic phrases that
> he uses in his stories might well make a Celtic scholar
> weep. Whereas a Carleton, by his own avowal, is con-
> stantly transferring oral Gaelic into written English, an
> O'Flaherty may translate visual images directly into the

written symbols of whichever language he happens to be using at the moment. Serious problems arise, however, when O'Flaherty has to write English dialogue for Gaelic-speaking Aran Island peasants. The reader will search in vain for the cadences which Synge put into the mouths of the same peasants. But Corkery, O'Connor, and O'Faolain are literate in Gaelic too; why do they not suffer the same handicap as O'Flaherty? The answer is that for all practical purposes these three are illiterate in Gaelic, in the sense that, not being native speakers, they would never dream of attempting creative work in that language. For them it is a tongue which one speaks and listens to, doesn't perhaps read very much, and almost never writes. Thus it can serve as a touchstone for the language which one writes constantly and speaks so habitually that one can no longer hear what one is saying.

Another problem which faces the native speaker of Gaelic when he writes prose fiction in his mother tongue is the absence of literary as opposed to oral native models. Gaelic society died or fossilized before emerging from the feudal stage, so that there never was a middle class to demand or supply the realistic novel. Sustained narrative prose of any kind in Gaelic was until recently a desperate venture: a celebrated eighteenth century attempt at autobiography can only be described as allegorical romance, while a political satire of the same period almost inevitably took the form of a burlesque hero-tale. These are not clever devices, as they would be in English writers of the same period; the Gaelic writers simply cannot present their own experience more directly because they know no precedent for doing so. As the late Professor Gerard Murphy has written: 'Though our knowledge of ancient Irish story-telling comes mainly from manuscript versions of the tales, there can be little doubt that Irish narrative tradition has on the whole been essentially oral.'[6]

A few remarks may be made by way of clearing the ground for further discussion. Firstly, Mercier is here specifically dealing with the short stories. However, there can be no doubt but that he would hold that his description applies equally well to the longer works ' . . . the least oral in his approach to *narrative* . . . ' It is certainly true that within the limits of what is considered 'oral' by Mercier (the relationship between the storyteller and audience being the indispensable component) O'Flaherty is not outstanding, despite his direct access to and use of oral material. His second point is less valid. O'Flaherty does indeed write 'as naturally for the eye as the mature Joyce for the ear' but this quality of 'pictur-ization' is as old as Gaelic narrative itself: *Once the girl's (Deirdre's) foster-father was skinning a calf on the snow out-side the house in winter to cook it for her. She saw a raven drinking its blood and said to Leborcham: 'I should love a man with these three colours — hair like the raven, cheek like the blood and body like the snow.'*

O'Flaherty develops this quality to an extraordinary extent, so that much of our discussion of these romances will be in the cinematic terms stressed by Mercier. Our critic's final point — that the Gaelic writer lacks literary as opposed to oral models is largely true (Keating's *History* not except-ed). He fails however to bend the argument back to O'Flaherty. Since this is so, is it not likely that he would have recourse to many of the procedures (apart from narrative) of oral liter-ature? The paradoxical and rather brilliant insight that O'Flaherty is *less* oral in his use of words than O'Connor, O'Faolain *et alii* because of his proximity to the oral Gaelic tradition need not be extended beyond this matter of the rhythm and idiom of the spoken tongue (in all other respects he is certainly more). There is the final observation that must be made: we are speaking of degrees of proximity to oral tradition. Our unquestioned assumption is that such a prox-imity exists.

This concludes our introductory review of the romances as regional fiction. We turn now to examine them separately and in such detail as their worth and interest demands. *The Wilderness* is not by any means as great a work of art as *Skerrett* and hence it will occupy less of our attention.

Thy Neighbour's Wife[7]

O'Flaherty's first published novel is set on Inishmore ('Inverara') a few years prior to the Great War — about 1910. In many respects it is apprentice work, but it is important as his first critique of island life (and, by implication, of Irish life generally), and as revealing future possibilities.

Something of the greyness and heaviness of this work — as indeed of all the works treated in this section — derives from the time and place of its setting. The years between 1891 and 1916, between the death of Parnell and the Rising, have, on the surface at least, a dull, uneventful character. The enigmatic quality of this period has been well caught by Conor Cruise O'Brien:

> It was a time in which nothing happened; nothing except (as we find when we look into it) a revolution in land ownership, the beginning of a national quest for a lost language and culture, and the preparation of the two successful rebellions which were, among other things, to tear Ireland in two. Yet despite these momentous events it is not only to us with our memories of school history that the period seems empty: it seemed so to many contemporaries. For James Joyce, as we know, the seething Dublin of 1904 was 'the centre of paralysis', a place in which the maudlin mumbled helplessly about 'poor oul Parnell'. From its own very different point of view, the Ascendancy saw things in a rather similar light: the native Irish and especially the *Babus* were squabbling interminably among themselves, showing their unfitness for self government.[8]

Thy Neighbour's Wife captures much of this squabbling and something too of the emerging cultural and social revolution, however dulled and blunted by the surrounding ignorance and apathy. The protagonist, Fr Hugh McMahon, is depicted as a poet of sorts, and his obviously Celtic Twilight poem, *The Death of Maeve,* has been a critical success ('as good as anything from the pen of Mr. Yeats'.) The representatives, lay and clerical, of the United Irish League who come to the island to 'rally Inverara to a man behind the Home Rule Programme' have to brook the opposition of the Irish Republican Brotherhood, 'later known as the Sinn Feiners'. The steamer which connects the island with 'The Big Town on the Mainland', brings over, in the course of this work, temperance preachers, Congested District Board Inspectors, Home Rulers, Gaelic League propagandists 'in kilts and spectacles and long hair', and Government officials. In short, the organizations and societies which were shaping the destiny of the nation all impinge on the island. The revolution in land ownership has already taken place prior to the action of the book and is attributed to the efforts of the parish priest, Fr O'Reilly: 'They claimed that it was due to his efforts that the Congested Districts Board purchased the land from the landlord, though of course it was the Land League agitation did that.' (*TNW* p. 14)

When the book opens, the efforts of the 'progressive' islanders are shown as directed at the industrialization of the island by means of a kelp factory and the maintenance of the fishing industry 'on a sound business footing' (O'Flaherty employs the cliches of business and journalism with deliberate ironic intent). Unmoved by such activity and giving the period in question its appearance of paralysis — Dublin, we remember, was, in Joyce's estimate, simply the *centre* of the general ailment — stand the peasantry: ' . . . spitting zealously while they discussed the weather, fishing and the price of pigs.' (*TNW* p. 12)

To a great extent, therefore, O'Flaherty's first book is rooted in the realities of its time and place. Indeed some of the characters are readily identifiable. The parish priest, Father O'Reilly, and his niece, Lily, with whom the protagonist falls in love, are, respectively, Father Faragher and his niece, Lily Faragher. Many of the minor characters, government officials and inspectors, are drawn from life. The earnest and, as presented, half lunatic Protestant minister ('Inverara had turned his intellect into incipient idiocy') is probably the Rev. William Kilbride, author of a learned article on the antiquities of the island. The two principal male characters, Fr McMahon and Hugh The O'Malley, have, however, a more equivocal relation to reality. To state it baldly, McMahon is a portrait of what O'Flaherty might have become had he accepted Holy Orders and stayed in Ireland; O'Malley is a portrait of what he would like to be. In a sense they represent two sides of a divided psyche, one passive, introspective, timid, the other outgoing, aggressive, courageous. In *Thy Neighbour's Wife* however, the balance between opposing forces, objective and subjective, action and contemplation, society and the individual, is not maintained. At the centre of the book, dominating it, is the priest protagonist, Fr McMahon. In essence it is the melodrama of the solitary soul working out its damnation from the point of view of the narrator's ironic stance. Held in the mind, the book breaks into two halves which remain, for the most part, distinct and unconnected. There is the torment of the young curate whose vocation is endangered on the one hand by the arrival on the island of a former girlfriend, and on the other, by the life of the island. The *vignettes* of caricature and incident in which *Thy Neighbour's Wife* abound are often simply 'background'. When the two halves do irradiate one another it is on the level of abstraction — a peasant is an emblem of Endurance, Fr O'Reilly of Power, McSherry of Lust. McMahon's *iter fabulosa* is beset by the traditional emblematic beasts. This is not to say that O'Flaherty is failing in the novelist's task of creating a complex web which illustrates man's social and personal relationships. Given the nature of his material and of his concerns, he could hardly do otherwise than adopt the romance form. To put it at its simplest, all the social and natural forces can only be made to act against the celibate, isolated priest.

Fr McMahon is not a native of the island where he serves as curate. Thus, from the beginning, he is a stranger to the islanders and their way of life. He is a Dubliner, a member of the rising middle class whose father has died of alcoholism (the hereditary drunkenness will be made much of). Just as the earlier nineteenth-century Irish novelists were in the habit of bringing a cultivated Englishman over to Ireland and describing his reaction to the wild natives, so O'Flaherty is faced with the problem of familiarizing his readers with a remote region. McMahon is a typical figure, at one with the younger clergy of the day in his secret sympathy with the

political and social aspirations of the people but afraid to express this openly in face of the Catholic Hierarchy's intrans-
igence. Jim Larkin's socialism, roundly condemned by his
superiors, is too revolutionary for his taste. Instead he owes
allegiance to a vision of ' . . . a great Irish Catholic Republic,
an Ireland that would again become the torch of learning and
sanctity for the whole world.' In him Religion and Nationalism form a nexus, a unified vision which he hopes can be
realized through the education and elevation of the peasant
people. Watching his parishoners coming to Mass he feels
' . . . a sudden surging of piety and zeal for his priesthood and
pride in himself and his flock. . . . Those peasants, they were
his to train, to educate, to rouse, to make the vanguard of the
great Catholic Republic of Ireland.' (TNW p. 40)

His belief is identical with the messianic idealism that
animated the poets of the 1916 Revolution. But he does not
yet know his peasants as the ironic narrator does. The action
of the novel, his passionate involvement with the heroine,
Lily McSharry, and the dirty game of local politics will
destroy the vision and drive him to seek a more fruitful soil
for his messianic zeal.

O'Flaherty presents him as an intellectual and poet steeped
in the notions and outlook of the Celtic Revival. Here too, it
is suggested, there is a contradiction. In a moment of crisis
when he seeks to draw solace from his conception of himself
as poet, all other roles having failed, he is reminded of the
words of a Dublin critic: ' . . . that a priest could not write
poetry, since his imagination was carped by reverence for
dogmas.' (TNW p. 202)

Like many intellectuals of his day Fr McMahon is interested in Irish folklore and history and he contributes learned
articles on these subjects to clerical magazines. As he moves
through the island on his priestly duties, he is haunted by the
shattered remains of Early Christian Ireland. The ruined
monasteries and oratories inspire him to the task of rebuild-
ing what has been lost through centuries of oppression. But
he is unaware of another, older and stronger tradition
symbolized in the novel by the ruins of the pagan fort of
Coill Namhan (Dun Aengus) and the fires lit by the peasantry,
ostensibly to honour St John but in fact to placate the pagan

god, Crom Cruach. Only painfully does he come to a knowledge of the pagan world without and the equally unchristened
world within of his own passions. Throughout, McMahon is
harshly treated; his intellectual arrogance and egotism are
everywhere contrasted with the simple lives and values of the
common people.

The seeds of his ultimate failure are to be found not only
in the falsity of his ideals but also in his ignorance of his own
nature. He is described and portrayed as a man of strong
passion and of a highly sensitive nature. His passion and sen-
sitivity make him vulnerable to the beauty and desires which
his training and role as a priest would demand that he abjure.
Early in the novel, in a flashback, he is shown to us as a man
who followed the abstract call of religion and personal
ambition rather than that of human love and contact. The
return of Lily McSharry as a young bride to the island
awakens old memories. She had been in love with him during
his student days and his renewed love for her precipitates the
events of the novel. The flashback is instructive of the kind
of connections which O'Flaherty makes and maintains
throughout — that paganism, nature and the life of the senses
are one, and over against these stand religion, abstraction and
spiritual aridity. Lily and the young clerical student are
shown standing on the brink of a cliff looking over the sea:
'It (the occasion) was like an opium dream, beautiful and yet
with the suggestion of sin and impurity that made it hateful.'
(*TNW* p. 24)

The beauty of the girl and the sexual feeling she arouses
are associated by the young man with sin and the devil. Lily,
on the other hand, is linked by the author, through the
imagery used, to the sun and the sea. As the setting sun
spreads a long phallic gleam on the water, so the girl's blushes
make her radiant. McMahon turns his back on the sea and
Lily, rejecting her love through what is known in the casuistry
of the Church as 'human respect'. He endeavours to forget his
own nature by means of the time-hallowed practice of the
seminarian — a novena to St Joseph and a pilgrimage to
Lough Derg.

The arrival of Lily on the island where he is now curate, in
the company of her middle-aged husband, introduces a new

and unprepared-for factor into McMahon's stable world. Sexual passion for Lily revives and becomes the third driving force of his existence. It is in terms of these three impulses — Love, Nationalism and Religion — that O'Flaherty treats the fate of his protagonist. Stated thus, they are on the level of abstraction and it is precisely on this level that McMahon tries to wrestle with and unite them. It is his fate to discover that they are not amenable to such a process, that in the ordinary and everyday life of man, categories and classificat-ions do not maintain the clear lines of demarcation they maintain in thought. Thus the leading Republican on the island, Hugh O'Malley becomes Lily's 'lover' (though in an a-sexual, 'Irish' sense of that word). McMahon's devotion to the Republican cause is complicated and finally erased by sexual jealousy. As a celibate priest he abhors the notion of adulterous love, so his priesthood is called into question. O'Flaherty plots the priest's agonized vacillation between the three impulses until finally, driven by drink and despair, he abandons himself to the sea.

The love theme is central to the book; for by rejecting Lily, McMahon has, in O'Flaherty's terms, rejected life. His celibacy is literally unnatural and nature takes its revenge. With the exception of a few comic peasants, Lily is the only character in the novel to survive unscathed from the shafts of irony which the narrator directs liberally at everybody else. Character is, perhaps, the wrong word to apply to Lily. She is more a cipher, the Fair Lady of myth and folklore imprisoned by an ogre. She refuses to allow her husband, always referred to as a beast, his conjugal rights and is dis-gusted by his libertinism. He is — in Aran terms — of monstrous parentage, as is revealed at the end: 'I'm a priest's bastard, curse you, you devil's breed, you, Reilly and your whore of a niece.' (*TNW* p. 335) In O'Flaherty's Manichaean world the sexes become emblems of salvation and damnation. Here Lily, as Persecuted Maiden, is at once a saviour and tempter. The bringing together of these opposing archetypal roles is exemplified in the following passage that contains an echo from yet another Manichaean world — that of Hawthorne' *Scarlet Letter:*

But the impulse of love at last gained the mastery, for
its object was there in the flesh, striking his senses by its
presence, appealing to him with the force of reality
that neither religion nor patriotism could muster in their
own defence, and even though his love was clothed in
the repulsive garment of sin, clothed in scarlet and
labelled in letters of fire 'Thy Neighbour's Wife' it was
the strongest passion of all. In that smile on Lily's lips,
when she looked into the face of Hugh O'Malley, the
curate thought he saw the smile of the Devil, mocking
his victim. (*TNW* p. 76)

McMahon's relationship with Lily is developed on a pattern
of melodramatic scenes followed by agonized interior monologues. It is not our purpose to follow the ups and downs of
the relationship in any detail, only a few salient features call
for comment. First there is the extreme melodrama of
presentation and description. The central episode takes place
on the cliff top, dominated by the ruins of the pagan fort,
Coill Namhan. The ruins, through an accumulation of
imagery and allusion, have become a potent symbol of the
pagan 'natural' life. There is even a cliff fisherman, ' . . . the
spirit of the Tuatha De Danaans . . . ', hardly distinguishable
from the surrounding rock in his grey homespuns, to provide
a mute commentary on the action. McMahon and Lily meet
by accident-on-purpose outside the fort. A wordless battle of
wills ensues that reads like the worst excesses of Victorian
romance, ' . . . waves of thought clash and founder against
one another, . . . waves of accusing thought, waves of scorn-
ful thought, turbulent eddies of mockery and deep rolling
breakers of revenge . . . ' (*TNW* p. 204) The priest realizes
that he has lost her love irrevocably as she walks past him.
Once inside the fort, which the priest has never entered, Lily
meets O'Malley, and the two, caught in the sensuous music of
youth and the magical circle, make their first shy approaches
to each other.

The final love scene is stagey in the extreme and represents
an interesting failure of nerve on O'Flaherty's behalf. At the
island sports meeting Lily and O'Malley confess their affection while being overheard by Fr McMahon. Lily hesitates to

go off with her lover while her despised husband lives. Promptly a messenger arrives to announce his death. O'Flaherty in this melodramatic fashion avoids the crisis to which the logic of the story is bringing him. Had Lily committed herself one way or the other, one could point to some significance. But the *deus ex machina* which absolves her from a choice draws our attention to the author and prompts questions about him. It is noticeable that at this point there is a very definite closing of the ironic gap between the narrator and the lovers. Irony is abandoned and the narrator shows sympathy for their plight. In so far as the novel has a moral centre this is it. Our difficulty, however, lies with the fortuitous death of McSherry. The term 'subversive imagination' is usually used to refer to that power of the imagination to subvert a publicly proclaimed moral scheme, usually the Christian. In, say, Richardson's *Clarissa* one sees readily enough that the laboured and lengthy condemnations of unchastity are in fact a dwelling on and a loving sympathy with the facts condemned. It is the 'pagan' glorification of body and sensuality which by implication O'Flaherty proclaims. Yet it would seem that at a deeper level the code of the Catechism constrains and thwarts the development of such a creed, at least its imaginative development. One might with some justice speak of O'Flaherty's subversive, Catholic conscience. A further contradiction is worth noting — that the novel depends for its full melodramatic effect on an audience which is riddled with the very prejudices, narrowness and puritanism which the ironic narrator condemns. Otherwise the emotion demanded is vastly in excess of the deed, the horror expected absurdly out of proportion to the evil narrated. A novel creates its own audience. The ideal audience of *Thy Neighbour's Wife* must contemplate the violation of clerical celibacy, drunkenness and any form of extra-marital sexuality with extreme horror and repulsion. That such an audience was available to it, at least on Aran, is revealed by O'Flaherty's nephew, Brendan O hEithir:

B'amhlaidh a leigh cailin a bhiodh i mbun an ti, le linn do mo thuismitheoiri bheith ag muineadh scoile, ceann da chuid urscealta. Chuaigh se ag faoistin ina dhiaidh sin agus duirt leis an sagart gur leigh si droch-leabhair. Mar chuid da pionos aimsire duirt seisean go gcaithfai an leabhar seo a scrios. De thimpist glan a thainig mo mhathair uirthi agus i ar ti cead eagran, sinithe, de *Thy Neighbour's Wife* a chur sa tine. Coinniodh na leabhair faoi ghlas ina dhiaidh sin.[9]

(It happened that a girl who was in charge of the house while my parents were away teaching read one of his novels. She went to confession after that and told the priest that she had read a bad book. As part of her penance the priest told her to destroy the book. By pure chance my mother came on her and she about to put a signed first edition of *Thy Neighbour's Wife* into the fire. After that the books were kept under lock and key).

Politics bulked large in the imaginative prose of nineteenth-century Ireland. True to that tradition, O'Flaherty also debates 'The Irish Question' but with a voice grown cynical and weary. The diverse political strands of the novel are neatly brought together at a public meeting held to support the Home Rule Campaign. Once more the scene is a 'scene' in the most literal sense. Characters are grouped dramatically according to their political allegiance or lack of it. The resulting tableau is best described in terms of a stage set. Centre-stage, in the village square, is the main platform containing the Home Rulers, chaired, inevitably, by the parish priest. In dramatic opposition to the main group Hugh O'Malley and his physical-force nationalists begin a counter-demonstration to one side. Between both platforms are the peasantry and residents of Kilmurrage with a hapless force of three Royal Irish Constabulary men trying to keep the King's peace. The scene thus conceived offers plenty of opportunity to show dramatically the clash of political opinion and expose the bad rhetoric of political debate on both sides of the Irish Question. The narrative description directs the reader's sympathy at every point to the peasantry whom both platforms harangue to no avail. Unsure of what King or Queen is on the throne of England, they can only appreciate those powers that affect them intimately — namely the powers, spiritual and temporal, invested in the parish priest. Only once have they been deeply stirred by political agitation, when the question of ownership of the soil of Inverara was at stake during the Land League campaign. Their solution to the problems raised at that time was brutally direct. Disdaining rhetoric, they simply shot the landlords. Their single tradition of political action is assassination. The present meeting is enjoyed as a mere spectacle and they are prepared to applaud the best actor. The break between platform and populace is further emphasized by the fact that the peasants speak only Irish while the people on the platform, with the brief exception of O'Malley, speak only English. It is perhaps the most terrifying image of Irish politics in action in all our literature. Hugh O'Malley comes closest to representing the aspirations of the people, not on the basis of any political philosophy but by right of heredity. His analysis of Irish society has at least the virtue of simplicity. Two classes retard the advance of the nation. Firstly the Gentry ('dissolute, roystering, ignorant scoundrels'), secondly, the priests and politicians. The solution: shoot them. O'Malley's eloquence draws on all the cliches and tired maternal imagery of nationalistic rhetoric. The narrator places his eloquence in its true perspective when he moves into O'Malley's mind as he descends from the platform. Ignoring the admiring glances of Lily, O'Malley sees instead ' . . . serried ranks of soldiers, shouting 'Mailleach Abu' with himself in front on a black charger, leading them to victory.' (*TNW* p. 76) By-passing Lily he grasps the withered hand of Dr Cassidy who congratulates him: 'That's what they want, men to bare their bosoms to the bullets with a song on their lips.' (*TNW* p. 76) Dr Cassidy is suffering from senile decay. By implication so are the ideals he shares with the young Republican.

The platform party of priests and politicians is designed to show that Ireland is indeed a country where God and Ceasar go hand and hand. They are united more by a common hatred of Socialism and Republicianism than any dedication to Parliamentry methods of solving the national problem. Considine, the principal clerical speaker, views all opposition to the Home Rulers as the work of the devil. Socialism, in particular, is ' . . . trying to quench the sacred lamp of Holy

Religion on every holy hill of holy Ireland.' (*TNW* p. 81) The
tone throughout is sentimental, pious and self-congratulatory.
The political content of all the speeches, lay and clerical, is
monotonously the same. The priests have been in the vanguard of every movement for Independence and are to be
trusted with the present one.

Father McMahon attends the meeting and is alienated by
what he sees and hears. The intellectual curate is revolted by
the shabby rhetoric, and confused as he becomes aware of
Lily's growing infatuation with O'Malley. When the square
empties as the meeting draws to a close, we are left with a
final image of such barren politics. It is deserted except for
the solitary figure of an old peasant, ' . . . who sat under the
monument smoking his pipe, like another Rip Van Winkle,
left aged and lonely amid the relics of the forgotten past.'
(*TNW* p. 88)

The religious theme is all pervasive. It is best considered in
terms of two crucial episodes; the curate's Sunday Mass and
the final episode of the book, his putting out to sea in
a currach. First, the curate's Mass. The ironic narrator begins
by drawing attention to a monument in the church grave-
yard, emblematic of the conflict he will show dramatically.
It was erected in memory of a temperance preacher 'who had
converted the whole population of Inverara to teetotalism
for three days, or the duration of the mission.' (*TNW* p. 38)
The monument, and the transience of the preacher's effect
illustrate the contrary feelings: while reading the 'prayer
before Mass' the curate wonders:

> . . . whether, after all, religion had any real hold on the
> islanders, beyond the reverence they had for it as some-
> thing they could not understand, and which was supp-
> osed to help them without much effort on their part.
> There were the old pagan customs they still maintained,
> relics of the pagan religion that St. Patrick found in the
> country, the worship of Crom Dubh, who still had a
> special Sunday to himself in early autumn. (*TNW* p. 44)

The narrator arranges the visual details in such a way as to
leave us in no doubt that Crom Dubh has bested St Patrick.

Once more the scene is stylized and exploited for dramatic effect. The priest, isolated on the altar, thinks of Lily; the congregation beneath him, which includes Lily and her husband, follow their own wayward thoughts and on a wooden gallery the men of the parish indulge in obscene conversation. The narrative technique throughout is cinematic and there is an attempt to render the priest's psychological tensions in terms of montage — the chalice over which he spreads his hands in blessing becomes Lily's head and her face hovers on the page of the open Bible. Torn between love of Lily and his religious ideals, the priest is reduced to a state of animal torpor which the narrative compares to that of ' . . . a bullock being herded to the slaughterhouse, that rushes wildly hither and thither in an effort to escape, and then giving up the effort succumbs wearily and stands with downcast head and foolish look, waiting for the death-blow.' (*TNW* p. 53) This is the kind of metaphor which has no place in the novel of manners. It finds a context for human action on the level of animal life. It is a context invoked again and again in O'Flaherty's works.

Like the protagonist of a morality play, O'Flaherty's heroes are poised between heaven and hell, the ministration of grace and the temptations of Satan. Their immortal souls are at stake rather than any mere social consideration. It is characteristic of them to magnify and distort everything they touch. The quality of McMahon's emotions at this point in the narrative may be gauged from the following representative passage:

He was trying to empty his soul of the wild torrent of passion that he felt was going to overwhelm him. He was crying aloud, like a prophet in the wilderness, casting his voice to the four winds of heaven, appealing for help against his temptation. His soul was contracted in an agony of pain, fearful of the chasm that stretched before it, magnifying the chasm, so that if it did fall, if it did succumb, if it were defeated in the struggle with sin, its conscience would understand that it did not fall without a superhuman struggle. (*TNW* p. 58)

The imaginative decor is that of high melodrama; the repitit-
ious rhythms of the passage emphasize the excess. The effect
of such tension is to drive the curate to drink, which takes
on all the melodramatic connotations of that villain of the
Victorian stage, the Demon Gin, breaker of homes, cancer of
the realm. This use of drink as a device to heighten tension
and call forth the wildest emotions is repeated in most of the
succeeding novels.

We can perhaps hear some of the author's uncertainty
about the final scene of the novel when he moves into
McMahon's mind as the latter contemplates a way out of his
difficulties: 'Ridiculous he murmured, melodramatic,
vulgar. . . . ' and later: 'I should have been an actor.' (*TNW*
pp. 306, 308).

The presence of the omniscient narrator alone saves the
denouement from being ridiculous, melodramatic, and vulgar.
Driven to despair, Fr McMahon decides to put God's will to
the test in the manner of the monks of the Golden Age, *the
peregrinationes pro amore Dei*. In a frenzy of religious
emotion, and stupified with alcohol, he puts out to sea in
what he imagines to be an oarless currach. A storm arises and
he recites aloud to the rising wind and sea the *Dies Irae, Dies
Illa*. Again it is a powerful, if hysterical, image of what
O'Flaherty loathes. The storm has the effect of bringing him
to his senses; he discovers that there are oars in the boat and
with the help of some fishermen he pulls to the shore. The
discovery of the oars seem to him a miraculous intervention
by God whom he has promised to serve in China, if spared.
Next morning he tells the parish priest of his decision and
asks to be released from the parish in order to join the
foreign missions: 'He became again the priest, the intellectual.
But he was a cleansed priest now, a purified priest. He had
passed the test . . . His poetry, his nationalism? Nothing
mattered but the Church.' (*TNW* p. 348) The narrator spares
no irony to reveal the emptiness of the curate's decision.
There is a strange contradiction at the heart of this final
episode. It seems that, in the course of the storm, McMahon
is on the way to a transformation, that O'Flaherty will
release him into a more authentic existence: 'The curate died.
The intellectual died. The visionary died. The drunkard died.

The lover died. The pious shrinking priest . . . they all died. There remained but Hugh McMahon the man, the human atom, the weak trembling atom. . . . ' (*TNW* pp. 342-43)

Yet our last view of McMahon is of him standing dripping wet, announcing to Father Reilly his intended mission to China. It is a contradiction of the same order as we noticed in relation to O'Flaherty's treatment of the love affair. The novel is torn apart by contradictory impulses, at once pro-Christian and anti-Christian, moving in the same breath towards rejection and acceptance. O'Flaherty's next work, *The Black Soul* resolves these contradictions to some extent, only to discover other, perhaps more abiding ones.

The Black Soul[10]

In *A Portrait of the Artist as a Young Man,* Stephen Daedalus, conscious of an Ireland and a tradition he has never known, notes in his diary for 14 April:

> John Alphonsus Mulrennan has just returned from the west of Ireland — European and Asiatic papers please copy. He told us he met an old man there in a mountain cabin. Old man spoke Irish. Mulrennan spoke Irish. Then old man and Mulrennan spoke English. Mulrennan spoke to him about universe and stars. Old man sat, listened, smoked, spat. Then said:
> — ah, there must be terrible queer creatures at the latter end of the world. I fear him. I fear his redrimmed horny eyes. It is with him I must struggle all through this night till day come, till he or I lie dead, gripping him by the sinewy throat, till . . . Till what? Till he yield to me? No. I mean him no harm.[11]

Liam O'Flaherty, in the person of his protagonist, 'The Stranger' of *The Black Soul,* grips that sinewy throat and makes the symbolic old man yield his life. The European (though hardly the Asiatic) papers which noticed his return were, like the young Stephen, and with some justice, derisory. But for O'Flaherty himself it remained 'the song with which

I hoped to storm the highest heavens.' The collocation of 'song' and 'storm' typify the work. It is at once his most lyrical and confused evocation of the struggle for life on 'Inverara'. Set beside *Thy Neighbour's Wife,* it presents a more abstract, naked appearance showing, as it does, the interaction of a few emblematic figures against a background of symbolic scenery. The world of the first novel is a half-forgotten memory: 'Gone to hell. Gone and forgotten. There isn't a trace of them. The last of them (The O'Malleys) devil take him, he had queer notions in his head, I hear, ran away to America with a slip of a flighty woman. And there you are.' (*BS* p. 58) Only the peasantry have survived, if anything more brutalized and degraded than in *Thy Neighbour's Wife.*

The Black Soul is divided into four sections corresponding to the four seasons of the year. In Winter, season of death and sterility, *The Stranger* arrives at Rooruck (the isolated village whence Father McMahon made his dramatic voyage). He has come to stay with the beautiful Little Mary and her savage husband, Red John. Their marriage, need it be said, has not been consummated. Red John is impotent. The time is a few years after World War 1 and the achievement of national independence. 'The Stranger' — Fergus O'Connor by name — is suffering from shell shock and acute depression. His body is wasted by debauchery and he has come to Rooruck for a rest cure. Little Mary falls in love with him. Laden with repressed guilt and the residue of his war experience, he refuses to respond to her and turns to heavy drinking. He is briefly attracted to the intellectual and puritanical daughter of the local magistrate, Kathleen O'Daly. In Spring, the season of awakening, his lust is roused. He makes love to Little Mary but is subsequently disgusted that an intellectual, such as he, has been brought low by an ignorant peasant woman. In Summer, his lust flowers into love and he begins to loose pride in intellectual attainment ('I am a part of nature'). Their mutual love reaches fruition in Autumn when Red John goes mad and, in a struggle with O'Connor, dies of a heart attack. The lovers, like all of O'Flaherty's island heroes, flee to the mainland. Thus, in a blatantly obvious way, there is an analogy drawn between the seasons and O'Connor's return to physical and psychological health. There is further a correlation, not sustained at the very end (we will discuss this later) between the protagonist's growth in sexual awareness and fulfilment and his spiritual rebirth. It is the most Lawrencian of O'Flaherty's books, but to say that is to be aware of the difference. O'Flaherty, by comparison, is gross, mechanical and, except where he writes of nature, insensitive and self-indulgent. If it is a 'Song to storm the highest Heavens', it is also a 'Song of Myself'.

Reference to the autobiographical volumes establish the point. There is an almost exact similarity between the character, career and theorizing of 'The Stranger' and the O'Flaherty of the Autobiographies. (Significantly, there is no ironic gap between the narrator and protagonist as there was in *Thy Neighbour's Wife*). The figure of Red John, the mad peasant who is exorcized at the end, is particularly interesting in this regard. It would seem to be a case of character-doubling in the sense that Miss Havisham and Estella of *Great Expectations* or Ahab and Fedallah of *Moby Dick* are not two characters but a single essence. Red John is O'Flaherty's 'madness' incarnate. This, taken in conjunction with the strange, atavistic strain of the novel in which human identities sometimes seems to merge with the forms of nature, point to what W.J. Harvey calls 'psychic decomposition':

> This process, wherein our sense of duality between self and world is diminished and in which discrete identities merge, we may call psychic decomposition. By this I mean that process whereby an artist's vision of the world is such that it decomposes and splits into various attributes which then form the substance of disparate characters. But the relative solidity of individual characterization does not quite conceal the fluidity of the original vision so that the characters exist not merely in the context of normal human relationships but also unite in them common reference back to a single imaginative vision from which they emerge and which, so to speak, still envelops and overflows their individual outlines.[12]

The 'single imaginative vision' from which all else emerges in

The Black Soul is the Stranger's education into the knowledge that: '... the only real thing in the universe was life itself, the act of living. Nothing else mattered. No particular expression of life was important but life itself.' (*BS* p. 47) An analysis of the novel must oscillate between the 'relative solidity of individual characterization' and the 'fluidity of the original vision'.

The character of Fergus O'Connor is in many ways similar to that of Fr Hugh McMahon. They are both intellectuals and writers, alienated by the ignorance and materialism about them. Unlike McMahon, O'Connor despises both Nationalism and Christianity as relics of the childhood of human thought. His 'Black Soul' is the civilized, intellectual part of himself which wars with 'instinctive' life. The conflict between an intellectual-rational ideal of man and a mindless abandonment to nature which tears the protagonist apart is objectified and rendered dramatic by his vacillation between two women, Little Mary (the flesh) and Kathleen O'Daly (the spirit). The personages translate easily into allegorical figures, because O'Flaherty makes little effort to humanize them.

Little Mary is the illegitimate daughter of Sir Henry Blake of Blake Castle on the mainland. Her mother, Blake's housekeeper, is herself the illegitimate daughter of a Breton smuggler. She is a 'natural child' twice over and her wild longing for love and life breaks through all social restraint. Despising her repulsive husband, she turns to the stranger from the mainland for fulfilment and release: '... her primitive soul was as merciless as nature itself. The tender growth of civilization had never taken root in her mind. Her love raged mightily. Like an ocean wave there was nothing either within her or without her to stay its progress. It must satisfy itself or shatter itself in death.' (*BS* p. 132) She is Lily of *Thy Neighbour's Wife* born again as a peasant woman, the myth incarnate of Woman as saviour and protector: '... his weary brain stared at this new sensation ... of being purified by the presence of a beautiful woman, of being cared for, of being protected spiritually.' (*BS* p. 74) She has magical powers of healing and possesses a charm of remarkable ancestry (from a Tuatha De Danaan warrior *via* a Firbolg princess!). Something of the grotesqueness, largely if not wholly unconscious, of the novel is caught in the fact that the charm is used to assist O'Connor to recover from a hang-over. Spring has a predictable effect on Little Mary, transforming her and filling her young body with vitality. Relentlessly it drives O'Connor to make love to her and she gives herself to him: ' . . . freely, like nature. She received from nature the clean gift of satisfied womanhood.' (*BS* p. 131) There is no attempt to individualize their lovemaking or place it on the basis of a personal decision. Rather is it the outcome of an impersonal process, above and beyond choice.

Little Mary's rival for the heart of O'Connor is the university educated Kathleen O'Daly. She stands to Little Mary as Red John to O'Connor, an alter-ego, the embodiment of other possibilities. She too has her magical attributes, a siren whose violin ('thats classic music!') draws O'Connor with hopes of intellectual companionship and understanding. No real balance, however, is maintained between the two girls: 'She was the emblem of what he had left, of what he had thrust from him . . . she was almost a spirit. She was the personification of memories.' (*BS* p. 115)

It is part of the disagreeable tone of the book that Kathleen is made to fall in love with O'Connor after he is sure of Little Mary. O'Connor/O'Flaherty is God's gift to women it would appear. The stark dualism of flesh and spirit lends, as might be expected, an hysterical aspect to the sexual relations portrayed. O'Connor, filled with remorse after he has made love to Little Mary 'tore his hair and bit the bed-clothes with his teeth.' Only at the end, in the penultimate climax of the book is there a moment of peace when, locked in one another's arms, they find the 'enduring love of mutual necessity.'

In many ways the most interesting relationship in the book is that obtaining between Red John and O'Connor. Red John is a grotesque uncouth figure, the first of O'Flaherty's inarticulate madmen. As O'Connor grows in sanity and recovers his manhood, Red John sinks into madness and terror. The cuckold tries to grapple with the change in his wife in terms of superstition. O'Connor is the devil, Little Mary is enchanted by the fairies. In marrying her he has violated not only the laws of nature but also the wisdom of

the folk: ' . . . don't make your house on a hill; don't marry
a beautiful woman.' (*BS* p. 48) Caught in a situation beyond
his comprehension, he reacts with violence, first against his
enemy and finally against himself. In the course of one of
these struggles O'Connor comes to a realization of the true
nature of their conflict:

> He was not afraid of physical hurt from Red John. He
> was not startled by seeing him standing naked against
> the wall. It was not that made him horror stricken. It
> was a sudden thought that flashed across his brain, when
> he looked into Red John's insane eyes. It was the
> thought that there was a kinship between his own soul
> and that of Red John, that he himself was mad like Red
> John. It was like seeing a photograph of himself taken
> during a nightmare . . . . 'I am insane,' he muttered. And
> he was seized with a frenzy that made him stiffen
> against the grinning idiot opposite him, who had torn
> the devilish secret from his breast. He raised his hands
> and hissed, about to grasp Red John by the throat.
> (*BS* p. 225)

Red John escapes and races, half naked, towards the cliffs.
The long final scene of the book the pursuit of Red John by
O'Connor, deserves some attention. It is a second climax,
coming after the climax of the love relationship and points
to some uncertainty on O'Flaherty's part as to the real nature
of his concern. It is not in the arms of his beloved that the
'Stranger' comes to rest and insight but astride the dead body
of Red John.

The narrative description of the concluding episode is
laden with images of crucifixion, resurrection and rebirth.
The whole village sets off over the crags towards the Hill of
Fate in pursuit of the lunatic. O'Connor takes the lead and
eventually is left in sole pursuit of Red John who leaps from
ledge to ledge demoniacally brandishing a knife. Scenically
the chase is very melodramatic and reminds one of nothing so
much as the cliff-hanging episodes in Boucicault's *The
Shaughran*. Unlike Boucicault, O'Flaherty makes very good
use of his stage props, investing them with a symbolic

significance. A convenient bulge in the cliff-face halts
O'Connor and the narrator moves into his mind to reveal his
thoughts. If nothing matters but life itself, purposeless
motion, why rescue Red John? The obstructing boulder
grows in O'Connor's mind to be a symbol of the mental
blocks that have kept him from living to the full. He moves
forward: ' . . . neither because of honour, morals, principles,
religion or sense of duty. It was merely instinct that said "Go
ahead and you will feel clean. Go back and you will have to
keep arguing all your life in order to prove you are not
dirty".' (BS p. 240)

The structure of his decision is remarkably similar to
that of Father McMahon. O'Connor closes with Red John,
they struggle, and Red John dies, his throat 'shivering like the
gills of a dying fish.' Astride the corpse of his alter-ego
O'Connor affirms his belief in life: 'He doubted no more. The
nightmare that had haunted his soul had vanished. He feared
life no more.' (BS p. 248) What, we are forced to ask, of the
philosophical broodings which have so tiresomely occupied
O'Connor for much of the book? Stated briefly they are that
man is a part of nature and life is motion without purpose:

> It was clear to him now that the only real thing in the
> universe was life itself, the act of living. Nothing else
> mattered. No particular expression of life was important
> but life itself. All expressions of life were transitional
> and ephemeral, like the star-fish fighting the periwinkle,
> or the embrace of the crabfish, on the building of the
> Pyramids, or the death of Christ, or the conquest of
> Gaul by Ceasar. (BS p. 187)

As stated, it is not a very remarkable philosophy and receives
more convincing treatment in the Autobiographies.

On the whole, The Black Soul is a disappointing book, for
many reasons. Even in the purest romance, 'the action begins
invariably in the solid world of actuality before it moves into
a divergent region.'[13] Here we begin with a symbolic landscape and return to — what? Little Mary and O'Connor flee
to Dublin but Dublin is simply a cipher for the unknown.
The Stranger's vision of what constitutes society is hysterical

and gross — it is a lunatic asylum. Is he then returning to madness and worse, bringing Little Mary with him? The unsatisfactory ending teases the mind with such questions but provides no answers directly or indirectly. O'Flaherty has settled for a conventional 'happy ending' that fails to do justice to any of the issues he raises.

The virtues of *The Black Soul* are largely those of *Thy Neighbour's Wife* — close and often very beautiful descriptions of the natural life of the islands. Since the second novel is set against a cosmic rather than a social background, these virtues are especially marked. Nature becomes dynamic, actively involved in the fate of the characters. The novel looses a great deal, however, in the portrayal of character in action. The 'character doubling', previously commented on, frequently results in rather simple allegory in which the characters are little more than personifications of spiritual and psychological forces. Structurally *The Black Soul* is a much more unified and coherent whole than *Thy Neighbour's Wife,* which tended towards episodic intensity. Both novels share a common debility — the weakness of the central figures. Father McMahon and Fergus O'Connor are presented as intellectuals in an inhibiting environment. Yet the reader can never quite believe the claims they or the narrator make for them. In a moment of insight O'Connor speaks of 'cheap cynicism and intellectual piffle' and the reader, regretfully, notes it as an accurate description of much in both novels. Taken together they do, however, represent a basic dialectic in O'Flaherty's treatment of the human condition — man as a social being and man isolated against the great primeval backgrounds of earth and sky. His work moves between these two poles and his best novels — *Skerrett* and *Famine* — represent a synthesis of the opposing views. Here they are held in isolation. Fr. McMahon moves against a tapestry of social life. Fergus O'Connor, The Stranger, is silhouetted against the earth and sky.

The House of Gold[14]

In the course of a discussion on Mr Eamon De Valera's

policies recorded in the autobiography, *Shame the Devil,* Liam O'Flaherty remarks: ' ... his (De Valera's) present economic policy was detailed by me in my novel The House of Gold.' 'Economic policy' needs a very large interpretation indeed if the phrase is to do anything like justice to the variety and scope of the novel. It is a broad, greatly flawed canvas, portraying the emergence of the middle class from the peasantry in post-revolutionary Ireland, about 1929. To accomplish this O'Flaherty has, perforce, to leave the restricted community represented by the Aran villages of his first two novels. He moves to the 'Big Town on the Mainland' which he calls 'Barra' (Galway City) and his principal characters are newly urbanized country folk. The islands are now a pawn in the game of mainland politics and commerce, their people an object of curiosity for their strange dress and customs. 'They looked alien'.

The House of Gold represents, in some respects, a considerable step in O'Flaherty's development as an artist. Hitherto one character held a dominant position and the other characters tended to fade into insignificance or become merely allegorical. Here he introduces four main characters and integrates them into an extremely complex plot. The novel is no less than an attempt to give a complete picture of all the social elements – the Church, the professions, the shopkeepers (better, the gombeenmen), the peasantry – that are struggling for power in the Irish countryside. The historic backdrop of the novel is the change from the aristocratic, almost feudal society of pre-revolutionary days to the sour 'grocer's Republic' of the 1920s. Consequently it is crammed full of the most varied life, and since it is so dramatized that the action takes place in one day, perhaps there is too much of it. The basic characterization and situation is reminiscent of that portrayed in *Thy Neighbour's Wife:* the beautiful, fatal young woman, the dashing young rebel, the rich, sexually frustrated husband, the drunken priest. They are involved in a plot so complex and in the end, where the plot gets out of hand, so banal, as to seem absurd in summary.

The House of Gold belongs to what is almost a *genre* of Anglo-Irish fiction – The Big House Novel. From Maria Edgeworth's *Castle Rackrent* (1800) to Aidan Higgins's

Langrishe Go Down (1967), Irish writers have used the great houses of the Protestant Ascendancy as a focus for their exploration of history and the rise and fall of social classes. Thomas Flanagan remarks that: 'Land and the great houses were at the core of the Irish question. Grievances over lands lost, the guilt attached to the possession of land, social status, religion and political loyalties, even the issue of personal identity were bound together: and in consequence, a plot involving land, houses, titles and heirs had an intrinsic social relevance.'[15] Indeed the social and cultural history of Ireland from 1800 forward can be plotted, emblematically, by the rise and fall of the Big House. The successive tenants — Ascendancy landlord, impoverished rake, upstart agent and finally a peasant proprietor risen from the turmoil of the 1920s — is an image of that history. Many of the novels and plays dealing with the theme came to an end actually and symbolically with the burning of the houses during the revolution and Civil War.

A few great houses survived and the emblem was given a further lease of artistic life as an ironic setting for the *gaucherie* of the new men who came to wealth after 'the Troubles'. The demesne of the de Burgo's where Ramon Mor Costello of *The House of Gold* now lives with his unwilling wife, withered mother and lesbian sister is one of these:

> The drawing-room was very large. It was cluttered with furniture. The furniture did not suit it. Everything lay about pell-mell. Colours contrasted violently. There were too many photographs on the mantlepiece. The walls were covered with pictures that are sold by the dozen in furnishing shops. Over the mantlepiece there hung an enormous portrait of His Holiness The Pope of Rome. The Pope had his hand raised, as if he were blessing Ramon beneath him on the hearthrug. As this was the room where Ramon received his guests, the parlour of the house, all the heirlooms of the family were ·therein gathered, including a spinning wheel and the blackthorn stick brought from Dublin by Ramon's father, as a souvenir of Daniel O'Connell's Birth Celebration. The head of O'Connell was carved on the knob

of the stick. (*HG* pp. 90—91)

Ramon is, in the vivid language of the countryside, a
'grabber'. He took possession of the lands and house when
those who actually fought the revolution had to emigrate.
This then, is the first meaning we have to ascribe to the
rather enigmatic title of the book. There is another meaning,
held in ironic juxtaposition to it. The phrase *House of Gold*,
as already pointed out, derives from the litany of the Blessed
Virgin. By an accumulation of image and symbol it also refers
to Ramon's wife, the golden-haired Nora. In this novel, as in
no other, O'Flaherty succeeds in bringing together his
obsessive sexual theme of impotent husband, beautiful wife,
lover and the larger social issues which concern him. If the
social history of nineteenth-century Ireland can, to some
extent, be bodied forth in terms of the fortunes of the Big
House, there is also a crude sexual metaphor. The sons of the
Great House raped the daughters of the peasantry. In better
(or worse?) times the rebel peasant climbed the walls of the
estate and had a midnight assignation with the daughter or
lady of the House. Or it could work the other way, the son of
the House stealing out to meet his village mistress, frequently
with disastrous results as we know from *The Lily of Killarney*.
In part symbol, in part wish-fulfilment, the ladies of the Big
House have played a large and unexplored part in our literature. One could hardly begin such a study with a more
luminous example than Nora, wife of Ramon Mor. She is the
symbolic flame that burns at the heart of the emblematic Big
House, Jung's *anima* whose fair locks turn to 'golden snakes
as thin as hairs' in the moonlight over Galway. The four
main, male, characters of the book revolve round her, seeking
to grasp and hold her. Despite adultery and a bastard child,
she remains, like her sisters in American fiction, inviolably
innocent.

Nora, unlike the other characters, belongs to the world of
the Big House. She is a daughter of a midland landlord who
hoped to restore his fallen fortunes by marrying her to
Ramon. He attracted her by his sheer brute energy as a member of the new parliament in Dublin: ' . . . this picturesque
figure, this dour business genius, the ruthless type that was

going to put the country on its feet after the revolution.'
(*HG* p. 24) She comes to live with her impotent husband in
the great empty house and from here on her life is mythical.
She lives more in the minds and imaginations of those she
draws to herself than for anything she actually says or does.
Life is a romance, even to herself: ' . . . a glorious tragedy, in
which she acted as the heroine.' (*HG* p. 231) The four main
characters — Ramon Mor, Francis O'Neill, Dr Fitzgerald and
Fr Considine — willingly succumb to her fantasy and are
brought, with her, to perdition. Danvers, the degenerate poet
of Barra, sums up in doggerel verse this disruptive force that
the provincial town cannot contain:

> . . . When you set foot within this town and all the press
> Of admiring eyes fall upon your golden hair
> . . .
> A passion was unbound which boded a menace to the
> town.
> Gold to gold comes running as moths come to the flame
> And lust's dark anger does stain love's holy face.
> (*HG* p. 287)

As mentioned earlier, the plot of *The House of Gold* is a
very complex one and a brief summary is necessary to indicate the relationship between event and character. It is
divided into three unequal sections which the author labels
'Passion', 'Disintegration', 'Nemesis'. The titles indicate the
general direction of the action. Our summary will touch on
the main points only.

On a moonlit cliff whose sepulchral glow is suffused
throughout the novel, Nora Costello meets her lover, Francis
O'Neill. She persuades him to rob her husband, Ramon Mor
Costello. They will meet in the same place the following
night and go off together with the aid of Ramon's money.
O'Neill is the familiar O'Flaherty young rebel, generously
endowed with the author's own background. Ex-clerical
student, ex-revolutionary, ex-journalist, etc., he is at present
living off his father, an aged peasant. As dawn breaks the
two make love and part. Nora, while stealing back into her
husband's estate is accosted by the drunken parish priest and

sexually assaulted by him. Father Considine is not only
drunk but mad, driven insane by his lust for the golden body
of Nora. His vows of Poverty, Obedience and now Chastity,
have all been broken. Nora faints in his arms. Back at the Big
House, Ramon Mor dreams of coming catastrophe and
wakens in an apoplectic fit. Nora is carried in and the doctor
sent for. She tells Dr Fitzgerald about the assault, her
husband's impotence, and that she herself is virtually a
prisoner in the house. There is no mention of her tryst with
O'Neill. Fitzgerald, who is secretly in love with her, agrees to
help. He is a well-meaning fool who has not courage equal to
desire (Nora) nor the courage of his convictions (Communist).
He hopes to seize on the rape and Ramon Mor's cruelty as
ways of exposing the twin oppressors of Barra. As the first
section 'Passion' concludes, we see that Ramon Mor's authority is under attack from another direction. The parish priest
of the islands where seven generations of the Costello's are
buried wants to replace Ramon's gombeenism with George
Russell's (A.E.) co-operatives.

'Disintegration' is largely taken up with a series of blackmails. Fr Considine learns of Nora's infidelity with O'Neill.
He tries to blackmail Ramon Mor into sending her away.
Ramon blackmails him in turn into silence. The priest then
moves to silence the only other person who knows of his
indiscretion with Nora; Dr Fitzgerald. Using Fitzgerald's wife
as an ally, and a threat to denounce him off the altar, he
cows Fitzgerald into submission. Meanwhile Nora is being
threatened by her mother-in-law and is about to flee when
Ramon arrives home from his store. He is still, and despite
everything, hopelessly in love with her. He wants to make a
new start. They drive together into the town in what is to be
a triumphant progress through Ramon's business empire and
a public display of their affection. Ramon has another
apoplectic fit in his office and Nora escapes, ending up in a
church, asleep on the mausoleum of a dead priest. The
section ends with the public meeting organized to set up the
co—operatives. All is going well until Ramon Mor, miracul-
ously recovered from his attack and at the head of a band of
followers, takes over the meeting and wins the people from
the co-operative ideal. Shots ring out as O'Neill and his gang

make good their escape with Ramon's money. Ramon, desolate, goes in search of Nora.

'Nemesis', a brief thirty-seven pages, brings the vengeful goddess in a fury of retribution into the story. Back in the church, Nora awakens, watched from a confessional by Fr Considine. She sets off for the Black Cliff to keep her assignation with O'Neill, followed by the priest. He throws her over the cliff. O'Neill on his way to meet her stops at a pub for a drink. His behaviour alerts a police agent. He is followed to the cliff where he finds blood and fistfulls of hair at the edge. The police carry him away screaming. Ramon Mor, in turn, goes in pursuit of the lost Nora. He finds Fr Considine praying to God for an assurance that in murdering the *femme fatale* he was an instrument of God's Holy Will. Ramon strangles him, has a third apoplectic stroke and dies.

The plot is a piece of hokum but no more so than Tomas O Cathasaigh's story *Lord Wilcaun* where there is a similar blend of the detective novel or thriller with the folklore proper.[16]

Francis O'Neill, despite his superficial characterization in terms of the author's own past, is first and foremost a figure out of legend and fairy-tale — the dark lover of the golden girl. Francis and Nora have a distant but real kinship with Heathcliff and Catherine of *Wuthering Heights*. Their kinship lies in a common ancestry except that O'Flaherty's lovers have little of the dark power possessed by Emily Bronte's. Speaking of the 'two children' figure as it operated in Emily Bronte's consciousness, Dorothy Van Ghent says:

> The *type* of classic form of this figure is a girl with golden hair and a boy with dark hair and shadowed brow, bound in kinship and in a relationship of charity and passion, and with a metamorphosis of some kind potential in their relationship. The beautiful dark boy will be brightened, made angelic and happy, by the beautiful golden girl; this apparently is what *should* happen.[17]

A somewhat similar figure emerges from O'Flaherty's fiction but with qualifications. Rather than kinship between a boy and a girl his obsessive image is of adulterous love between the dark boy and golden girl grown older. The girl is tied to an impotent husband who is presented as a monster or imprisoning ogre.

O'Neill feels himself to be 'followed by a damnable curse', he is 'a waster . . . a cursed fellow'. Lying beside Nora he ' . . . offered a striking contract to the voluptuous repose of her golden body. Black-haired, with flashing, brown eyes, a dark skin taut upon bony cheeks . . . ' Nora's beauty is sinister:

> Her whole body had a golden sheen and, like that precious metal which has aroused the madness of conquest in countless men, her beauty was almost evil in its turbulent influence on the senses. She was terrible in her beauty, like the lovely, golden sea-plants that wind, swaying languidly, around the limbs of a white swimmer and drag him down into their bed, caressing him with many twisting arms. (*HG* p. 13)

There is, as the imagery constantly implies, something deathly about their love. A study on the lines of Leslie Fielder's *Love and Death in the American Novel* would find rich material in this book. Nora and O'Neill make love:

> The moonlight shone upon their enlaced limbs with the sinister yellow glare that candles in the sconces of a bier throw upon an outstretched corpse, decked for the tomb; golden no more, but yellow, the sick colour of corruption. (*HG* p. 31)

O'Neill, true to his mythical role, hopes for salvation through the golden girl. It is a role made grotesque by being played out in Catholic Ireland: ' . . . he had a clear vision of himself, purified and holy, receiving the Blessed Sacrament of the Eucharist. A voice said to him: "Keep her. She is your salvation."' (*HG* p. 32) The lovers made their tryst on a haunted cliff-top. At cock-crow they part, like ghosts, about their separate ways. The *liebestod* theme is pursued to the grotesque end when O'Neill is found 'grinning like an idiot' with a tress of Nora's golden hair clutched in his hand.

The disharmony between the lovers, implied by the emblematic use of colour, is brought further into relief by their different backgrounds. O'Neill has spent his youth in the service of Republicanism and the peasant nation from which he has sprung. Yet it is Nora, child of the world which he sought to destroy, who embodies his deepest wishes 'the riches of the earth which he had never enjoyed'. The political allegory which lurks behind the relationships portrayed is a frightening one.

If Nora represents salvation of a kind to O'Neill, she is a demon in the imagination of the parish priest, Fr Considine. He is, quite simply, mad. As such he could not hold our attention for long were it not for the fact that his madness is a general condition which in him is brought to a high pitch of intensity. The revulsion from sexuality and horrified fascination with it, which is a feature of our literature, is especially acute in O'Flaherty. His priests in the throes of lust exemplify the condition at its most hysterical. That they can so easily and with a certain degree of fidelity invoke the prayers and litanies of the Church in their struggle against the flesh points to the origin of the dilemma. Fr Considine prays against temptation:

> 'Lord have mercy on me. I am being swallowed in the abyss of lust. My will is weak. Take this apple of evil from my sight. Crush this demon. I am unclean like a leper. I dare not raise my eyes to Thy Holy Face. Save me or I perish. . . . Christ! God! Crush this yellow viper. Her arms are about my neck. Crush her or I perish.' (HG p. 37)

Again:

> He talked of serpents and of golden hair and of a tower of ivory and of a virgin. (HG p. 38)

and we remember that the next invocation in the litany after 'Tower of Ivory' is 'House of Gold'. Religion, or at least Irish Catholicism as presented in the figure of Fr Considine, is shown as leading to madness. It seeks to exclude rather than contain sexuality. Nora's death at the hands of Fr Considine is at once a human embrace and a union with the devil. O'Flaherty invokes an image out of folklore — golden hair turning into snakes under moonlight — to bring his themes together: *He drew in his breath through his clenched teeth and then saw golden snakes as thin as hairs, passing back and forth through his teeth, that bit at them, tearing their heads off, until their bodies became limp and swayed backwards, and he lowered his hands to encircle them about the waist and savagely kissed them on the open lips, and then flung them from him . . .* (*HG* p. 322) Considine is also important in the book because of his relationship with Ramon Mor. It is the old and tired relationship of God and Caesar. He is the power behind the throne, preaching in Ramon's interest, inculcating a passive attitude in the people who would otherwise have revolted against the gombeen. In short the priest is a figure straight out of O'Flaherty's demonology, *A Tourist's Guide to Ireland.*

The characters of Francis O'Neill and Dr Jim Fitzgerald are twin studies in failure of a kind different from that represented by Fr Considine and Ramon Mor. In a sense the latter two, imaginatively and actually, never had a chance, overwhelmed as they are by the stereotype of Priest and Gombeen. O'Neill and Fitzgerald, however, are new men, representative figures of the educated and idealistic sons of the peasantry who came to their majority during the revolution. The reality of Irish life after the high rhetoric and idealism which had fed their youth has left both men bitter and cynical. Indeed the young men of *Thy Neighbour's Wife, The Black Soul* and *The House of Gold* are, among other things, imaginative explorations of the quality of life and the lifestyles available to an educated man in the rural areas of Ireland in the first two decades of this century. The gallery of faces — McMahon, the Stranger, O'Neill and especially Dr Fitzgerald — is not a happy one. One hundred years earlier, Maria Edgeworth in *Ormond* (1817) had explored the possibilities open to her young man, Harry Ormond, and found that Irish society presented three possible alternatives to which he might give his allegiance — in Flanagan's summary:

Young Ormond has been raised in a fosterer's cabin, and his quick, generous temper has received no chastening discipline. When he comes to manhood, however, he encounters three possible models. One of these is Sir Herbert Annaly, a resident landlord of English stock. The second is his own uncle, Sir Ulick O'Shane, one of the government's 'Undertakers' and an important figure in the management of national affairs. The third is a second uncle, 'King' Corny O'Shane, a kind of chieftain who leads in the Black Islands the half feudal, half out-law existence of the proscribed Catholic gentry. Ormond lives, for long stretches of time, with each of these and becomes immersed in the three worlds which they inhabit. The worlds are various and they are richly created. . . .[18]

In O'Flaherty's Ireland of the '20s no such variety or diversity of choice is possible. 'King' Corny, less the manners of a gentleman, has moved into town and set up shop. No viable alternative to the middleclass Catholic republic exists and those who fight against its personification, Ramon Mor, are reduced to impotence. O'Flaherty expresses his sense of the aridity of this life through the figure of Dr Jim Fitz-gerald, dispensary doctor to Barra and environs. In many ways he is the most solidly grounded character in the book — if only because he has a wife, children, and a profession and is not afflicted with nameless diseases. His background, too, is credibly sketched in a piece of 'telling' which elaborates in detail on the narrative comment that the 'unknown spirit' who creates souls 'sometimes . . . joins to an uncouth and servile body an alien soul whose dreams are a torment to the flesh that covers it.' In brief, Fitzgerald, son of a poor family, sees with compassion the sufferings of the people and deter-mines to be a doctor in order to help them. When the revol-ution breaks out he joins up. The revolutionaries, having gained their limited objectives, are satisfied but he continues to revolt against social injustice. He is jailed by the Govern-ment, recants and signs an undertaking promising to take no further part in political agitation. Released, he falls ill and is nursed back to health by his future wife. Marriage forces him more and more to deny his convictions in order to keep his job. He sinks into a sour apathy: 'Then Nora came and her coming inspired him with a strange exaltation that sent him preaching to the people of the ideal world which would one day come into being, when mankind should be free from superstition (Fr. Considine) and the oppression of the greedy (Ramon Mor).' (*HG* p. 27)

For Fitzgerald, Nora by her grace and beauty is the embodiment of that ideal world which haunts his imagination and makes him unfit to deal effectively with the ordinary and everyday. When he is first introduced — at Nora's bedside — the narrator explains on his behalf. His face bears a melancholy expression which is ascribed to 'our barbarous provincial life': 'For no punishment can be greater for a refined intellect than to be forced to live in an Irish provincial town. . . . barbarous companionship, an entire lack of social morality, of culture and of intellectual tolerance cause a melancholy that corrupts the strongest mind.' (*HG* p. 76)

Nora has the power of involving him in her imagined world where she is an imprisoned heroine and reawakens his idealistic dreams. But twice in the course of the day he fails to act on information — Considine's rape, Ramon's cruelty — that would expose the oppressors of Barra. His House of Gold collapses when he is made aware of Nora's duplicity: 'Suddenly he hated Nora; . . . He saw how beautiful it was to be a person without the instinct towards revolt, a weak acceptor, living a dull life. He saw the folly of being opposed to Ramon Mor and the priest.' (*HG* p. 226)

Worse, as a doctor, he must attend Ramon, seek to keep alive the monster that crushes him. He is given to philosophizing, and the day's events, coupled with his own inadequacy to meet them, drive him to a view of life similar to that expressed by the Stranger in *The Black Soul.* Chapter XVI, where he arrives at his conclusions, is important for a number of reasons. It is, firstly, the single most sustained piece of analysis in the novel and this analysis and its conclusion are in line with everything we know of O'Flaherty's thinking already. Significantly, it is here hedged round with irony, as if O'Flaherty were seeking to objectify and disassociate himself from his most familiar thought, to 'place' it. Finally, the 'objective co-relative' of that thought is the figure of the struggling insect or minute creature. In *The Black Soul,* as

indeed in *Shame the Devil*, O'Connor/O'Flaherty broods on a
starfish struggling with a periwinkle and leaps to large conclusions about life. Here Fitzgerald watches a spider and
'some kind of insect' struggling for the mastery.

The doctor is alone at the window of his dispensary,
watching the crowds gather for the public meeting to condemn Ramon Mor's system of exploitation. A spider's web
on the window pane catches his attention. An insect has been
caught in the web, spider and insect alternatively attack and
repel one another. Visually, the image of the web and its
combatants is superimposed on the scene outside where
political factions struggle for power. The doctor's attention
shifts cinematically from long-shots of the meeting to close-
ups of the web. In both he discerns a similar pattern of
pursuit and conquest leading to exhaustion. He, as passive
observer of both, is granted the supreme satisfaction of
understanding and insight: ' . . . it became manifest to him
that the desire to appreciate the full sensuous and mental
pleasure to be derived from a phenomenon, by means of
wonder, was probably the main instinct in life.' (*HG* pp.
296–97)

As the spider and insect rest from their struggle with each
other, he compares the anarchy of the crowd unfavourably
with the natural world represented by the creatures in the
web. The creative faculty in man which idealizes human
relationships and, worse, tries to realize the ideal, is seen as
an aberration. The doctor decides on the inward journey of
self-realization (compared to the spider moving about his
own web) as against the outward journey of social action
(compared to the insect who invades the spider's world). All
his relationships are reviewed in the light of this decision. It
was false to have tried to remedy the disharmony of Nora's
life, to have adopted any attitude to Ramon Mor other than
a disinterested wonder at his qualities. Ramon is viewed as a
creative being with the power and energy to match the
creative impulse and thus, in him, it is not an aberration.
Henceforth his attitude to Nora will be one of simple admiration, the kind of static attention awarded to a beautiful
statue. His attitude to life will be to regard it as a work of art,
passively noting colour and contour. The kinetic impulses are

dead in him, all passion spent:

> He would be henceforth indifferent to fame, to the
> opinions of his enemies, to the irritations of society.
> Henceforth he would see that life was good and beauti-
> ful in all its manifestations, when absorbed by the senses
> without fear and judged by an unprejudiced intellect.
> Henceforth evil would cease to have a meaning, since
> even fog, rain and hail were really useful contrasts to the
> sun's heat and light, and therefore a measure of the
> sun's beauty. Existence itself in its simplest form, the
> act of inhaling air into the lungs, would be as beautiful
> as its most complex manifestation, the act of love, fully
> enjoyed both physically and mentally. All human beings
> became beautiful and lovable, each after its kind, one
> by the beauty of its body, another by its wit, another
> by its gentleness, another by its courage, another by its
> ferocity; others acting as contrasts by their cruelty, ugli-
> ness, stupidity, by being diseased, criminal, insane,
> perverted. All their activities became beautiful, their
> marriages, their drinking, their dancing, their sowing,
> their reaping, their dying, their birth, their wailing, their
> laughter, their games, their love, their hatred, their wars;
> all the many-formed movements of their collective life.
> After them came the animals, the birds, the insects, the
> earth itself, the sea, the firmament with its countless
> worlds and its milky way, where the spawn of unborn
> worlds float in space, waiting for the spark of life. From
> whom? That did not matter now, to his mind, ruminat-
> ing on beauty, right to the dissolution of his existence,
> his disembodiment, his decay, his return to the earth,
> the earth's bursting, becoming spawn, which, in its turn,
> floats in space, waiting for the spark of life. From no-
> body. A circle has no beginning once it is completed.
> (*HG* p. 301)

The narrator follows the doctor as he leaves the dispensary
and in a long sentence, scored by subclauses, marches him
out of the story. The narrative description with which he was
introduced was at least indulgent. His exit is made to the

mockery of a few minor characters with the obvious collus-
ion of the narrator. There remains, however, the uncomfort-
able feeling that it is the doctor or somebody very like him
who has written *The House of Gold.*

'Knowledge' or 'insight', then, is the leading term of the
doctor's aesthetic. 'Greatness' is the rubric of the life and
work of Ramon Mor. (Mor = Big/Great). Throughout, the
narrator's attitude towards Ramon is to regard him, not as a
man subject to the moral categories of good and evil (as the
characters do) but as a natural force. (One recalls Marvell's
similar treatment of Cromwell in the *Horation Ode*).
Ramon's power, energy and tenacity is that of the a-moral
stallion, great oak and bull to which he is so frequently
compared. The times are evil, confused by warring political
philosophies and contrary allegiances. Ramon, in one perspective, is the only man to possess the qualities of leadership
and the sheer physical energy to hold this broken world
together. Defending himself against the moral censure of the
priest, he will say:

> 'I have been all my life chained to the wheel, slaving to
> earn my bread. I have built up this business, like my
> father and mother before me, by hard work and by
> denying myself every pleasure in life. . . . How did I find
> the people living? They were living in houses worse than
> pigsties on bread and salt. They were no better than
> savages. It's I put them on their feet. . . . ' (*HG* p. 129)

Dr Fitzgerald has typified him as a Shylock, but Ramon is
rather a Creon who speaks and acts with authority at the
expense of being known and loved. (One might say of
O'Flaherty's fictional world in that it contains many Creons
but no Antigone). The analogy with Greek tragedy is a useful
one, as the peasants who pass under the walls of Ramon's
estate on their way to the fair form themselves into a chorus
commenting on the rights and wrongs of his rise to power.
They fall into two groups, expressing opposite sentiments.
The womenfolk are grateful for all that Ramon has done and
admire his success. ('They were great managers,' said the old
woman, 'They denied themselves and they have the benefit

of it.') The menfolk are envious and hate the materialism and meanness that made it possible ('a fine benefit it is,' cried the big man, 'to be eating their own flesh'). Ode and epode are supported scenically by the great wall and lush fields of Ramon's estate and, opposite, the broken-down cottages of the peasantry, once the out-houses of the estate. A small farmer puts forward the peasant case against the new establishment. The priests and bishops have allied themselves with the new rich. The new rich gain their wealth from owning large tracts of good land ('Drop your stick there at night on bare ground and it will be hidden with grass in the morning'). They raise cattle for export and invest the returns abroad. The common people have gained nothing. The old woman replies succinctly:

> You'd be better off if you minded your land and put a stitch on your wife's back, instead of listening to bladherskite spouted by Republicans from Dublin. (*HG* p. 110)

Authorial silence, unusual with O'Flaherty when such issues are at stake, maintains the balance and tension between the opposite views. Shortly, however, the omniscient narrator uses his privilege to reveal the price Ramon has to pay for his power. Assured in the public world of men and affairs, he is pathetic in the private. He can keep the peasantry loyal by appealing to his blood relationship with them and by promising future benefits. Nora is impervious to such promises. She is purely a creature of passion and Ramon cannot satisfy her. He loves her — but after his own fashion. She is a piece of valuable property, doubly valuable since others desire her. Intent on demonstrating publicly his ownership of her, the two are driven slowly in Ramon's open car through the main streets of Barra. Ramon acts the attentive husband, utterly insensitive to his wife's true feelings. Arriving at his offices, he dismisses her. He is on his own territory. The mental anguish and insecurity which had tortured him is obscured by visions of a glorious future. The narrator follows Ramon about his shops and yards where everything Midas-like turns to gold. The gombeen successor to the departed landlord reaches an almost tragic dignity in his effort to transform the dross of Barra into a golden world — a House of Gold.

The character of Ramon Mor functions at a number of levels — indeed we can often read O'Flaherty as we might read a medieval text. Literally, he is a gombeen man — perhaps the most striking in our literature. Morally, he is a figure of avarice. Symbolically, he is a monster, son of a witch, who enthralls the fair lady, (Nora: 'He is really terrifying. He is a genius. I always know when he is in the house, even though I don't see him or know that he has come in'). It is, perhaps, a mistake to describe the symbolical/mythical level too precisely — although it is only at this level that one can view the work as having any coherence. At the risk of reading too much into the text, it could be suggested that the basic mythical pattern harks back to the classical myth of Polyphemus, Galatea and Acis — a story, incidentally, of which there are numerous Irish folk versions. In Ovid's rendition of the tale (*Metamorphoses,* Book XIII) the ungainly cyclops, Polyphemus, tries to hold the nymph Galatea by a vulgar display of his wealth, but she prefers the poor shepherd Acis. Gatatea is one of the Nereids, beautiful sea maidens, and in some versions of the story she marries Polyphemus after he has killed her lover. Without going into detail it is perhaps sufficient to point out the emphasis in *The House of Gold* on Ramon's single vision ('One of his eyes was closed. The other was wide open and fixed') and on Nora as a creature from the sea to which she ultimately returns.

The chief characters of *The House of Gold* are supported by a host of minor characters, ranging from the wild peasants who descend from the mountains to vivid portraits of civil servants and business people of the town. The whole tone of small-town life is caught in the portrait of Mr Lawrence Finnigan, the leader of local society since the revolution. He is proprietor of the Railway Hotel (today the Great Southern) and his claims to lead Barra society are based on the fact that he is ' . . . chairman of the local branch of the Gaelic Athletic Association, member of the Barra Golf Club Committee, chairman of the local branch of the Licensed Vintners' Association, member of the Third Order of St. Francis and formerly handball (soft) champion of the county. . . . ' (*HG* p. 189)

The bracketed 'soft' places him and his society perfectly. Small town life is portrayed as dull and enervating in contrast with the richness of peasant life. Every time the peasantry enter on the scene – for a fair or a public meeting – the narrator reaches after exotic imagery to point up their vivacity and strangeness. Indeed their arrival into the ugly town of Barra is described by means of an epic simile: 'As when, on the desert wastes of Arabia, the caravans encamp and camels kneel upon the burning sands to drop their loads of spices and of silk, and turbanned merchants sit cross-legged on their carpets and gems are passed from hand to hand . . . ' (*HG* p. 112) Their life is the norm against which we are to judge everything and from which the other characters deviate. In one of the few poignant moments allowed to Ramon he is described as looking:

> . . . with longing at a life of obscurity, at the peasant life from which he had dragged himself, goaded by ambition. The silence of the mountains. The sombre quiet of great uninhabited cliffs. The murmer of summer bees. Village smoke rising straight into an empty sky. The whispering of women huddled by a well at dusk. Silence. Peace. Bowed heads. God. (*HG* p. 62)

As in *The Black Soul*, lyrical descriptions of nature carry a large freight of commentary but here they tend to be overdone and melodramatic in the pejorative sense. The Black Cliff in particular resembles a piece of elaborate stage property which the author has constructed at Enormous Expense and wishes to display over and over again. It shares too the worst feature of *The Black Soul* – great clumsiness and lack of subtlety in the description of inner mental states. A whole troupe of devils, a flail-carrying hunchback and other weird creatures act out a dumb show to portray the tensions that afflict Fr Considine. The glowing sparks and red arrows which afflict Ramon are hardly less crude. The novel as a whole, however, represents a generally successful attempt to show provincial society at work. O'Flaherty's metaphor for that society is the spider's web, used not as in Dickens or George Eliot to denote a network of relationships, but rather a trap, the trammelling cords of which inhibit freedom and happiness.

Skerrett[19]

On 28 February 1914, the following letter appeared in the *Galway Express:*

> *Oatquarter, Feb. 17th, '14.*
> *Dear Mr. Editor, — I was evicted from my residence on yesterday, 16th. inst. at the suit of Rev. M. Farragher, P.P., Aran Islands, for the recovery of his legal expenses in the case of Callaghan v. Farragher. I came to the Aran Isles as teacher in September 1880, and had during my teaching period the following managers: (lists clerical managers) with all of whom my relations were amicable. The late Mr W.E. Gladstone styled an eviction 'a sentence of death'. These sentences were carried out in the past by a few evicting landlords, but it is rather a novel incident for a priest professing national sentiments to play the role of evictor. Trusting you will kindly insert this — I am, yours respectively,*
>
> *David O'Callaghan.*

This letter to the local Unionist paper was the last pathetic shot in a battle that had raged on the Aran Islands since the turn of the century between the parish priest, Fr Farragher, and the schoolmaster, David O'Callaghan. Liam O'Flaherty, who served Mass for Farragher and was taught by O'Callaghan, made their rivalry the subject of what is, with *Famine*, his greatest work. The story, too, entered the folklore of the islands. Elizabeth Rivers in her *Stranger in Aran* records a version of it, and various fantastic elaborations on the same theme have also been noted. There were also two ballads and a mock—epic, now forgotten but preserved in part in the pages of local newspapers, which celebrated the prowess of the various factions involved. The series of events which precipitated such a creative outburst in Galway is of interest to the student of regional fiction for its own sake but our particular interest lies in the aspects which O'Flaherty seized on and the kind of significance he attributed to the leading characters. O'Flaherty builds up the character of Fr Farragher ('Moclair') as an embodiment of 'the will towards civilization' and Master O'Callaghan ('Skerrett') as 'the enemy of society' who 'aimed at being a man who owns no master'.

The following are the facts on which O'Flaherty based his fiction, insofar as we can piece them together. As the letter quoted above reveals, David O'Callaghan came to teach at Oatquarter Boys' School in 1880. Tom 'Flaherty's praise of O'Callaghan's work, especially the fact that he learned Irish and taught his pupils to love and respect their island traditions, has already been quoted (Part 1, p. 45). The general direction of his interests can be gauged from his contribution on Irish folklore to Haddon and Browne's survey of the Aran Islands. It reveals a close knowledge and affection for old ways and old beliefs. He co-operated for some time with Fr Farragher in his efforts to improve conditions on the island, and was secretary of an agricultural bank of which Farragher was chairman. The priest first came to Aran from Mayo in 1887 (hence the gibe 'the beggar from Mayo') and was curate there until 1897 when he was appointed parish priest, a position he held until 1920. If it is indicative of O'Callaghan's interests that we should find him among the recorders of folklore, it is equally indicative of Farragher's that we find his work recorded in the pages of the *Statist,* a London financial paper. He was partly responsible for establishing the fishing industry on the islands and organizing the Aran people into a work force with division of labour rather than the traditional *meitheal.* On his invitation, the Congested Districts Board surveyed the islands, eventually purchased them, and redistributed the land to the landless fishermen — thus breaking down the old system of land holdings. Again, on his initiative, Galway County Council built roads and a large number of County Council houses on the island. He led various campaigns both to pay and not to pay county rates, one of which resulted in the islands being disfranchized. Earlier he had used his influence on the islanders to force

his own importance that when Fr. Farragher would go into the school he would turn his back on him and when he would meet him in the street he would do the same. Talk about autocracy! There was no greater autocrat than the village schoolmaster.

They are classic figures from the Irish countryside involved in one of its most typical struggles.

In 1908 an event occurred on the Aran Islands which drew national attention and shocked headlines — 'The Aran Outrage':

Explosion at Aran Island — Parish Priest's house wrecked — Narrow escape of the inmates — Remains of a bomb discovered — Islanders Indignant — Resolved to find the Perpetrators, etc. etc.[21]

In a dispute over the division of the Digby estate on the island Fr Farragher had earned the enmity of a land-hungry family who, in retaliation, blew up the parish priest's house with a bomb placed in a saucepan. The perpetrators of the 'outrage' were brought to trial and their leader, one Roger Dirrane, sentenced to penal servitude. Fr Farragher had recourse to a more traditional method of bringing his enemies to their knees. He forbade the islanders, from the altar, to have any contact whatsoever with the relatives of those convicted and refused confession to anybody who sided with them. The local branch of the United Irish League was used to enforce the boycott. Dirrane's relatives and friends in the closed community of Aran formed a sizeable proportion of the population. One and all they ceased to practise their faith or pay clerical dues. The enormity of such a step can only be appreciated by those familiar with the strong bonds that bound the peasantry to the Church at the time. The dissenters became known as *'lucht tin-canna'* or 'Saucepans' and were boycotted for upwards of ten years. Divisions and dissensions in a closed community go deep and are long lasting. So much so in this case that the high percentage, even for Aran, of spinsters and bachelors among *lucht tin-canna* is still put down to their isolation from the rest of the community.

Several people were forced to leave the island and in at least two cases attempted suicide and subsequent transfer to a lunatic asylum were attributed directly to the boycott. Master O'Callaghan, too, was one of its victims. He refused to observe the sanctions imposed by the parish priest on his former pupils. Hostility between the two men had come into the open the year before the bombing incident, when Farragher, in an effort to have O'Callaghan removed from the school, resigned as manager. In the years up to 1911 numerous further efforts were made to drive out the schoolmaster but he survived with the help of the inspectors of the Board of National Education. Farragher once again had recourse to his old tactic; he denounced the schoolmaster from the altar and advised parents not to send their children to Oatquarter School:

> ... I would not recommend parents to send their children to that school if they had any other; not telling you not to send them there, but if you take my advice you won't. As you know I have not visited that school for some time, and when the Parish Priest does not visit the school there is something out of place, and I believe the fault is not mine.[22]

When O'Callaghan opened his school in January 1911 none of his 100-odd pupils turned up. He continued to open the school every morning and remained seated at his desk in the empty schoolroom during class hours for several months. In March 1912 he took a slander action against the parish priest for the words quoted above. Efforts to have his case tried in Dublin, away from the influence of Galway clergy and the United Irish League, failed, and at Galway Assizes the jury found that the defendant, Fr Farragher, spoke the words in good faith and without malice. The recovery of Farragher's legal expenses left O'Callaghan a broken man with the results described in the letter which opens this account.

On a number of counts it is interesting to see what O'Flaherty made of this rather sordid incident. In the brief coda to *Skerrett* he reverses the decision of the Galway Assizes or rather points to local legend as reversing it. History dissolves into legend and legend enshrines the greater truth:

> Thirty years have now passed since Skerrett's death and
> already his name has become a glorious legend on that
> island, where his bones were not allowed bleach and
> moulder into the substance of the rock, that was so like
> his spirit. His enemy Moclair, who left Nara two years
> after Skerrett to become bishop of the diocese, has also
> become a legend; but his legend grows less with the
> years, while that of the schoolmaster grows greater. In-
> deed, both men are now only remembered for their
> virtues, while the evil in their natures is forgotten. And
> as Moclair's virtues were of the body, allied to the cunn-
> ing which ministers to the temporal body's wants, so do
> they wither quickly into nothingness. Whereas the
> nobility of Skerrett's nature lay in his pursuit of god-
> liness. He aimed at being a man who owns no master.
> And such men, though doomed to destruction by the
> timid herd, grow after death to the full proportion of
> their greatness. (S p. 274)

Again, since O'Flaherty writes of events and characters which
have a solid existence outside his imagination we would
expect a greater realism than heretofore, and a subordination
of romantic elements. This is indeed what we find but there
is also in evidence a peculiar straining away from the mere
facts. Two sentences from the first page point up the tension.
The novel opens:

> On a wild day in February 1887, the hooker Carra Lass
> brought David Skerrett and his wife from Galway to the
> island of Nara.

A few sentences later we read:

> . . . the sky grew *sudden* clear . . . the wind-filled bellies
> of the sails *near* touched the waves and she seemed *like*
> to founder at each careering plunge. (S p. 5)

The first with its factual statement of time, place and name,
the very essence of realism, is counterpointed by the arch-
aism and biblical tone of the second. The two styles will

merge in the course of the novel, the one lending dignity, the other restraint, to produce O'Flaherty's best-written book.

There is a further respect in which the historic, 'real' events and characters bring pressure to bear on the novel. More than any of the works we have considered so far *Skerrett* is concerned with external conflicts rather than with crises of conscience or soul searching. There is, for instance, no character in the book that we can readily identify with the author or who acts as a surrogate for him. O'Flaherty's personal exploration of life and its meaning, projected into the characters of MacMahon, the Stranger, Dr Fitzgerald, *et alii,* find no place in *Skerrett.*

What of O'Flaherty's obsessive sexual pattern? Do the facts on which he builds his novel resist it? Skerrett is married and in the early part of the novel his wife gives birth to a son. Yet he sees himself moving 'through a dark loveless world, a *gelding* chained to unrewarding toil'. In view of this it is not altogether surprising that in the course of the work his only son dies and his wife becomes successively a drunkard and lunatic. (In fairness it must be added that both these events fits perfectly into the overall pattern of the book). Skerrett, however, remains another impotent hero haunted by a consummation he can never enjoy. Watching a peasant couple, 'He ached at the thought of their beautiful young bodies locked in an embrace at night loin to loin and chest to paps that already swelled with the milk of pregnancy, while he himself lay supine and silent beside one who was repulsive to him.' (*S* p. 30) It is left to his friend, Dr Melia to run away with the fair, faceless Maiden. Melia is an interesting character in that he is purely fictional, created to fill out yet another set of O'Flaherty oppositions, that between action and contemplation. Unable to act himself (except in the matter of the uncharacteristic elopement) he drives Skerrett on to realize in action his vision of primitive socialism.

Finally, it is worth remarking that this is the least *dramatized* of the novels we have considered so far. Apart from two or three wonderful scenes, much of the action and character is given in narrative summary — often very close to the press reports and court records of the events.

Two contrary and contradictory movements are at war

within the imaginative world of *Skerrett*. There is, first and foremost, the life and times of Skerrett who is stripped of everything he possesses until he 'stood alone in a tiny cabin on a lonely crag by the edge of the sea.' His way is the *via negativa* which leads to the 'dark wisdom' that there is 'nothing beyond this unconquerable earth but the phantasies born of man's fear and man's vanity.' (*S* p. 262) The opposite direction, the way of affirmation, is followed by Fr Moclair who waxes as Skerrett wains and whose final achievement is not wisdom but power ('he was undisputed ruler of the island'). Skerrett is a dreamer whose pet subject is a Utopian vision of Irish society based on what he has come to know and love of primitive life. The 'subtle priest' on the other hand is an expert manipulator of men and affairs — 'The islanders prospered with him' — who leads his flock on 'a march towards civilization'. Both men are, in some respects, mirror-images of one another. As the doctor points out, they both want to be king of the island and bring its people in their chosen directions, Skerrett to lead them back to the ancient verities, Moclair to lead them forward to the new opportunities. Again and again we are made aware of the islanders as living in a half-way house between primitive life and civilization — sometimes with grotesque effect, as in the case of the rate collector who 'wore a swallow-tailed coat over a white frieze shirt' and who, when addressing his fellow Gaelic-speaking islanders, ' . . . in almost every sentence inserted an English work or phrase; just like a slightly educated African negro posing before his fellow tribesmen on his return to the bush from a Christian settlement.' (*S* p. 10) There is, further, a rather naive division of the peasantry into the corrupted and the uncorrupted, the minions of Skerrett and Moclair. Before going on to deal with the novel under the three headings of Schoolmaster, Priest and Peasantry it is necessary to notice one large difference between Skerrett and the other characters portrayed. He is dynamic while the others are static. He is capable of change and does change under the stress of inner and outer compulsions. The others are fixed, oppressors or oppressed.

Skerrett's life on 'Nara' falls into two very unequal parts. Indeed the first five chapters, describing his integration into

island life are in the nature of a prologue to the main action.
He arrives, with his pregnant wife, on an island already
dominated by the parish priest and sets about taming (and
cleaning) by brute force the wild schoolchildren of Ballincarrig. Disgruntled and unsettled, he is hostile to the islanders.
Then, when his wife gives birth to a son, his attitude changes
completely. He is filled with love and hope and accepts the
life of Nara. Chapter V gives a narrative summary of seven
years spent in peace and prosperity during which he co-
operates with Fr Moclair for the betterment of his fellowmen.
The tone of this chapter is very elevated. Skerrett is more
patriarch than family man:

> Yea! They were great years for Skerrett, with his school,
> where children learned from his mouth, and his four
> hamlets, whose people treated him as a wise chief, and
> his garden and his house and his little son.

and again:

> It seemed that the fierce soul of Skerrett had found
> permanent peace. From his high hill, he looked out with
> pride on the sphere of his influence, which kept contin-
> ually widening, like the spreading branches of a tree; so
> that even the island, which at first appeared cruel and
> barren to him now assumed a darling beauty. (S p. 41)

It is interesting to note that, given the opportunity to
describe or dramatize domestic life, O'Flaherty turns away
towards the romantic and heroic. Skerrett builds his house on
a hill, makes a garden on the naked rock, teaches his people
by example. There are many biblical echoes, not least in the
language employed ('And lo! The other men of the village,
seeing that the stye was good . . . made similar little houses
for their own pigs'). This marks the high point of Skerrett's
career; hereafter he becomes the familiar O'Flaherty figure
of the Hunted Man. His son dies and he looses faith in life
and in his mentor, Fr Moclair. At the 'offerings' for his son:

> . . . the demon of jealousy found voice in Skerrett.
> Suddenly it appeared evil to him that the priest, whom
> he had thought good and pure . . . should stand greedily

watching coins in the house where his beloved son was dead. (*S* p. 55)

The rivalry and hostility between the two men date from this moment. On the level of moral allegory, never far from the surface, it is a struggle between Avarice (Moclair) and Pride (Skerrett). Everything conspires to pull down Skerrett's pride. His wife, who teaches in the girls' section of the school, disgraces him and is warned by Moclair that her work is unsatisfactory. Later he finds her dead drunk and is unable to prevent her sinking into alcoholism. His friend, Dr Melia, is unwilling to support him openly and he has only one resource left: 'He now tried to come closer to the Gaelic speaking peasants of the West, according as Moclair fortified himself more strongly in the anglicized village of Ardglass. . . . ' (*S* p. 160) The peasants regard him as a crank. He is caught up in the cess agitation and sides with the people against the priest. At a public meeting to decide the issue Moclair calls Skerrett a cur and wifebeater. Heretofore a reformer, the schoolmaster decides to become a revolutionary. For two years he carries out his plan to become one with the farmers and fishermen. He buys a cow and a currach, identifies himself in all things with the people and prospers. But the fates only raise him up to cast him down again. The cow dies, the currach sinks. Skerrett in the eyes of the people is accursed. His wife goes mad and has to be taken to an asylum but not before she has administered a blow to her husband that will eventually drive him to the same place. He comes to blows, literally, with the parish priest at a confirmation examination when he tells his pupils:

> You will grow up in the love of God more by learning to till your land well, to be good fishermen than by learning these (Catechism) answers like parrots. (*S* p. 209)

Dr Melia, his friend and adviser, runs off with the local landlord's daughter, an action that is contrary to all that Melia seemed to stand for: 'Childless, without a wife, tied to a lunatic, unable to remarry, a failure at his profession, scoffed at by the people, watched at every step by an implacable enemy who never let slip an opportunity to wound, he again became surly and brutal in his treatment of the school-children.' (S p. 223) In the course of the perennial land agitation on the island one of Skerrett's former pupils blows up the parish priest's house. A boycott is imposed on any-body who has any contact with the culprits. Moclair seizes on the event to direct popular anger at Skerrett, darkly hinting that he is responsible. Deftly he turns the islander's belief in sympathetic magic to his own account:

> We must treat every one in any way connected with the perpetrators of this crime as social lepers. We must shun them like the plague. And if any man or woman even nods to them in the road, we must treat him or her in the same manner. Band yourselves together and watch day and night. The devil is in your midst, people of Nara. A wolf in sheep's clothing in your midst. Of him, even more than of the misguided scoundrels who threw the bomb you must be aware. It was his teaching that planted the poison in the minds of the criminals. Until we shun this devil and treat him as a Pariah, God will turn His divine face away from us. He will be deaf to our prayers and our land shall be barren. Our seas will refuse us fish. Disease will destroy our cattle. Brother will turn against brother and son against father. We'll be visited by all the horrors that are foretold with the coming of Anti-Christ. (S p. 262)

Skerrett falls ill and begins to rave. He is dismissed from his school and while still a sick man is ordered out of the school residence. He moves to a cottage he has built on the crags at the extreme west of the island: 'For the first time, his arrogant soul took wing into complete freedom and he decided that henceforth not even a belief in God would make him subservient to Moclair.' (S p. 262)

In his own house, at his own hearth, surrounded by the simple people of Cappatagle he experiences a brief moment of peace. But soon his arrogance alienates the villagers and he determines on one last foolish bid against his tormentor. He sets out for Moclair's house determined to strike him down but he is seized as a lunatic and brought to the asylum on the mainland. The final, brief chapter of the novel evaluates these events in the light of thirty years afterwards.

Skerrett is a romance in the modern application of the term. The schoolmaster is the solitary, alienated hero who discovers his identity and the reality of his own existence, not through involvement in society but by asserting himself against it. It is legitimate to ask, what other values does he find or create beyond the purely negative ones of being against society, against religion, etc.? The sequence of Skerrett's deprivations bring him, in a banal phrase, 'back to Nature'. Like the Stranger of *The Black Soul,* what he finds and briefly holds is a mindless (at least non-intellectual) communion with that large abstraction, Nature. What, in O'Flaherty's terms, does this mean? Here we should call on the evidence of Dr Melia, Skerrett's friend and the man who, to a large extent, shapes his thinking:

> Under the doctor's influence he absorbed the doctrines of philosophic anarchism, which have been made popular in Prince Kropotkin's work. The doctor mixed this philosophy with a mystical worship of the earth and the old pagan gods of the island. Indeed he worshipped the island itself. (*S* p. 161)

Melia's panacea for the ills of life is the gospel of mutual love. Capitalism which puts men into competition with one another and makes the pursuit of wealth the end of existence corrupts and destroys life. Love is only possible in a village commune because 'It is only in villages that people can live without money.' Skerrett, under Melia's influence tries to turn the people against the use of money and trade:

> Money is no good to you. Instead of selling your pigs, kill them, cure them and eat them. Kill your lambs and eat them. If you join together, you can have beef all the year round, by killing one beast at a time and sharing the meat. What good is the money to you that you get by selling these animals, or your fish? You use it to buy tea, sugar, flour, drink and tobacco. You don't need

these things and they are harmful to you. You become
slaves of the shopkeepers. You are in debt all your lives.
You can get all you need from the land and the sea,
without ever going to a shop. You were free before
shops came to the island. Keep away from Ardglass.
Ardglass is the headquarters of the devil. (*S* p. 282)

Ardglass v. Cappatagle, Capitalism v. Philosophic anarchism,
Moclair v. Skerrett, Reason v. Nature, Body v. Soul. The
scheme is simple, too simple, as we find when Skerrett builds
a cabin in remote Cappatagle. He is regarded as little better
than the village idiot. There is a further complication which
this simple scheme fails to take account of and that is the
suggestion, scattered throughout the book, that Nature itself
is hostile to man. Skerrett is defeated, in the end, by both the
natural *and* social environment. The heart of the book, the
central dilemma is to be found in the sentence 'He (Skerrett)
wanted to commit some violence in order to assert himself'.
(*S* p. 282) All the springs of action and thought have dried
up. Skerrett is, as the narrator points out, a wounded creature
and violence, frenzy, is the only way he can assert his humanity. Because he is the man he is, his *non serviam* is expressed
on the level of brute action, the chargings of a 'wounded
bull'. His final words are an assertion of freedom — 'I defy
them all. They can't make me bend the knee' — but the man
who speaks them is now 'one of the most vicious and un-
controllable inmates' of an asylum. It is a peculiarly modern
situation: brute violence as an assertion of humanity and
madness as more truly sane than conventional sanity. The
legend which grows about him after death readily accommodates the paradox.

   Skerrett's opponent, Fr Moclair, need not detain us for
long. He is a flat character, the embodiment of rational
discipline and materialism, a brother to Fr Reilly of *Thy
Neighbour's Wife* and the parish priests of *A Tourist's Guide
to Ireland*. He is, above all else, efficient and effective:

   He had come at the very height of the Land League
   agitation and he had at once taken command of the
   people as a soldier and statesman as well as a Priest.

Roads, piers, lighthouses, fishing boats came in his trail rapidly and in Ardglass a native trading class came into being, together with a little group of petty officials, a rate-collector, a sanitary officer, a harbour master, all tending to give the people an idea of their new importance and dignity. (*S* p. 33)

O'Flaherty does not allow the priest to develop in any direction other than his role of symbolizing materialistic society. The balance between him and Skerrett is not maintained, so much so that the reader is conscious of another possible novel, viewing these events from Moclair's perspective. There is a sense, however, in which one can justify O'Flaherty's handling of his principal characters. It is part of his thesis that the Roman Catholic religion is false, artificial and inhuman. By counterpointing the dynamic characterization of Skerrett with the flat characterization of Moclair he is making a major point about both. And in a sense, and certainly in the popular imagination, the priest was inviolate, a man above and beyond all conflict:

He saw how Moclair stood alone and impregnable, with the powerful structure of the Church standing behind him like an army, placing him beyond reach of all attack. His priestly clothes seemed to have magic in them, making him inhuman and occult, for all bowed down in reverence before them and yet, within their shelter he was free to exercise all the human passions, except concupiscence of the flesh. (*S* p. 78)

What of the people whom both men seek to dominate? The narrator, or the author's 'second self' displays great confidence and sureness when dealing with them. They exist in a way that Skerrett or Moclair never exist. We can translate the protagonists into allegorical or symbolic terms but they simply *are*. From one point of view *Skerrett* is a novel about the hopelessness of political action in a peasant society:

. . . for peasants are the least prone to conviction of all human beings on matters that affect their material lives.

It is only on matters dealing with the supernatural that
they are credulous. (*S* p. 270)
and again:
The new gospel of love for their language and traditional
mode of living, together with a longing for national
independence, which he began to preach to them, made
no appeal to these peasants, who, like all peasants, were
only too eager to sell any birth-right for a mess of
pottage. And Father Moclair the man of progress and
materialist, had the pottage. (*S* p. 161)

To focus our argument we will take up at some length
O'Flaherty's portrayal of the cess agitation on Nara. The
payment of the county cess is not simply a personal issue
between Moclair and Skerrett. It involves all the islanders
who are divided into two opposing camps. As is usual in
O'Flaherty's work, a cause or creed is characterized and
evaluated not so much by its intrinsic worth as by the calibre
of the men it attracts. When the issue is first raised in Chapter
X, Moclair is supported by the 'Trickster Finnegan' and
opposed by the honest farmer Michael Ferris. Finnegan is a
respected figure among the people 'because of the cleverness
with which he earned his living without tilling the soil' or
'scalding his thighs with brine'. He runs a shebeen which
supplies the islanders, including Skerrett's wife, with poteen.
Michael Ferris, who threatens to shoot Finnegan if the
opportunity should arise, is a model of excellence. His physical prowess is matched by his moral integrity. What he signifies
in the narrative, and to Skerrett, is best revealed by the
following description of his moving over the crags:

In his raw-hide shoes he hardly made any sound moving
over the flat rocks that had been polished as smooth as
glass by the impress of human feet for hundreds and
hundreds of years. He moved rapidly, tall, lean, erect,
with sudden jerks of his shoulders as he lengthened his
stride now and again to cross a fissure between the
rocks. His walk was like a dance, a movement perfect in
rhythm and significant of some mystic bond between
this beautiful human energy and the wild earth over

which it passed. (S p. 108)

The 'mystic bond' is in direct contrast to the commercial bond which binds the huckster Finnegan to those around him.

The public meeting held at the church gates to decide on the cess question is one of those set-pieces which evoke O'Flaherty's best powers. This is the third occasion on which he has used such a meeting to bring political and social conflicts into sharp focus. The narrator moves cinematically over the scene, picking out significant details and relating them to the larger issues of the novel. The whole congregation, with the exception of Skerrett and Moclair, is gathered on the sloping ground that leads from the church to the road below. The narrator groups the participants dramatically. The wild, colourful peasantry occupy the church grounds. Beneath them, on the road, a group of Ardglass men, led by the upstart Colman O'Rourke, who has seized control of the anti-cess agitation for his own selfish ends, strut up and down. They differ from the peasantry by their crude dress, speech and deportment. The police, representatives of the 'distant and unconscious imperial race that held the island in subjection', stands apart. Further away still Dr Melia is actually and symbolically sitting on the fence. The church door forms the backdrop to the scene. From it will emerge villain and hero. Description of scenery conceals commentary. The wind presages events as it comes 'in sudden rushes and crookedly, whining as if in pain and curling on its tracks like a demented thing which can only vent its anger on itself.' The description of each group, apart from its intrinsic merit as a fine piece of writing, is interesting for the kind of emphasis it makes. The peasantry attract the narrator's eye by their colourful costume, the quick, nervous movement of the men and the quiet passivity of the women. Only the paintings of Jack Yeats capture a similar colour and movement:

> They moved like dancers, making no sound in their rawhide shoes on the silken grass, now here, now there, now on bended knee, listening, now erect with arms waving in gesture. Their faces, blood red with wind and

sun, were of a sudden slit with white as their teeth
showed in the outrush of their passionate speech.
(*S* p. 138)

The men with O'Rourke are, like him, 'characteristic of the
social changes that were taking place on the island.' They are
heavy and clumsy in movement and have none of the vivid
colour of the peasantry. They speak a bastard English and
despise the Gaelic speakers above them. The narrator compares them to a 'wretched knock-kneed English trader'
building an empire by cunning on the backs of magnificent
Zulu warriors. His values are clear: colour, movement diversity as against the dull sameness imposed by civilization.
The impossibility of rational public debate in these circumstances is demonstrated by two incidents which sway
the people in opposite directions. O'Rourke, determined to
demonstrate his patriotism, spits while passing the police. A
wag remarks: 'Tis no good him spitting on the doorstep, for
Twig has pressed the button long ago and gone inside the
house.' He refers to the exploit of a Constable Twig who ran
away with O'Rourke's fiancee. The peasantry, eager to find
an excuse that will absolve them from taking action seize on
the joke as a way out — 'tis poor comfort for us to get evict-
ed by the red soldiers, so that fat-gut O'Rourke can get
satisfaction out of the peelers.' Fortunately for O'Rourke the
local landlord's landau appears round a corner and he diverts
their anger against its occupants. The county cess is being
levied to pay for damage committed against Athy's property.
There is hostility and incomprehension on both sides. The
shabby landau grows in the peasant imagination into a royal
carriage. The daughters of Athy himself can only scowl and
look shamefacedly at the people of whom he is genuinely
fond. Rank and history have placed him in a false position
and he has not the strength of character to break through
their trammelling bonds. The narrator takes the Athys away
from the scene on a comic note, as if to say that such complexities of history and personality cannot be resolved in any
other way.

The public meeting begins with Fr Moclair's speech, the
substance of which is contained in the injunction: 'Give unto

Caesar what is due unto Caesar and to God what is due unto God.' Otherwise the islanders will loose all the benefits of civilization that have come with Government grants: 'You'll be left without any help from outside. You'll have to go back to your rocks and your fishing lines.' (S p. 146) It is a crucial moment in O'Flaherty's imaginative history of rural life. The decision to go back into isolation or go forward and accept 'civilization' with its good and ills hangs on it. Yet 'decision' is the wrong word, as the main point of the narrative is to show that nothing like a rational decision is possible in the broken world of Nara. The meeting begins to break up in disorder, like the wind that could only vent its anger on itself. Moclair and O'Rourke abuse one another roundly while the people cry out their misery. Dramatically, Skerrett appears at the church door (he has been teaching catechism within) and the people hail him as their deliverer. Called on to speak both by the crowd and Moclair, Skerrett hesitates. Whichever side he speaks on will bring his personal ruin. The issue is decided by Moclair who begins to abuse Skerrett as a cur and wife-beater. Once more political debate is deflected into personal animosity and the meeting turns into a riot, both sides blaming Skerrett.

The first part of this study of regional literature dealt with the 'spirit of place'. The following quotation shows how in O'Flaherty's Galway novels this spirit operates. The narrative voice of *Skerrett* tries to account for the vacillations and disharmonies we have noted:

A peasant's memory is short when it has to deal with benefaction; more especially in a place like Nara, where the struggle of life was terribly intense. There, not only extreme poverty, but the very position of the island, foster in the human mind those devils of suspicion and resentment, which make ingratitude seem man's strongest vice. The surrounding sea, constantly stirred into fury by storms that cut off communication with the mainland, always maintains in the minds of inhabitants a restless anxiety, which has a strong bearing on character, sharpening the wits and heightening the energy, but at the same time producing a violent instability of

temperament. The fear of hunger becomes an evil
demon, whose horns are emblazoned on the bright face
of the sun as well as on the drooping bellies of the
thunderclouds, that belch a blight upon the meagre soil,
washing from the half-clad rocks the budding seeds and
throwing a barricade of mountainous waves over the
sea's rich treasure. So it comes to pass that a good catch
of fish can send a whole village into a frenzy of excitement, while an outbreak of swine fever may cause a
panic comparable to that caused by an earthquake
among people differently placed on the earth's crust.
This instability, in the same manner, turns friends into
foes and foes into friends with startling suddenness. It
corrupts the dictionary of human qualities, making the
stolid neurotic in their spleen and showing by fits a
goulish barbarism in natures ordinarily of sweet temper.
(S pp. 135-36)

The Wilderness[23]

The Wilderness is an extraordinary document. It is a piece of
allegory, almost unrelieved by realistic elements, concerning
the life and death of an Irish Messiah. That early tradition of
Messianism in Anglo-Irish life and letters sketched by Herbert
Howard here reaches a remarkable and unexpected climax.
Nietzsche, folk and fairy lore, current notions of a coming
apocalypse and the manifestation of Anti-Christ, all coupled
with Liam O'Flaherty's characteristic obsessions, fuse to
form what must be at once one of the most outlandish and
revealing documents in Irish literature. It is particularly
interesting in the context of our study of the regional
romances. Reading it, one has the sensation of coming on the
prototype of all the works we have studied so far, as if
O'Flaherty were saying here completely through allegory and
symbol what he fitfully says elsewhere. Unhampered by the
demands of realism and history, he pushes his typical characters and the ideas which animate them to their final, logical
conclusion. Each character in the novelette is separate, a pure
type. Looked at figuratively, The Wilderness is a constellation

of types and meanings, each radiating its own energy, connected only by the thin lines of allegory. Elsewhere these elements are embedded in a social context. Here they have a radiant simplicity.

Henry Lawless, the son of a landlord, comes to live in isolation in the remote Fairy Glen. He has set himself the task of finding God. After a month of solitude he is visited by a land-hungry peasant named Patrick Macanasa. Macanasa claims a hereditary right to the valley and to Lawless's farm. Lawless, eager to be loved and trusted, gives Macanasa and the people of the Fairy Glen the right to graze his land — thereby causing strife among them. He meets a fellow recluse, Dr Edward Stevens, son of a peasant farmer, who has become a successful scientist and an agnostic philosopher. They recognise one another as natural enemies yet are strangely attracted. Much of the book is taken up with their disputes over the claims of science and religion. Lawless has moments of mystical illumination but these give way to madness as he starves himself and retreats further from contact with his fellows. He believes himself to be the bearer of a new Gospel and that his hour is at hand. He falls ill and is nursed by the beautiful but ill-omened dark lady, Mrs Dillon, the wife of a 'degenerate' peasant. He invites the Dillons to come and live with him and hands over all his money to them. Mrs Dillon becomes his mistress. The Catholic curate hears about Lawless and interprets his actions as an effort to proselytize the people. He preaches against him, visits Lawless and is routed by him and finally institutes a boycott to drive Anti-Christ out of the parish. Only Mrs Dillon continues to visit him. She hopes Lawless will take her away to Dublin but his pursuit is of no earthly city. Disillusioned, she leaves him and her family and heads for Dublin. Lawless divides everything he possesses among the people and awaits Armageddon. In the morning he is found stabbed to death, and nearby the cuckold, Mr Dillon, swings by the neck from a tree.

This is, to say the least, a rather bald summary of *The Wilderness,* but it does provide a point of departure and reference for our analysis. This will be, unashamedly, an investigation of the various symbols and allegories at work in the novelette. The re-discoverer of the text of *The Wilderness,*

Angeline Kelly, in a brief note, points the direction which any analysis must take:

> The three men (Lawless, Stevens, Macanasa) represent beauty, evil and truth imperfectly represented as Abstracts in human terms: and they stand for the three-fold qualities of mysticism, violence and creativity found in Nature herself which are complementary but which war continually in Nature as in Man. The love of the woman for Lawless is based on physical attraction and greed, and the love for the Parish Priest for his religion is vitiated by fear. The thesis behind the novel is a complicated one, as a social criticism of the Irish situation is also involved.[24]

Five areas in particular call for comment and we will treat of these briefly in turn — the valley and its native inhabitants, Macanasa and Mrs Dillon, and finally the conflicts involving Dr Stevens and Lawless.

The valley or Fairy Glen functions on a number of levels. It is, first, the wilderness of the title which Lawless regards as a 'natural cloister'. He has come here to prepare himself for his mission. Like Christ, he spends forty days and forty nights in the wilderness undergoing temptation. More generally, within the symbolism of landscape, the valley 'represents a neutral zone apt for the development of all creation and for all material progress in the world of manifestation. . . . In short the valley is symbolic of life and is the mystic abode of shepherd and priest.'[25] Symbolic sun and moon (with values close to those of Yeats) rise over it in the course of the narrative and in the end the storm clouds of the apocalypse gather overhead. Its name, the *Fairy Glen,* indicates that it is the abode of spirits and of a long departed race:

> In the glen there are relics of the Druids, where the hawthorn bushes grow in a circle around a cairn of smooth stones. There are green mounds by the river where their kings were buried. There are dim tracks among the ferns that once were chariot roads. On flat stones there are strange signs engraven which nobody

can read, and which the illiterate glen dwellers hold in
superstitious fear. These Gaelic lords have become fairy
phantoms. Their habitations are a wilderness. . . .
(W, chap. II, p. 3)

It is interesting to note that Lawless's house is reputedly
haunted, that it has seen fairy activity (the previous owner
was stolen away) and that his family have been cursed by a
dying tenant. Magical trees, hawthorn bushes and rowans
grow close to the door. Finally, the valley is an image of rural
Ireland and it is on this level that it evokes O'Flaherty's
greatest power. The ghost which haunts it is the memory of
a fuller life that existed before the Great Famine and the
breakdown of the old organic community:

Although the glen is ten miles long and two miles wide,
there are now no more than fifty little houses in it.
There are no villages, no shops, and each house stands
remote from its fellows. Before the great famine there
were many villages and the glen was merry in the evening with the laughter of young lovers courting on the
roadside in the moonlight. Then in their last mountain
refuges our persecuted people were pursued by famine
which almost entirely destroyed them. The glen is
thickly strewn with the ruins of their houses. And on
the mountainside the fields they cultivated have again
sunk back into the wilderness, overgrown with ferns and
briars, with only the earthen mounds of their fences left
to show that they once were tilled. (W, chap. II, p. 3)

A number of new people have moved into the valley from the
city that lies to the east. They are all alienated individuals —
Lawless, Dr Stevens, ladies interested in the occult — who
have fled the corruption and materialism of modern life.
Ironically, Mrs Dillon, the only native inhabitant of the
Glen who displays any dash or courage, wants to flee away
to the bright lights. The intellectuals who have 'invaded' the
Fairy Glen are utterly unaware of its true nature: for Lawless
it is a 'holy place', but as Macanasa points out 'It's not the
place. It's the people that's in it.'

Foremost among these people is Macanasa himself. He is 'hidden Ireland' incarnate, a paradigm of the peasant type as we find him in all O'Flaherty's work: 'This unseemly peasant was the descendant of Gaelic lords who had conquered the glen and enslaved its inhabitants: so long ago that their names, their exploits and their very gods are quite forgotten.' (*W*, chap. II, p. 3) Dispossessed in turn, the Macanasas have become predatory creatures, still believing that the Glen is their property. The narrative description of Macanasa makes clear through mataphor and simile that the valley is flesh of his flesh, bone of his bone. He is earth, gross matter, the antithesis of the spiritual and intellectual (air and fire) principles embodied in Stevens and Lawless. O'Flaherty writes finely of his love for the land and the peculiar nature of that love:

> A peasant's love for the land is fanatical because it is his only love. His children, his wife, even his own life, are simply dear to him in relation to the soil, for whose benefit alone they are used and squandered freely. It is a lust without the emotion of passion. It is cold because it lies so deep, deep in his nature that even when a manifestation of it reaches his consciousness it comes with a dull flicker of pure joy that almost immediately is overcome with fear and perishes in a brooding hatred of something unknown. He is only happy when he is rooting the earth or tending his flocks; or while resting in apparent idleness, his dull mind ponders on the growth of herds and crops and the movement of their enemies, blight, storms, rain or drought. (*W*, chap. II, p. 4)

Macanasa and his kind have survived for generations by skill and cunning, yet 'they too see visions.' The valley is a 'gentle' place. Macanasa is in contact with the fairies and ghosts which haunt it. He performs magical rituals, sees that there is a 'dark shadow' on Lawless' house. His curse is effective. The first impulse of both Lawless and Dr Stevens is to kill him. For both he is an obscenity, a figure they would like to destroy or forget. They in turn, with their theorizing, are irritants on the surface of his life. He achieves his purpose and gains possession of Lawless's farm but we are not to presume that peasant Ireland has come into its own in the end. He is old, his sons are unmarried or diseased. The endurance of the Macanasas is contained within the greater endurance of nature. It is the wild flowers and weeds which inherit the earth and not the 'risen people'.

Mrs Dillon is the female counterpart to Macanasa, though in terms of the symbolism of *The Wilderness* she leads a more complex existence. If Lawless is Christ, she is Mary Magdalen. She is a loose woman and at one point kisses the feet of her Master, Lawless. On another level she is the dark lady of myth. Unlike her fair sister (Lily McSharry, Little Mary, Nora Costello) who leads her devotees to salvation, she is a figure of instinctual life and uncontrolled passion:

> The young men of the neighbourhood had gathered in Mrs. Dillon's cottage. Although none of them was definitely aware of it, they had all come in pursuit of Mrs. Dillon. She was the only attractive young woman in that part of the glen; and being married to a degenerate husband, who maintained her in dire poverty, her restless soul vented its spleen on society by arousing the passions of all the males in her environment. The result was that she and her husband were most unhappy mates; their house was in a filthy, ramshackle condition; their land was becoming barren; and their two children unhealthy and cross. (*W*, chap. VII, p. 17)

She sees Lawless and/or Dr Stevens as offering a way out of the narrow world of the valley and gives herself to both. Stevens, the practical man, simply wants to satisfy his lust. Lawless, the visionary, wants to reach, through her, 'some hitherto unsuspected form of consciousness'. Painfully he comes to see her true nature:

> Raising himself on his elbow, he looked at her with wonder in his eyes, and he thought: 'What do I expect of this? This is no sister soul.' Coldly now, with remorse, he saw his vision as that of a deranged mind, dreaming of an impossible godliness, detached from earth and flesh and the insatiable lusts that bring death with the

satisfaction of desire. He saw her as a she beast, caress-
ing him with velvet paws, with white teeth bared to suck
his blood. (*W*, chap. XIX, p. 44)

The horrible image of the vampire reveals yet again the
Manichaeism that bedevils O'Flaherty's world. The sexes are
images of salvation or damnation, God or devil. One is
reminded of Leslie Fiedler's comment on the treatment of
women in American fiction. 'There are only two sets of expectations and a single imperfect kind of woman caught
between them: only actual incomplete females, looking in
vain for a satisfactory definition of their role in a land of
artists who insist on treating them as goddesses or bitches.'[26]
Dr Stevens makes the connection between the hysterical
view of sex held by Lawless and the society which fosters it:

> We are an accursed race, like the ancient Jews. There is
> that same mark of slavery on our brow. We are born in
> hatred and we live like fanatics seeking God. Why can't
> we become rich and pompous, and love luxury and find
> joy in fornication and all the forms of lechery that other
> races imbibe into their systems with their mother's
> milk? No. We rush from a house of sin howling in terror
> lest a bolt might fall from Heaven on us. (*W*, chap. XIV,
> p. 34)

He proposes a *menage a trois* that will unite body, soul
and passion. Lawless is horrified. ('Devil'!). Mrs Dillon
abandons her husband and children for a life of prostitution
in the city.

The two central figures of the allegory are Lawless and
Stevens. They form a complementary pair, two halves of a
divided consciousness. At odd moments of exhaustion in the
strife which divides them they recognize their kinship:

> You and I are very alike. . . . for each of us God
> is a terrible reality. (Stevens)

and again:
> Can't you see that my despair is the complement of
> your fanatical enthusiasm? (Stevens).
> > (*W,* chap. XIV, p. 34; chap. XXI, p. 52)

But this is Ireland and O'Flaherty and hence it is the divisions
and differences that are stressed. The life history and ideals
of both men are starkly opposed. Lawless is the son of a landlord, Stevens of — as he insists on describing himself — a serf.
If man and woman in *The Wilderness* have a predatory,
vampire-like relationship, so too do the social classes. Stevens
tells Lawless: 'You were born free, but we have dragged you
down and we'll suck your blood because you have trodden
on us for centuries.' (*W,* chap. X, p. 26)

Lawless, in a moment of lucidity as he listens to the litany
of wrongs inflicted on the poor, realizes that history, from
which he had thought to break free, enchains him too:

> I see why I have done all this. Afraid of their hatred.
> The wise teacher sits in the valley among the people, for
> in the high places the wind distorts their voices into
> strange forms. (*W,* chap. X, p. 26)

Indeed 'history' — in its largest sense — is a vital concern of
both men. Stephen Dedalus, we remember, sought to wake
from the nightmare that is history and for both Dr. Stevens
and Lawless the problem is equally urgent. Lawless shares a
belief, common in the 1920s that the earth is growing old,
worn out. The 'one beautiful thing' for him in human history
is 'the soul of man struggling towards the light'. The great
prophets and seers (Christ, Buddha) are the real makers of
history because they have led men to the gates of Heaven. He
is himself a prophet in this tradition:

> I have hopes of bestowing a great blessing on humanity,
> on all life. I have come to purify my soul in this wilder-
> ness, and . . . . . I am going to know God, to find the
> road to Him, and then we'll travel that road and there
> will be no death for anything that lives. (*W,* chap. II, p. 6)

Stevens will have none of this. The great mass of men of all ages and times has been robbed again and again of 'the fruits of science and civilization' by 'fanatics who are bursting with egomania.' Stevens opposes a different concept of God and mankind's search for him:

> It is curious that Nietche *(sic)*, having joyfully announced that God was dead, later put on a white sheet and announced that he himself was God. Poetry is impossible unless there is a God. And God is good. There must be such, for it seems that life is an arch and God the centre-piece. But that God is the God we make and civilise, the mirror of our own perfection. Not the vision created by half savage minds, starved bodies and unsatisfied ambitions. He is an imperial God, of Rome, Egypt, Persia, Greece, England, the apex of great civilizations, a forebearing God, with scales of justice and respect for knowledge. He is an accumulation of properties. But always it seems that somebody rises and overwhelms all that; just as the fanatic Christ roused the slaves against Rome. (*W*, chap. IX, p. 25)

Lawless (Law-less!) is a local instance of the same thing: he has come to the valley preaching love and has only succeeded in causing strife. Stevens, the scientist, concentrates on helping humanity in any way he can. His efforts take a rather banal form — he leaves the valley triumphant, having taken out a patent on a new invention to prolong sexual potency in old age! ('It does not ensure immortality. It ensures possession of amorous power while life lasts'). Need we add that he is impotent?

How, finally, are we to understand Lawless/Christ? He is Alyosha Karamazov grown mad in the Celtic twilight. As Messiah he is surrounded by a plethora of appropriate images. On the table of his study lies a skull and votive lamp, above them a painting of Christ in his last agony. He is accompanied by two goats, one of them with only one horn, always referred to as 'the unicorn'. The unicorn, we remember, is a traditional symbol of sublimated sexuality (the beast will turn from him when he has relations with Mrs Dillon). He dresses in white and eats only natural food. His speech is incantatory with a biblical ring ('you herd of gluttonous swine', etc., etc.). Indeed he frequently paraphrases the words of Christ. The parallels with Christ's life are confused and crossed with others from the lives of the saints. One can pick out obvious references to Christ's temptations, the transfiguration, the Sermon on the Mount, the Crucifixion and St John of God's 'dark night of the soul', but this is the least satisfactory aspect of *The Wilderness*. Since this is an ironic gospel, Lawless in the final tableau is more thief than saviour.

It is perhaps, more fruitful to notice that Lawless, initially at least, has reached the condition which all O'Flaherty's heroes aspire to:

I am free, I am free. Eternal beauty, I approach thee. I come trembling with love. (*W*, chap. III, p. 8)

The Wilderness works out the implications and results of that freedom which McMahon, the Stranger (Lawless is frequently described as 'the stranger'), Dr Fitzgerald and Skerrett so ardently sought. Such absolute freedom, naked of time and circumstance, leads to madness and death. Lawless clarifies many of the impulses and motives behind these characters — and how strange that O'Flaherty should posit this figure as the apotheosis of the Anglo-Irish, Protestant nation! Anglo-Irish and Irish have brought equal ruin to one another. Lawless's class created Macanasa and Stevens, and they in turn have created Lawless. One thinks of the image of a snake eating its own tail and Kant's comment (in, of course, a different context) that objectively the snake is eating, subjectively being eaten.

PART II: 2 THE HISTORICAL ROMANCES

CHAPTER 10

THE HISTORICAL ROMANCES

Liam O'Flaherty's historical romances cover the period in Irish history from 1845 to 1922. The first three volumes — *Famine, Land* and *Insurrection* — form a trilogy, consciously composed as such. Included in this section is a fourth volume — *The Martyr* — which is placed in imaginative rather than chronological order with the others. Composed before *Famine* it deals with the Civil War period in ways similar to the historical romances and sheds an interesting light on them. It bears much the same relationship to this group of novels as *The Wilderness* bears to the regional romances, clarifying, both in method and intention, what is less obvious in others of the same group.

We will confine ourselves, in this introduction, to a discussion of the historical period with which O'Flaherty deals and the particular perspective in which he sees it. *Famine* is the only really important novel of this group (*Land* and *Insurrection* are largely commercial ventures, an effort to cash in on the success of *Famine*) and hence we will devote most of our attention to it.

O'Flaherty begins his imaginative survey of modern Irish history, appropriately, with the Great Famine. All historians are agreed on its importance both as fact and symbol. 'In Irish social and political history the famine was very much of a watershed. The Ireland on the other side of those dark days is a difficult world for us to understand, the Ireland that emerged we recognize as one with problems akin to our own.'[1]

Four basic elements go into the making of *Famine*. There is, first, O'Flaherty's intimate knowledge of peasant life on the Aran Islands which in many respects had not changed since the 1840s. As noted in the opening section ('Early Background'), famine was not uncommon on the islands and occurred periodically right up to the first decade of this century. Thus the world of the Great Famine was, in essence, not very different from the one that he had experienced as a child. The *minutiae* of ordinary everyday life were the same and one gains a lively sense of this in the way, to take but one small example, O'Flaherty has his peasant characters enter a room. It is not simply that they do not knock or observe the manners of 'polite' society. On entering a room they move towards the nearest wall and crouch there 'on their hunkers', before stating their business. It is from such particulars as this that he builds up a vivid and compelling picture of life at the time.

Secondly, there was available to O'Flaherty — and especially on the Aran Islands — a great body of folklore about the famine years. Much of this finds its way into *Famine*. A good example of this is O'Flaherty's portrayal of the circumstances under which the potato blight strikes. In the Black Valley where *Famine* is set the people are startled by a white cloud which overhangs the valley:

It was like a great mound of snow, hanging by an invisible chain, above the mountain peaks. It was dazzling white in the glare of the rising sun. . . . 'Snow', Mary said 'Its like a big heap of snow.' 'How could it be snow?' said the old man. 'And this the middle of summer? Its a miracle.' 'Or would it be a bad sign, God between us and harm?' said Thomsy. Other people came from their cabins and stared at the cloud. There was a peculiar silence in the Valley. The air was as heavy as a drug. There was not a breath of wind. The birds did not sing. And then, as the people watched, the cloud began to move lazily down upon the Valley. It spread out on either side, lost its form and polluted the atmosphere, which became full of a whitish vapour, through which the sun's rays glistened; so that it seemed that a fine rain of tiny whitish particles of dust was gently falling from the sky. Gradually a sulphurous stench affected the senses of those who watched. It was like the smell of foul water in a sewer. Yet, there was no moisture and the stench left an arid feeling in the nostrils. Even the animals were affected by it. Dogs sat up on their haunches and howled. Not a bird was to be seen, although there had been flocks of crows and of starlings about on the previous day. Then indeed, terror seized the people and a loud wailing broke out from the cabins, as the cloud overspread the whole Valley, shutting out the sun completely. (*F* pp. 299-300)

O'Flaherty is here drawing on a 'tradition of an ominous season of mist, of storms of rain and wind alternating with periods of vast and terrible stillness. . . . '[2] Our quotation comes from Roger J. McHugh's survey of 'The Famine in Irish Oral Tradition' where much of the folk materials used by O'Flaherty is mentioned. Indeed McHugh remarks that *Famine* itself 'has something of the simple and forceful quality of these oral accounts.'[3]

The third source — and the one which provided O'Flaherty with the great bulk of facts and material on the Famine — is, undoubtedly, the Rev. J. O'Rourke's *The History of the Great Irish Famine of 1847 with Notices of Earlier Irish Famines.*[4] Of all the early histories of the event, O'Rourke's is by far the most concerned with the plight of the ordinary people. He prepared himself for writing his book by speaking to many of those who had lived through the terrible years of '45 — '47 and includes vivid details from their accounts. Among other matters, his description of people eating dogs and dogs eating people is dramatized in *Famine*.

We come finally to what is, we think, the source of O'Flaherty's attitude not only to the famine period but to the subsequent land war as well. More correctly we should say the source of one major attitude to this history, because there is another which is at variance with it and which will be discussed later. The source is that classic of Irish socialism, James Connolly's *Labour in Irish History*.[5] We will deal with this matter in some detail as it is an important and hitherto unexplored aspect of O'Flaherty's work.

O'Flaherty was a socialist, if an inconstant one. During his sojourn in the United States (1917) he engaged in propaganda work for the Industrial Workers of the World of which James Connolly was a founding member. In 1922 he proclaimed an 'Irish Soviet Republic' and raised the Red Flag over the Rotunda. When we bear these matters in mind it is hardly conceivable that he could have been unaware of Connolly's socialist analysis of Irish history. Apart from the evidence afforded by the historical romances themselves, the only other direct evidence we can afford is the testimony of O'Flaherty's friend and contemporary, Peadar O'Donnell, in the *Bell* (August 1946, pp. 443-44):

> More than any other Irish writer he has *consciously* adopted Connolly's vision of the conquest as a bullock-whacking savagery under which the people were enslaved and degraded, and of the re-conquest as the struggle of those same people to fight their way back to their inheritance over a long and bloody road.

This is a general statement of Connolly's position: we will investigate more fully what he has to say on both the famine period and subsequent land war. As George Lucaks demonstrated forcibly in his study of the historical novel, a writer's suppositions about the nature of society shapes the kind of historical fiction he writes.[6] At its simplest, if one is writing a novel about the land war — as O'Flaherty is in *Land* — what kind of prominence should one give to the leaders of the day, Davitt and Parnell? Should they, as they largely do in the history books, dominate the scene? Or are the people whose aspirations they embody the real force in history and hence the centre of the novelists' concern? In *Land* there is a scene in which Davitt addresses the 'risen people'. It is seen through the eyes of a pair of young lovers who wander off after the first few sentences of Davitt's speech and the narrator follows them into the bushes. In *Insurrection* the reading of the Proclamation of Independence by Pearse is seen through the eyes of a simple Connemara man. He joins the revolutionaries largely by accident and the events of Easter Week are described as they effect him. Connolly bequeathed to O'Flaherty a concept of Irish history as the destiny of the people rather than of a few 'great' men. Reference to his analysis will go some way to explain and clarify O'Flaherty's historical novels (especially *Famine* and *Land*) and place them within their proper context.

James Connolly in the preface to *Labour in Irish History* makes the connection between Irish history and Anglo-Irish literature as *he* knew it:

> In the re-conversion of Ireland to the Gaelic principle of common ownership by a people of their sources of food and maintenance the worst obstacle to overcome will be the opposition of the men and women who have imbibed their ideas of Irish character and history from Anglo-Irish literature. That literature, as we have explained, was born in the worst agonies of the slavery of our race; it bears all the birth-marks of such origin upon it, but irony of ironies, these birth-marks of slavery are hailed by our teachers as 'the native characteristics of the Celt!'

he goes on:

> Hence we believe that this book attempting to depict the attitude of the dispossessed masses of the Irish people in the great crisis of modern Irish history, may justly be looked upon as part of the literature of the Gaelic revival.[7]

The two propositions upon which his study is founded are stated as follows:

> First, that in the evolution of civilization the progress of the fight for national liberty of any subject nation must, perforce, keep pace with the progress of the struggle for liberty of the most subject class in that nation, and that the shifting of economic and political forces which accompanies the development of the system of capitalist society leads inevitably to the increasing conservatism of

the non-working-class element, and to the revolutionary vigour and power of the working class.

Second, that the result of the long drawn out struggle of Ireland has been, so far, that the old chieftainry has disappeared, or, through its degenerate descendants, has made terms with iniquity, and become part and parcel of the supporters of the established order; the middle class, growing up in the midst of the national struggle, and at one time, as in 1798, through the stress of the economic rivalry of England almost forced into the position of revolutionary leaders against the political despotism of their industrial competitors, have now also bowed the knee to Baal, and have a thousand economic strings in the shape of investments binding them to English capitalism as against every sentimental or histor- ic attachment drawing them toward Irish patriotism; only the Irish working class remain as the incorruptible inheritors of the fight for freedom in Ireland.[8]

Connolly treats of the Great Famine in a chapter with the resounding title *Our Irish Girondins sacrifice the Irish Peas- antry upon the Altar of Private Property*. The famine, he maintains, brought to a head class antagonism in Ireland and ' . . . revealed the question of property as the test by which the public conduct is regulated.' (p. 127) Conventional his- torians, both Irish and English, have obscured the real issue by concentrating their attention on such matters as the split in Daniel O'Connell's Repeal Association between those who advocated physical force and those who counselled parlia- mentary methods as a means of solving the nation's ills. The Young Irelanders, who favoured physical force, seceded from O'Connell on a false issue ' . . . the majority on either side being disinclined to admit, even if they recognized, the real issue dividing them. That issue was the old and ever-present one of the Democratic principle in human society versus the Aristocratic.' (p. 120)

It is part of ultra-Nationalist mythology that England was solely responsible for the Famine, indeed that she used it in an attempt to exterminate the 'Celtic People' of this island (O'Rourke's history by-and-large adopts this attitude).

Connolly and Fintan Lalor before him, placed the emphasis
rather differently. It was the social system rather than the
Government that was at fault. 'No man who accepts capitalist
society and the laws thereof can logically find fault with the
statesmen of England for their acts in that awful period.
They stood for the rights of property and free competition
and philosophically accepted their consequences upon
Ireland; the leaders of the Irish people also stood for the
rights of property and refused to abandon them even when
they saw the consequences in the slaughter by famine of over
a million of the Irish toilers.' (p. 130) The only revolutionary
movement within society at the time was the Young Irelanders and they were, as a body, interested in force 'as a subject
for flights in poetry and oratory'. They preached the moral
righteousness of rebellion 'learnedly in English to a starving
people, the most of whom knew only Irish'. (pp. 131-32)
Connolly exempts a few men from what he scathingly calls
the 'comic opera' of Young Ireland activities, notably John
Mitchel and James Fintan Lalor who developed a plan for
guerilla warfare against those who were taking cattle and corn
crops out of the country. Finally, he describes the limitations
placed on famine relief by the capitalist system within which
it was undertaken:

> Early in the course of the famine the English Premier,
> Lord John Russell, declared that nothing must be done
> to interfere with private enterprise or the regular course
> of trade, and this was the settled policy of the Govern-
> ment from first to last. A Treasure "Minute" of August
> 31, 1846, provided that "depots for the sale of food
> were to be established at Longford, Banagher, Limerick,
> Galway, Waterford and Sligo, and subordinate depots at
> other places on the western coast" but the rules provid-
> ed that such depots were not to be opened where food
> could be obtained from private dealers, and, when
> opened, food was to be sold at prices which would
> permit of private dealers competing. In all the acts
> establishing relief works, it was stipulated that all the
> labour must be entirely unproductive, so as not to
> prevent capitalists making a profit either then or in the

future. Private dealers made fortunes ranging from
£40,000 to £80,000. (pp. 135-36)

Connolly considers the next revolutionary period after the
Great Famine to be the days of the Fenian Conspiracy and
the Land League, " . . . the same coincidence of militant class
feeling and revolutionary nationalism is deeply marked.'
(p. 158) One of his criteria for 'the really dangerous revolut-
ionists of Ireland' is that they should be concerned not
simply with 'the incidents of the struggle of Ireland against
England' but with the 'creed of the democracy of the world.'
(p. 148) The leading Fenian conspirators, notably James
Stephens, were deeply involved with revolutionary activities
in France — indeed the whole Fenian movement grew out of
a meeting in the Latin Quarter of Paris. Connolly is greatly
impressed by the fact that ' . . . the General chosen by
Stephens to be Commander-in-Chief was afterwards Commander-in-Chief of the Federals during the Commune of Paris.'
(p. 159) Numerous quotations from contemporary accounts
are presented to demonstrate that the *personnel* of both the
Fenian and Land League movements were drawn from the
Irish proletariat, thus 'bearing out our analysis of the relation
between the revolutionary movement and the working class.'
(p. 161) Both movements were opposed, not only by the
Anglo-Irish ascendancy class but by the Catholic clergy, the
middleclass Catholics and the larger farmers. The most telling
quotation, for Connolly's purposes, is the comment of a
French aristocrat who toured Ireland in 1866 and met many
of the Land League leaders:

> For in fact, however they may try to dissimulate it, the
> Irish claims, if they do not yet amount to Communism
> as their avowed object — and they may still retain a few
> illusions upon that point — still it is quite certain that
> the methods employed by the Land League would not
> be disowned by the most advanced Communists. (p.164)

The Land League, however, was only partially successful and
its final dubious achievement was to convert Ireland 'from a
country governed according to the conception of feudalism

into a country shaping itself after capitalistic laws of trade.'
(p. 164) This, in summary, and in his own words, is
Connolly's analysis of modern Irish history which leads up to
the Rebellion heralded in the concluding paragraphs of
Labour in Irish History. There is much to quarrel with in this
document — for instance he places, in the last quotation, the
conversion of Ireland from a feudal to a capitalist economy
subsequent to the land reforms brought about by the Land
League while earlier he discussed the events of the 1840s in
terms of capitalist exploitation. It is interesting to note that
this confusion is imported into O'Flaherty's novels — at one
moment he speaks of a feudal society, at another of a capitalistic one. The point is perhaps a minor one. Both, in fact,
existed side by side.

We turn now to consider a few examples of the ways in
which O'Flaherty embodied these ideas in his historical
romances (the relationships between Connolly's analysis and
the romances, is not, of course, simple and direct). In
Famine, contrary to the common critical judgement that the
central conflict is that of Man against Nature, it could be
maintained that it is rather Man against Society, against the
political, economic and religious forces which maimed the
lives of the people. O'Flaherty is one with Connolly in his
embittered attitude towards Daniel O'Connell and the middle-
class leadership of the Catholic people. Chapter XII of
Famine describes a public meeting addressed by ' . . . our
distinguished representative in Parliament . . . Mr. McCarthy
Lalor'. (*F* p. 94) It is one of these set-pieces at which
O'Flaherty is so expert. The meeting is held actually and
symbolically in the chapel yard between the church and
Hyne's shop (the local gombeen). The Parish priest, Fr Roche,
opens the proceedings and introduces the speaker, whose
well-fed appearance contrasts with that of his starving con-
stituents. O'Flaherty's venom drives him to caricature:

At a time when big men were the rule rather than the
exception, Mr. Lalor was beyond the ordinary in size;
one of those rapacious giants, unknown in our puny
generation, who could devour a leg of mutton at a
sitting. Still on the right side of fifty, he would be in his

prime if he were not so fat. His fat, however, had not
gone to his belly. It was evenly distributed, as on a
mammoth bull, the neck, shoulders, chest and gullet
offering a greater proof of his appetite than his abdo-
men. His full, florid countenance was scaled like a fish
and his little eyes had that ferocious expression often
seen in the eyes of fat men, who are by no means ferocious because of their fine condition. He exuded
consciousness of his importance as a henchman of the
great Daniel O'Connell and his dress imitated that of the
liberator. He wore the great frieze cape of the leader and
he carried it loose about his shoulders, as the leader had
the habit of doing. (*F* p. 94)

McCarthy-Lalor's speech is eloquent if cliche-ridden. He
buoys up the people (or those of them who can understand
him, his audience consisting largely of Irish speakers) by
empty promises and plans for reform. At the end of the
meeting, when the cheering is over, the people troop into the
local rent office 'with the money they had received for that
food which was being driven down the road for export,
together with the jaunting car of Mr. Lalor, the saviour of
the people.' (*F* p. 97)
    Fr Roche, who symbolizes the role of the Church in Irish
affairs, recalls this meeting when, later in the book, he leads
the starving people to demand the opening of a food store. In
a moment of insight he realizes that:

    . . . it was the policy of 'peace at any price', preached by
    him and by all the other priests and politicians in
    command of the great Repeal Association, that had pro-
    duced this catastrophe, a disillusioned, disheartened,
    disorganized people at the mercy of the tyrannical
    government. A few short months ago, less than a year
    ago, if the bugles of war had been sounded, a million
    men would have been ready, armed with the frenzy of
    revolutionary faith, to crush the feudal robbers that
    oppressed them. But the demagogue O'Connell had
    professed himself a pacifist and a loyal subject of Her
    Majesty. The bishops also preached peace and obedience

to the laws that gave them fat bellies and rich vestments
and palaces. All those in command said that life must be
spared and that no cause was worth the shedding of a
single man's blood. Now that blood was going to rot in
starved bodies; bodies that would pay for the sin of
craven pacifism the punishment that has always been
enforced by history. (*F* p. 327-28)

O'Flaherty links the rise of the Irish middle class with
O'Connell's political career, through the family history of
John Hynes, the gombeen shopkeeper of *Famine*. Hynes'
grandfather had been one of the first settlers in Black Valley
following the 'Act For Reclaiming Unprofitable Bogs' (1742).
The dispossessed Catholic peasantry who became landholders
as a result of this act increased and multiplied so that one
hundred years later the population of Ireland had increased
by four millions. Competition for possession of the bogs
became so intense that many secret societies were formed
and one of these was responsible for the death of Hynes'
father who had given some information to the authorities.
The local landlord gave the informer's widow a cabin in the
Catholic ('Irishtown') part of the local town ('Crom') and a
sum of money to set up as a huckster. Since the people
would not trade with an informer's widow her precocious
son, John, took to the roads with a travelling shop. He
'married money' and expanded his business:

He got better premises and procured a licence for the
sale of wine, spirits and ale. Things went well with him
and he wore down the hostility of the people by taking
an active part in the nationalist movement under
O'Connell. In this, of course, he was guided by self
interest rather than by patriotism. For it was the purpose of this movement, which was really economic
although it was religious on the surface, to support the
rising Catholic petty middle-class traders against their
Protestant competitors. . . . During the thirty years that
had elapsed since his marriage, his power and prosperity
had kept pace with that of his class all over Ireland,
under the leadership of the great demagogue O'Connell.

> . . . His younger son was the local doctor. One of his
> daughters was a nun. . . . In a word, he had made him-
> self, next to the landlord, the most powerful man in the
> parish. (*F* pp. 79-80)

The scenario of the action in which he is involved, his insistence on the rights of property and private enterprise in the
face of a starving people, could have come straight from
Labour in Irish History.

The protagonist of *Famine* is the Irish peasant class as
represented by the Kilmartin family. Here we wish to touch
on two matters, O'Flaherty's portrayal of the revolutionary
potential of that class and the significance he attributes to
the Young Irelanders. His peasants do rebel, in Chapter XXX,
and it is a rebellion after Connolly's heart. Fr Roche preaches
a violent sermon 'warning the people against being influenced
"by agitators and physical force men," saying that nothing
but disaster would result from violent conduct and they must
"give unto Caesar" what was Caesar's; meaning that the rent
should be paid.' (*F* p. 236) The sermon produces the opposite
effect on his starving people. At this point, O'Flaherty interr-
upts the third-person narrative, in a way that destroys the
dramatic illusion, and speaks out in his own person, as if to
reinforce the point he wishes to make:—

> . . . I am certain that, apart from whispered propaganda
> by a few militant republicans from the town, no definite
> organisation had been established in the parish. It was a
> spontaneous movement on the part of the people; one
> of those silent and sudden movements of rebellion that
> spring from the earth itself. The peasant can endure
> tyranny longer than any other class of the community;
> but when the moment arrives for him to revolt, he needs
> no outside force to rouse him. His rebellion is instinctive.
> (*F* pp. 236-37)

The rebellion, of course, fails, but throughout the book there
is portrayed a growing consciousness among the people of the
necessity for revolt. ('The people will rise again.')

The Young Irelanders are present in *Famine* very much as

they are present in *Labour in Irish History* as spinners of fine
words and as holding out a vague hope for a resurgent Ireland.
One of the characters in *Famine* joins them but their activities, as presented, are confined to getting wanted men out of
the country so that they can continue the struggle in America.
Another character, Thomsy, who meets them, returns to his
expectant family with 'nothing but a tale told by a strange
man in a barn at night.' (*F* p. 389) Yet he dies with a dream
of the promised land in his head, a man with yellow hair on
a mountain top, 'his naked sword flashing in the spears of the
rising sun', leading the people to victory.

Land adopts a similar perspective to *Famine* on the period
of history with which it deals. Two brief quotations from the
novel will indicate its relation to Connolly's views. Captain
Butcher, the resident landlord, declares: '... I'm no fool in
business matters. I could see how things were going. With
industry developing in England at a colossal pace, a man
didn't have to be a wizard in order to see that rural Ireland
would become England's cattle market. So I decided to clear
Mainister of peasants and raise cattle.' (*L* p. 39) Fr Costigan,
the parish priest of *Land,* condemns the Land League in the
following terms (the League was founded, in actual fact, in
1879 at Irishtown, county Mayo, at a meeting held to oppose
a rackrenting landlord — the parish priest, Canon Bourke):

> 'The events at Irishtown on the nineteenth of last
> month,' he said, 'were an outrage against the Catholic
> Church. On that day, Michael Davitt and his followers
> tore off the mask of patriotism. They showed them-
> selves in their true colours as the Communist disciples of
> Karl Marx. They openly preached the dismal Commun-
> ist faith, that tried to drown Paris nine years ago in a
> welter of Christian blood. Naked savages could not have
> behaved worse than Irish Catholics did towards Canon
> Geoffrey Bourke, the saintly parish priest of Irishtown,
> on the nineteenth of April.' (*L* p. 91)

The reference to Marx, which would probably have been
highly unlikely at the time and place, reveals yet again
O'Flaherty reading Irish history in the light of Connolly's

analysis.

In the detailed examination of *Land* which follows, a precise theory of O'Flaherty's is studied, which is first enunciated in *Land* but is also important for a reading of *Insurrection* and *The Martyr*. From these three novels there emerge three fundamental types of men '. . . representing three distinctive responses to the absolute challenge that an occasion in history presents.'9 These are the soldier, the poet and the monk. Raoul St George, the Frenchified aristocrat of *Land* explains:

> 'The soldier, the poet and the monk represent what is finest in man. They represent man's will to power, to beauty and to immortality. They alone among men are capable of complete love, because they love the unattainable. Their love is never tarnished by possession. . . . '
> (*L* p. 53)

The three figures, representing absolute dedication to an ideal, impose in a mechanical way on the life of *Land, Insurrection* and *The Martyr*. Each of these novels has a character who embodies the aspirations of soldier, poet and monk, often in a very confused fashion. Further discussion of this matter will be postponed to an analysis of the relevant works.

Famine10

Famine has long been, and deservedly so, O'Flaherty's most popular novel. Its panoramic portrayal of the Great Famine combines the sharp pictorial clarity of his short stories with his best narrative skill. Alone of all his novels he accepts here a social pattern of norms and values against which to dramatize the lives and destinies of his characters — indeed, in this sense, *Famine* is his most realistic work. Characters are placed within a well defined and intelligible society and they are motivated by real human passions and concerns. It is interesting to note that a number of the multifarious characters of *Famine* appear in previous works by O'Flaherty but are seen here with a difference. In *Famine* they are shorn of their wildest excesses, rooted in a place and time which contains and defines them. Perhaps the most remarkable quality of this work is its feeling for the ordinary, everyday life of rural Ireland in the nineteenth century. The famine corrodes and finally destroys that life and the reader is left, not so much with a sense of the individual tragedies of the lives portrayed but with a feeling of loss for a whole society and a way of life:

> Feet rising and falling. Eating and
> Drinking. Dung and Death.[11]

Famine presents special difficulties in that it is the longest (about twice the length of the usual O'Flaherty novel) and most populous of his work.

On the level of plot and action the novel falls into three major sections. The first section (Chapters I to XV) deals with the domestic life of the Kilmartins, a peasant family and their relatives. One generation — Martin Kilmartin and his young wife, Mary Gleeson — takes over the running of the house and farm from old Kilmartin. The domestic theme of the conflict of father and son is played out against the growing ravages of the potato blight. In Chapters XVI to XL the theme is a much more public one. The scene broadens to include the whole of Black Valley and its village, called 'Crom'. At the centre of the section is the evil genius of the novel, the local landlord's agent, Chadwick. Famine drives the starving people to commit, in the language of the day, 'outrages'. Chadwick is assassinated by, among others, Martin Kilmartin. Chapter XLI to the end focuses, in the main, on Mary Kilmartin. Her husband is 'on the run' as a result of the assassination. In order to save herself and her child she plans to emigrate to America. The Famine is portrayed in all its horror in this section and it is against a background of death and pestilence that the young family makes good its escape to the New World. Vague talk of the Young Irelanders and coming revolution adds to the hopeful strain on which the book closes. The divisions we have marked out are rough, plots and characters overlap and cannot be understood in isolation from one another. The central, unifying factor in *Famine,* is the Kilmartin family — more accurately an extended

family which includes three generations and all grades of
peasant society. It is with this group that we first have to
deal.

The immediate family consists of the parents, Brian and
Maggie Kilmartin, their sons Michael and Martin, and
Thomsy, a drunken relative. Martin, the eldest son, has just
married Mary Gleeson and there exists between the old and
the young couple a largely unconscious struggle for mastery
of the house. Old Brian Kilmartin is O'Flaherty's peasant
farmer *par excellence* (there is some evidence to show that he
is modelled on his own father). He rules the house with an
iron hand and his rule is based on the customs of the people.
Two points are important about him — his total allegiance to
tradition and his love for the land. Both are shown to be at
once noble and, in the context of the times, fatal. There is
about his daily life, as O'Flaherty dramatizes it, a beautiful
ritualistic quality — rising at dawn, morning prayers, milking
the cow, his breakfast of bread and milk and so on to the
final little ritual of the rosary in the evening. Even his speech
has a ritualistic quality with its invocations to God, and wise
sayings:

> 'God doesn't send hunger for long. He sends it to
> remind us of our sins. But when we repent he sends
> riches. The earth is rich. God has blessed our earth.'
> (*F* p. 295)

There is too, as is revealed in small particulars, a fine delicacy
and gentleness in the way he manages his family — when the
old man, for example, wishes to surrender control of the
household to his son he does so by pretending to be sick and
taking to his bed until Martin is securely in command. It is
this life and its small ceremonies which is pitted against the
famine — rather as the household of Maurya is surrounded by
the brute sea in Synge's play. O'Flaherty through brief
vignettes of morning in the cottage, threshing the oats, spin-
ning flax, establishes a secure sense of what normal life is like
for the Kilmartins. The impression is reinforced by a complete
avoidance of sentimentality — the infamous pig is in the
kitchen and stinks, Michael spits mouthfuls of blood, Thomsy

is a drunken lout. Everywhere there are signs of the disaster
to come. A neighbour, Sally O'Hanlon, 'like a ghost' (the first
few chapters are stalked with ghosts) arrives with news of the
blight. The dying Michael is one with the rotting potatoes.
('Rotten? Are they though? Like me'). His stricken life is an
emblem of the life of his community:

> 'Poor Michael! Its not a land slave he should have been
> born, but a rhyming poet at the court of some high
> king. God gave him poor harness to drag the load of
> poverty, and what good to him is his dreaming mind,
> that would make your mouth water at the stories he
> tells?' (F p. 30)

Mary Gleeson, who has married into the family, provides an
interesting perspective on her in-laws. She tells her mother:

> '. . . They are queer people. They wouldn't sow a head
> of cabbage or an onion, for fear the other people would
> make fun of them. . . . Nor would they hunt a rabbit
> either. Everything like that counts, but they wouldn't
> do it. The old man nearly ate me when I talked about
> making a pigsty, or putting the hens in the barn. "A
> custom is a custom" he always says. But I ask myself
> what is going to happen if this blight gets worse. . . . '
> (F p. 63)

'A custom is a custom' — all the Kilmartins, at some point
invoke the tautology. Their ruinous inflexibility is first
shown when Michael dies. Old Kilmartin, as custom demands,
takes charge of the wake and orders twenty gallons of
poiteen which the family can ill afford: ' . . . I have always
lived as the customs of the people say I should live and I'll
die that way. There's no going against custom.' (F p. 199)
But the same traditions demand, as we are reminded again
and again, that nobody should be turned away hungry from
the door ' . . . the poor should take no credit for helping the
poor, for it was so that God ordained it.' The scene of
Michael's wake is, as the narrator points out, formal, cere-
monious. Rituals like these have held the people together in

the face of recurring disaster. By emphasizing this aspect of peasant life, O'Flaherty is able to convey in a way in which no mere narrative of the famine years (see Cecil Woodham-Smith's *The Great Famine*) could, the full horror of the times. As hunger and disease take their toll, custom and ceremony break down — 'Patsy O'Hanlon (a relative of the Kilmartins) was the first man in the Parish of Crom, within living memory, to be buried without a wake or a funeral procession.' (*F* p. 372) It is this, more than the simple fact of starvation, which destroys the people. Late in the novel, the flat, factual account of old Kilmartin burying his wife in a field gains its terrible force from what we remember of his insistence on custom.

Kilmartin's whole being is bound up with his ten acres of rocky land. For him it is something sacred and there exists between him and it what can only be described as a sacramental relationship. When his daughter-in-law first broaches the question of leaving the farm he is stirred to fury:

> ' . . . Stand by the land. You married into this house and into this land. A son has been born to you in this house. And while the sod is there and this roof, the law of God is against your going.' (*F* p. 341)

And again, expressing his attachment more fully:

> ' . . . Leave the land, is it, at the first sign of trouble? Where else would you get land, or the riches that comes out of it? It's foolishness and a temptation of the devil to dream of leaving it. Taking the good times with the bad, there's no more peaceful life on this earth. It's the life that God ordained, tilling the earth with the sweat of the brow. To be master of your plot of ground and of your own hearth. And making things grow, like a miracle, out of the cold earth. Tyrants come and go, but the landsman goes on for ever, reaping and sowing, for all the generations of time, like the coming and going of the year, from father to son. . . . ' (*F* pp. 257-58)

His statement of the sacredness of the land is echoed repeatedly by many of the minor characters in *Famine*. How then account for the blight? Kilmartin and his peers see in it the hand of God. The blight is a punishment for the sins of men. This general attitude contributes to the hopelessness and inertia of the people — for how can one go against the will of the Almighty? ' "It's the hand of God. God's will be done." Thereupon he crossed himself and bowed his head. Not troubling even to collect the potatoes he had pulled up with the stalks. . . . ' (*F* p. 304) Like the strict adherence to custom this is an attachment which can be fruitful and meaningful. But in a time of famine those who live by the land, die by the land. The old man stays on in the Black Valley when most of its inhabitants have fled and dies in a frost-bound field while making a last effort to dig a grave. The rhythms of the final chapter have the fall of James Joyce's *The Dead:*

> Hoar frost had fallen in the night. It shone in the morning light upon the mountain-sides and all along the Valley's bed. It lay in a whitish crust upon the sagging thatch of the empty houses and on the blighted fields that were already falling back into the wilderness. The stone walls, the granite boulders, and the gorse bushes were white with it. It had formed a thin crust of ice on the surface of the Black Lake. The river was the only thing that moved here beneath the grey sky. (*F* p. 477)

If old Kilmartin is a representative figure of the old order his daughter-in-law, Mary, is a representative of the new. He preserves his dignity and dies; she is ruthless and survives. On first acquaintance she seems a typical O'Flaherty heroine — beautiful, fertile, a cipher for the female principle. As the novel progresses O'Flaherty deepens and broadens her character until she becomes the most convincing and powerful of all his heroines. She is assigned a precise position in the social scale of *Famine* and this explains much about her. Mary is a daughter of 'the weaver Gleeson', not of the land-owning peasantry. In an Ireland where, as Yeats remarked, every man is a class to himself, her family is on a lower social scale than the Kilmartins. (Indeed, for this reason old Kilmartin is none too pleased with his son's choice of wife). She is thus free of the attachments to land and custom which bind her in-laws — almost vulgarly so. O'Flaherty treats her, explicitly, as a representative of 'civilization'. The first part of the book contains a series of emblematic encounters which reveal Mary's opposition to custom as observed by the Kilmartins. She asks her mother — 'what's the use of having land if you don't make money out of it? People always looked down on us because we had no land, but we lived better than they do.... If things don't change, I'll say to Martin: "Take charge here, or take me to America." ' (*F* p. 65) Driven by Mary, Martin does take charge. The house is cleaned and scoured (Maggie Kilmartin: 'The poor were born to be dirty'), a patch of ground is cleared for vegetables, Thomsy gets his first bath in years and a new suit of clothes. 'The household settled down to the new kind of life that Mary had introduced . . . allowing themselves to become inoculated with the germs of civilization which her weaver father had brought to the valley.' (*F* p. 115) The weaver has also brought his knowledge of Irish history and of the injustices of the oppressor. He preaches revolt rather than passive acceptance of God's will and becomes a 'notorious hero' when he strikes the landlord's agent and is deported. The exploitation by the landlord class has been brought home to him in a cruelly personal way, when his other daughter — Ellie, Mary's dark sister — is seduced by Chadwick. Mary carries on the tradition of revolt, first against the 'custom' of her in-laws, then against the social system which makes famine possible, finally against God. Her finest moment occurs in the scene where two Quaker gentlemen, Messrs Potter and Broadbent, come to the Black Valley on a 'fact finding mission'. Grasping at any straw, the starving people grovel before the Quakers. Mary, however, rebels against their 'charitable intentions' and replies to a remark on the fatness of her baby:

'If my baby is fat', she cried, 'he can thank God for it. It's little thanks are due to the powers, that took our stock and refused us work on the roads. It's not charity we're asking for, sir, but justice. We are not murderers either, sir, but honest people. . . . You have broad cloth on yer backs, so ye can look at our rags and our dirt. Ye are welcome to it. But maybe the day will come when the poor people of the world will make the tyrants pay

with their blood for these rags and this dirt.'
. . .
'A pretty exhibition of the unchristian spirit of rebell-
ion,' said Mr. Potter. 'Irish temper, I should call it,' said
Mr. Broadbent. (*F* p. 356)

One of the great emotional themes of *Famine* is the struggle
of mothers to feed and protect their children. Mary and her
son are in the foreground but beyond them are all the
mothers and children of the valley — Kitty Hernon who puts
her children in the Protestant Home after an unsuccessful
attempt to sell them to the parson, Sally O'Hanlon who feeds
her little ones on dog meat and then kills them rather than let
them starve to death. Just as a number of brief sub-plots
involving small landholders other than the Kilmartins reflect
and enlarge their fate, so here O'Flaherty achieves what Yeats
in a valuable essay describes as *Emotion of Multitude*.[12]
Yeats's example is Shakespearian drama; on, of course, a
lesser scale, and in the romance form, O'Flaherty strives for a
similar effect.

As the famine intensifies and fever spreads, the mask of
civilization is torn from Mary's face. She steals, lies, plans to
escape without concern for anybody save her husband and
child. When her mother dies she buries her in a 'common
hole, in a wild field, like an animal'. O'Flaherty handles her
degradation very well; what is less satisfactory is his portrayal
of her impulse towards life and liberty, symbolized as escape
to America. The New World appears to her in a vision, she is
directed by an angel to go to 'a rich land where the corn grew
taller than a man's head and there were no masters.' America
too is the land where, as a Young Irelander explains, 'the
fight for liberty must go on until it's won.' The whole weight
and direction of the novel however pulls against this 'happy'
resolution of the conflicts engendered. The 'weaver' Gleeson,
early in *Famine* offers a more realistic assessment of this
brave New World:

'. . . To hell or to Connaught, Cromwell the murderer
used to say. Nowadays, begob, the gentry are clearing
the people out of Connaught itself, into the grave or the

workhouse, or the emigrant ship. It's America now, instead of Connaught, to die of hunger in the New York dives, or to be thrown to the wild Indians on the plains of the west.' (*F* p. 52)

Artistically, one feels, Mary and her husband should not have been allowed to reach the emigrant ship.

O'Flaherty's ideological leanings are at variance with his artistic concern more than once in *Famine*. A lengthy episode in the third section concerns the search by Thomsy for Martin Kilmartin who is 'on the run'. Mary inspires him to undertake the search and O'Flaherty exploits his journey to bring the Young Irelanders into the novel. He comes upon them in a barn where a man with yellow hair, who will enter Thomsy's dreams as a symbol of liberty, addresses a group of conspirators:

> '... there were going to be clubs started all over the country, to fight for a republic in Ireland, to drive out the Queen's men and to get freedom for the poor people. Liberty, he said, was going to be made the law all over the world. He said that France would lead the way, same as she did before. . . .
> . . . .
> He said there are millions of the poor and only a few of the rich, and if the poor got together and made themselves into a proper army, with a proper plan, same as an army and knew what they wanted to do and stuck together, same as an army, they'd make short work of the tyrants. Then there would be liberty all over the world and no hunger on anybody. Landlords,' he said, 'would be shot down like rabbits when the moment came. . . . ' (*F* pp. 385-86)

Thomsy relates his adventures and contact with the rebels to Mary. His narrative is one of the best things in *Famine* — a story within a story that has many of the qualities of a folktale. It is nonetheless largely irrelevant — so far as the dramatic quality of the book is concerned. The episode does, however, find a place within the context we have outlined in our

introduction. It brings into the account of *Famine* the positive, revolutionary elements within the society of the time.

The oppressors and exploiters receive more convincing
expression than do the revolutionaries. To draw on the socialist terminology which lies aback of the character grouping in
Famine, they fall into two large classes. There is, first, the
foreign capitalist-landlord class represented by Captain Chadwick and the parson, Mr Coburn; secondly, the native capital-
ists, foremost among whom is Mr Hynes (a gombeen merchant,
to use more traditional terms), his son, Dr Hynes, and the
parish priest. While all of these characters play out their
assigned and expected roles of exploiters of the peasantry
they are yet portrayed as convincing human beings. It is one
of the strengths of *Famine* that characters operate on two
levels, both as the embodiment of class attitudes and as well-
developed characters in their own right.

Captain Chadwick of Crom House ranks highest in the
scale of perfidy. His relationship to the people is that of
torturer to victim, more brutalized himself by the violence he
inflicts than those on whom he inflicts it. When we first meet
him he is in bed, drunk, and in conversation with Mr Coburn:

> '. . . What has it (his agency) done to me? . . . I've just
> become a sot. This is no place for an Englishman . . . . . .
> Cut off here among a lot of howling savages. . . . no
> wife, no children, no prospects. Own up now. What
> would you do? Cut your throat or go to the colonies?'
> (*F* p. 71)

Outwardly he is hard, ruthless, brutal. He carries with him
that great symbol of Ascendancy power, a horsewhip, and
casts a lecherous, signorial eye on every pretty face in the
village. Ellie Gleeson is his personal servant and kept woman.
Expertly O'Flaherty manipulates these pieces of property —
the whip and woman — to reveal his true, inner nature.
Chadwick is impotent and a masochist (he has been castrated
in India). Ellie ('It's the master, he does be at me') whips
him. When Chadwick orders her to bed with him he 'acts like
a baby at breast.' The middle-aged Lord of the Manor, grotesque at the breast of a village girl, the horseman flogged

with his own whip to give him pleasure — these are the powerful if sordid images in which O'Flaherty bodies forth the social relationships of the nineteenth century. We must add to the last sentence 'in Ireland'. Dr Hynes, as he watches the retreating figure of Chadwick muses: 'Funny how they all like that awful looking drunkard.'

In many ways Dr Hynes is the most interesting character in *Famine*. We have met him before in the person of Dr Fitzpatrick of *The House of Gold*. Like Fitzgerald he is caught between two worlds symbolically represented by the cabin and the Big House. He is the son of Crom's gombeen shopkeeper, John Hynes, and a similar figure in many ways to Ramon Mor Costello *(House of Gold)*. The relationship between father and son parallels and contrasts with that obtaining between Brian and Martin Kilmartin. Their natural ties, however, fraught with difficulties and tensions, act as a foil to the mechanical, commercial bond which binds Gombeen father to Doctor son. Dr Hynes is, literally, a piece of valuable property in which his father has invested. The commercial metaphor which governs the Gombeen's relationship to the peasantry is also operative in his personal relationships.

O'Flaherty explores through the family history of the Hynes's, the rise of native capitalism in Ireland. Dr Hynes is both the product and victim of the new system. When he makes a sick call on the Kilmartins he realizes, for the first time, where his true allegiances lie. The people of Black Valley claim him as one of their own, 'you're one of ourselves, a Catholic and a son of the people.' Watching the beautiful Mary Kilmartin, he 'felt proud to be of their stock.' Yet he is repelled by the dreariness and squalor of life in the valley: 'What was to be had there by anybody whose demands on life were even slightly removed from those of an animal?' *(F* p. 131) His training as a gentleman has taught him to demand more:

> Now he cursed his family for having tried to turn him into a 'gentleman', giving him appetites which he could not satisfy, showing him the joy of brightness and then thrusting him back into the darkness of his native village.

They pretended to sacrifice themselves for his sake, sending him to school and college and now even living in the kitchen so that he might have a room to himself. A private room for the gentleman of the family! What advantage was there in his sitting here miserably alone, while they were having fun in the kitchen, listening to Reilly's account of a steeple-chase? A gentleman! They watched him as if he were still a little boy on apron strings. He couldn't take a drink like any other man, or have fun with girls. (*F* p. 131-32)

'The gentleman of the family' — he is one of the great enduring characters of Anglo-Irish fiction, the clerical student/ teacher/doctor whose morale is undermined by the giggling in the hedgerows and the taste of strong liquor. Hynes tries to escape from the narrow world of his father and the false personality it imposes on him by making friends with Chadwick. Hard drinking, gambling and the presence of Ellie Gleeson are the main attractions that Crom House has to offer. But if Hynes is a gentleman in the eyes of the people, he is a 'native' in the eyes of the gentry. Chadwick and his friends humiliate him, pointing out to one another his 'peasant' posture, his slow deliberation while playing cards which they regard as a 'native' trait. He is rescued from his dilemma by the local Catholic curate, Fr Gellan, who points the way forward for him. This curate is one of the few sympathetically treated clerics in O'Flaherty's novels and it is not difficult to see why this is so. He preaches revolution to the people and has a mystical love for the earth: in short he speaks with O'Flaherty's own voice. He counsels Dr Hynes:

'You can't change the blood in your veins. It will cry out in the darkness of night against your foolishness. I told you before to love this Irish earth as your mother. How? Ask the people. They know. It's in their veins. Listen to them. Feel with them. Bow down before them. It's only when we deny our instincts through greed or cowardice, that we sin. So humble yourself. Not in words, with the tongue, but down in your soul. The future is still pure and holy. Let people cast stones if they wish. The people are always right in the mass. For a moment they may be wrong or for a generation. A generation is only a moment in history. In the long run they are right. Turn your back on the marauders and your face to the people. They'll accept you with open arms. You've been chosen from many and trained at the people's expense to gain proficiency in the art of healing. At the people's expense. The pennies your father collected from the poor. The spades of poor land slaves dug those pennies out of the earth. The people's pence. We are all one family and each person in the family has his duties towards the rest. This house that shelters you and the chair you sit on are gifts to you from the people. The clothes on your back. Give them what you can in return.' (*F* p. 164)

Hynes burns for a brief while with enthusiasm for the cause of the people. He rejects Chadwick – 'you and your kind have ruined and degraded this country' – and turns away from his father ' . . . almost with hatred. For he could recall nothing that inspired tenderness; only that loathsome, furtive look, that constant mumbling about money, . . . ' (*F* p. 134) The doctor is in turn rejected because, as the narrator explains at some length, he is one of those who lack the moral courage to live up to an ideal. His death, from typhus, is absurd and meaningless.

O'Flaherty dramatizes the political and social mismanagement which exacerbated and in many cases prolonged the famine through his handling of the 'Relief Committee'. Its seven members are the parson, Mr Coburn, the parish priest, Fr Roche, three illiterate farmers and John Hynes. Fr Roche opposes any suggestion put forward by the parson whom he suspects of proselytizing tendencies. The three farmers object to all proposals on the grounds that 'they are not within the meaning of the act' – which, of course, they cannot read. Hynes keeps an eye on the 'commercial interest' – ensuring that nothing will be undertaken, such as the distribution of food, that will lessen his profits. The relief works themselves are managed by a small army of officials which costs more to maintain than is paid out to the starving workers. One of the many government restrictions placed on the works is that no useful projects be undertaken. (Digging holes and filling them in again was a not uncommon task for relief workers). Even Chadwick is repelled by the absurdity of it all — 'God Almighty. This army of clerks, gangers, overseers, and engineers, who are not engineers, all destroying our roads at our own expense!' (*F* p. 227)

The government reacts to the agitation for food and work in classical fashion, transforming a social problem into one of security, 'law and order'. The apathy and terror of the people increases while those who wish to help them are further disunited. Something of the thesis-and-illustration quality of *Famine* is caught in Chapter XLIII where the parish priest and curate lead their flock in an attempt to have the food store opened. The chapter begins with a statement of the general proposition which will be acted out by the characters involved:

> When government is an expression of the people's will, a menace to any section of the community rouses the authorities to protective action. Under a tyranny, the only active forces of government are those of coercion. Unless the interests of the ruling class are threatened, authority remains indifferent. We have seen how the feudal government acted with brutal force when the interests of the landowner were threatened (the death of Chadwick and subsequent repression), even to the extent of plundering the poor people's property. Now it remains to be seen what that same government did when those poor lost, by the act of God, all that was left to them by the police and Mr. Chadwick — the potato crop which they had sown. (*F* p. 324)

The police line up, bayonets fixed, to halt the advancing people. A district inspector orders the priest to disband their flock. Fr Gellan, revolutionary as ever, calls on the people to rush the police, 'God save Ireland'. But his superior, Fr Roche, prevents them, parleys with the inspector and both he and the people are browbeaten — 'Do your duty, Father Roche. Tell them to disperse quietly.' If people are looking

for food they should do so 'through their proper representatives'. Conversation reveals that the police have acted at the
behest of John Hynes, the gombeen, who fears an attack on
his shop. *Quod erat demonstravimus*. The rights of property,
in a capitalist society, are superior to human rights. It is thus
not true to say that the characters of *Famine* 'argue no thesis'.
This matter has been investigated more fully in the introduction, and suffice it here to say that much of the characterization and action of the novel is by way of illustrating a
thesis.

O'Flaherty, in his subsequent historical romances, never
achieved the range or power of *Famine*. There is, one feels,
something in the desolation and brute drama of the event
itself which struck a responsive chord within him. It emerges
clearly here and there where the stance of the omniscient
narrator is abandoned, and he speaks in his own voice,
identifying himself with the people and their sufferings.

Land[13]

Nine years after *Famine*, O'Flaherty published the second
volume of his trilogy based on Irish history. His themes are
the exploitation of the peasantry by the feudal landlords and
the coming to power of a new, capitalistic middle class. These
themes are loosely centred round the development of the
technique of isolation known as 'Boycotting', though
O'Flaherty portrays the origin and author of the idea rather
differently from the history books. *Land* differs from
Famine too in the fact that the peasantry are kept very much
in the background. This is a 'Big House' novel that by reason
of the protagonist's sympathies strays among the cabins.

As is usual in the historical romances there are two
opposing forces in *Land*. Broadly, these are the Fenians
versus the Landlords, with somewhere in between, vacillating
and unreliable, the common people and the representative of
the Church, the parish priest. As we might expect, the most
coherently and forcefully portrayed group are the Fenians.
The landlords and their supporters, the Royal Irish Constabulary are not convincingly portrayed. They are, one and all,

stereotypes and the novel is vitiated by this failure of imagination. The peasantry make fitful appearances in the guise of serving men, old women, etc., but they are largely pawns in the game played by their superiors. On the Fenian side these are the aristocratic intellectual, Raoul St George, just home from revolutionary Paris, the Fenian captain, Michael O'Dwyer, fresh from the United States, and an unfrocked priest, Fr Francis Kelly. Opposing the Fenians are Captain Butcher, the demon of the piece, the R.I.C. Inspector Fenton, and Fr Costigan, the parish priest. On the simple level of plot the novel concerns the vengeance of O'Dwyer on Captain Butcher who was responsible for the death of his father.

When we examine the Fenian group we see that they fit readily into the threefold division of worthy men enunciated by Raoul St George: soldier, poet and monk. Raoul is the poet, the man of contemplation who, Prospero-like, directs the action of the novel. O'Dwyer is almost purely a creature of action and Fr Francis readily accommodates the role of monk. It is perhaps worth noting that all three are, in a sense, traitors to either their class or creed. Raoul St George is a traitor to the Anglo-Irish gentry and is recognized as such by his peers — (so too was Parnell whose shadow moves across the novel). O'Dwyer is an interesting character in the light of contemporary events — he stands to the Fenians as the Provisional I.R.A. stand to the Officials today. Towards the end of *Land* he receives the following message which, as an advocate of physical force, he ignores:

> ' . . . A continuation of violence, by even a small group, would prejudice their (the Fenian's) chances of gaining land reforms from the English. . . . the Fenians, in every district except this, have obeyed Michael Davitt and renounced militant action of an illegal character. He (Father Costigan) said that you would be shortly outlawed by your own Fenian organization if you persist in your present conduct. . . . ' (*L* p. 209)

O'Dwyer goes ahead with his bomb attack on Captain Butcher and is killed in the resulting melee.

Fr Francis is an outlaw of a different sort; he is an unfrocked priest, deprived of his ministry because of his part in an earlier rebellion. Soldier, poet and monk then, receive rather special embodiments in *Land* and we will have to examine them more closely. When Yeats praises Major Robert Gregory as 'soldier, scholar, horseman', the terms have a solid social sanction. When Liam O'Flaherty, in the guise of Raoul St George, announces his epithets of praise and refers them to Fr Francis ('. . . Before all three of them I always bow low. When I bowed to you, I bowed to all three'), (*L* p. 53) the reader is conscious that the meanings of the terms are being strained. Similarly there is a certain sleight-of-hand in the treatment of social classes. The overall parable of the book is that a new generation, born from a union of the peasantry and the gentry, will liberate Ireland. To this end O'Dwyer marries Lettice, the daughter of St George, and the book closes to the squeals of a fatherless infant. The parable would have some force if the two classes were fairly represented. What O'Flaherty does instead is to scale down the gentry as represented by the St George's (the impoverished Raoul describes himself as *declasse;* Lettice undergoes a hasty conversion to Catholicism) and tone up the peasantry (O'Dwyer is educated and has a much despised uncle — Sir John Corcoran!). The author's treatment of the group of characters associated with Captain Butcher moves beyond simple unfairness; one suspects that the anthropologist rather than the literary critic might do it more justice. That fabulous figure, the Lady of the Big House, is revealed in all her naked terror. Barbara Butcher (golden hair and golden eyes like Nora of *The House of Gold*) is a nymphomaniac who seduces her groom and meets her lover, Fenton, dressed as a captain of Dragoons ('. . . The highly-ornamented tunic, the tight-fitted breeches and the shining jack boots made her sensual beauty more than usually alluring. At the same time, the warlike male dress brought the latent cruelty of her features into relief'). (*L* p. 190) Yet when she undresses herself for her lover the narrator dwells on 'the tawny beauty of her virgin breasts'. Virgin and nymphomaniac, half man, half woman, her ambivalence is not that of any real woman. She is a nymphomaniac because she has been assaulted many times and not only by O'Flaherty; she is eternally a virgin because the assaults have all been imaginary.

The aristocratic intellectual, Raoul St George, stands at the centre of the book. He is the one and only member of the Anglo-Irish aristocracy to emerge as a hero in O'Flaherty's fiction — and this because he is consciously opposed to his own class. He has returned with his daughter from self-imposed exile in Paris to take charge of his much diminished family estate. The connection with Paris is important on the level of political allegory. Raoul and Lettice moved in revolutionary circles there, they have met the Russian Bakunin and lived through the days of the Paris Commune. They are, on this level, emissaries of the revolution and establish a link, admittedly rather tenuous, between the Fenians and the Communards. More important than any link, however, is the hostility which the returned emigres evoke and the terms in which it is couched. The rhetoric images of social revolution are not available to the people of Manister; what is available and compelling is the authority and tradition of the Catholic Church. A conversation between the parish priest, Fr Cornelius, and his sacristan exemplifies the reaction and its peculiar terms:

> 'I can hardly believe it Pat,' he said . . . 'It must have been like this in Paris nine years ago.' The aged sacristan made the sign of the Cross on his forehead and looked at Father Cornelius in horror.
> 'The Paris Commune!' he gasped. 'The pagans came out of the slums and set up idols on the holy altars and murdered priests and threw the Blessed Sacrament in the gutter. The Communists spat in the face of God and set up Antichrist as King.'
> A wild look of suspicion came into his sunken eyes. 'Lord save us!' he whispered. 'Do you think Anti-Christ have come to Manister, Father Cornelius?'.
> 'He may have, at that,' . . .
> 'From foreign parts?' said the sacristan.
> 'From foreign parts,' Father Cornelius said. (*L* p. 95-96)

Raoul is elected leader of the people's committee because he has sheltered the rebel O'Dwyer and he proceeds to implement a plan, long meditated in Paris, of social revolution. Briefly, as he outlines it to O'Dwyer it consists of the following: 'the few' (presumably the revolutionary *elite*) first seek a mandate from the people to enforce discipline on 'the many'. Having achieved this the people can resist tyranny by the technique of social isolation. The method is given a trial run, so to speak, against a local publican and informer (ironically he is a brother-in-law of Fr Francis) who commits suicide as a result. A villager who breaks the boycott is flogged and flees to America. The undertone of hostility to Raoul and his scheme centres round a village girl (wife of the man who was flogged) who has begun to see visions of the Blessed Virgin. The Virgin's message is the catch-cry of the faction opposed to Raoul — 'Antichrist must go'. Despite the banality of the situation something interesting does emerge (and here one pauses, such visions — Knock was not an isolated case — were a feature of the times. As the parish priest remarks — 'These miraculous signs and apparitions have occurred mainly on the scene of revolutionary disorders, at places where the faithfull have been momentarily led away from God by wicked ideas . . . .') (*L* pp. 175-76) Raoul abandons his efforts to create what would be called today a greater political consciousness among the people. Instead he adopts one of the great symbolic roles of Irish nationalism — the martyr. Told by his servant that the people regard him as 'Antichrist himself sent all the way from Paris by the Devil', he decides to have himself arrested for making a seditious speech — 'It will be difficult to denounce a man who is in jail as Antichrist and an enemy of the people.' (*L* p. 278) He is duly arrested, imprisoned and on his release returns to a triumphant welcome led by the parish priest. The effective politics of *Land* function on the level of symbol and symbolic roles, couched in the terms of Christianity versus Paganism, Christ, antichrist and the martyr. There is, in the person of Raoul, an agonized sense of a different world. He defines himself early in the work as a free-thinker — 'That means that I adopt a purely personal attitude towards ideas and the phenomena of life.' (*L* p. 117) His fine manners and elegant, epigrammatic wit contrast with the blunt, often brutish world around him. He is clear-sighted and generous in his analysis, especially of religion:

> 'In a free society . . . religion is the poetry of the
> people. It is the dark ecstasy by means of which even
> the most lowly confront suffering and death with
> dignity. It ennobles all the incidents of daily life. Under
> tyranny, on the other hand, it becomes the monopoly
> of priestcraft, being tolerated by the ruling power only
> for the purpose of keeping the oppressed in ignorant
> awe. In the latter case, religion becomes an evil and
> mysterious force, to be approached by free man with
> the utmost caution.' (L p. 157)

In the end he has to compromise with that 'mysterious force'.
A little has been gained, the people are united, Raoul like the
Stranger of *The Black Soul* 'felt humbled and exalted before
the unending march of life.'

Michael O'Dwyer is a simple, enduring type in Irish life
and letters. Perhaps the most remarkable fact about
O'Flaherty's portrayal of him is that he is presented without
a shadow of irony. A few quotations serve to establish his
meaning:

> ' . . . he is unique, judged by our standards. I mean that
> he creates his own world and his own laws. . . .
> He sees beauty only in danger.' (Lettice) (L p. 57)

> 'He was one of those on whose forehead tragedy is
> written for even the least intelligent to read. . . . I knew
> instinctively that there never could be peace where he
> was and that to know him meant to suffer. . . . Of
> course, one cannot feel sorrow in the ordinary way for
> one so strong and so certain of his purpose. It would be
> like a common sparrow mourning a royal eagle, that has
> fallen in all its glory. The people certainly don't mourn
> for him. On the contrary, they feel proud and triumph-
> ant, as if they had won a great victory.' (Elizabeth,
> Raoul's sister, after Michael's death) (L p. 227-28)

> 'Oh! How I envy him the way he died.' (Raoul) (L p.229)

If there is something perverse in the imagination which dis-
figures Barbara Butcher as a representative of the 'Big House'
there is something equally perverse in the glorification of
O'Dwyer as a champion of the common people. His motives
are simple and chauvinistic. He wishes to kill Butcher in
revenge for his father's death. Revenge, as we know from
Jacobean drama, can be a forceful and compelling motive.
And single-minded pursuit of a plan of action is often admir-
able. What we sense in O'Dwyer, however, is the will-towards-
death, masquerading as high patriotism. This is particularly
evident in the brief love scenes he has with Lettice. His talk is
all of death and even his actions have a dark inflexion.
Lettice describes the high point of their honeymoon together
on a tiny island. On the morning of the fifth day a terrible
storm blows up and Michael asks Lettice to go sailing with
him through the storm. He lashes her to the stern:

> 'I felt certain that we had foundered, because a giant
> wave passed right over me. I was nearly carried over-
> board, in spite of the stout rope with which I was tied.
> I lay breathless and unable to see for several minutes. . . .
> At once I felt a greater joy than I had ever known
> before. He had opened the innermost door and allowed
> me to enter. Then I understood what he had really
> meant when he said that Cape Horn was beautiful. I
> understood why beauty could be found in danger and
> why rapture could be dark as well as bright. We fought
> the hurricane for six hours. . . . During every moment of
> that time we treaded the brink of death. . . . ' (*L* pp.
> 203-204)

On his way to the final assault on Butcher, O'Dwyer meets
an old woman who acts the part of soothsayer. He tells her,
'No sooner did I meet my love than I had to say farewell,'
and she replies — 'Before you met her,' . . . 'you were already
wedded to the dark stranger.' (*L* p. 215) The 'dark stranger'
is, of course, death, and O'Dwyer's death sets the final seal of
approval on his life and actions. What is disturbing about all
this — and it is a disturbing fact about Irish life — is the
simple acquiescence in the will towards death and destruction.

Again one reverts to American fiction and Leslie Fiedler's summary: 'Our fiction is not merely in flight from the physical data of the actual world, in search of a (sexless and dim) ideal. . . . . it is bewilderingly and embarrassingly a gothic fiction, non-realistic and negative, sadist and melodramatic — a literature of darkness and the grotesque in a land of light and affirmation.'[14] Taught by our novelists, we would have to change the last phrase to 'a land of darkness and denial'.

The monk of *Land*, Fr Francis Kelly, is a shadowy figure. He is present not so much because the plot or situation demands him but to balance with a spiritual principle the soldierly and poetic principles embodied in O'Dwyer and Raoul. He has been defrocked for his part in the rising of 1867 and, as Raoul describes him, 'He has remained fixed ever since in that single act of revolt. He can neither advance beyond it, nor regain the state of mind that preceded it. He wanders about the country like a lost soul, trying to rouse the people to a repetition of his own tragedy.' (*L* p. 59) As with Fr Gellan of *Famine* he is another of the few clerics who are sympathetically treated in O'Flaherty's fiction. Raoul, we remember, finds in him the threefold qualities of poet, soldier and priest. Poets, says Shelley, are 'the unacknowledged legislators of the world'; Fr Francis, who writes ballads, would amend the text to read 'balladmakers':

> 'Ballads are very important, because people sing them if they are any good. They are the poetry of the people. Poetry should be sung. That's the only way it can become part of life, what it should be, instead of being buried in books. Ballads can overthrow empires and bring new nations into existence.' (*L* p. 49)

It was a ballad on the death of his father, heard in a Dublin street, which drove Michael O'Dwyer to join the Fenians and exact vengeance on Captain Butcher. Fr Francis as monk is an equivocal figure. He retires to a *clochan* (an ancient monastic cell) when Raoul initiates his campaign of isolation, in protest against the alleged 'paganism' of the method. (Ironically the Church's refusal of the right to administer the sacraments to him is boycotting of a similar kind). He comes to see, under Raoul's influence that he is a 'terrible sinner for having deserted the people' and emerges from his *clochan* to fight with O'Dwyer and Raoul. O'Flaherty's 'monk' is something of the order of the 'guerilla priests' of South America today.

However we may qualify our assent to the character of Raoul, O'Dwyer and Fr Francis, they at least represent something new in O'Flaherty's fiction. The British side of the central conflict in *Land* is something else again. The intrigue between Inspector Fenton of the R.I.C. and Barbara Butcher is a rehash of that between Nora and Francis O'Neill *(House of Gold)*. Like Nora she persuades her lover to rob her husband and the only difference is that Fenton succeeds and the two make good their escape to America. Barbara, as remarked earlier, is an equivocal figure. In one of the few episodes where she is sympathetically treated she sums up the view of Ireland from the windows of the Big House:

'Sometimes I have the feeling that I am living in a lunatic asylum. It really is beastly, living in a state of permanent fear, among people by whom one is permanently hated.' (*L* p. 66)

Captain Butcher with his Cuban bloodhound and large oaths is an equally stereotyped and tawdry character. He tells Fenton:

'I'm just a plain Englishman, son of a Berkshire yeoman. My rank of captain is mere eye-wash. You know yourself that I'm just a captain of Irish militia. I'm a self-made man and I frankly admit it. Yet I feel that my work here in Ireland is more important to the Empire than what my sons are doing (fighting the natives in Afghanistan and South Africa). I'm defending the feudal system and the landowning gentry, on whom the power of England is based. If that system and that class are destroyed, then England is doomed with the space of a few generations.' (*L* p. 37)

Neither the plot of *Land* nor the subsequent characterization of Butcher, in the end, support the theme of landowners *versus* an insurgent peasantry. It descends to a cowboy-and-Indian shoot-out where one's interest is held, if at all, by the desire to see what will happen next. Butcher's wife makes the appropriate comparison when describing the effects of the boycott on her household — 'We have been living since then like people besieged by Red Indians, in one of Fenimore Cooper's frontier outposts.' (*L* p. 195) *Land* is written by one of the Redskins.

Insurrection[15]

An examination of *Insurrection*, O'Flaherty's last published novel, must begin with the admission that it is a very bad novel. The reasons for this opinion will emerge in the discussion of the various elements which go to make up the works. Carl Jung first established the principle that it is often inferior and sometimes downright bad novels which are the most revealing psychologically and culturally. It is in this spirit that we examine *Insurrection*.

Bartley Madden, a Connemara man, returns from exile in England to marry and settle down. In Dublin he is robbed of his savings while drunk and by a series of accidents is caught up in the Easter Week Rising. *Insurrection* is largely an account of the Rising as seen through the eyes of Madden. The character types of soldier, poet and monk first explicitly defined in *Land* are here further elaborated and confused. Madden is the soldier:

> He certainly looked the type of man that is ideally fitted by nature to be a soldier. He was twenty-four years old, over six feet in height, lean and finely muscled, with strong jaws and clear blue eyes set wide apart in a bony tanned face. (*I* p. 7)

In one perspective, the theme of *Insurrection* is the education of Madden into his true role as soldier. Just as in the *Playboy* Christy Mahon is presented with an ideal picture of himself which in the end he actually becomes, so Madden is trans-

formed from the destitute *spalpeen* of the early chapters to
the heroic freedom fighter of the last. His education or
transformation proceeds by way of a series of emblematic
encounters with the revolutionaries, notably Captain Kinsella
and George Stapleton who embody the roles of monk and
poet respectively.

It is important to establish the actuality which the Idea
(thus capitalized throughout the novel) transfigures. Two
elements are important here — Dublin on the eve of revolution and the position of Madden himself. Both are handled
very much in the manner of O'Casey's *The Plough and the
Stars*. The occupation of the General Post Office by the
Volunteers is seen through the eyes of bystanders, all of them
hostile:

> Those bloody rebels should be shot. . . . It makes me
> mad to see those bowsies go route-marching at a time
> like this, stirring up trouble while patriotic Irishmen are
> dying at the front. They are in German pay.
>
>   (a Dublin slum-dweller)
> You yellow swine! If you want to play at soldiers, why
> don't you go out there and fight the Hun?
> (a British Army Officer on his way to Fairyhouse Races)
> It's an outrage. . . . . I have been a civil servant for
> twenty-five years. Now I've been thrown into the street
> by a gang of hooligans.
>
>   (a G.P.O. official)
>   (*I* pp. 8, 10, 20)

An argument develops among the crowd gathered outside the
G.P.O. and it quickly turns into a faction-fight between those
traditional Irish enemies, townies *versus* bogman. ('Up
Castlebar . . . There's a Mayo man with you. Up Castlebar! . . . ' as opposed to 'Don't let it be said that two bog-
trotters from the west can lick the whole Dublin'). This is the
ironic setting for the reading of the Proclamation of Independence. The narrator makes explicit the dramatic analogy that
underlies his handling of the scene:

All eyes were turned towards the Grecian columns of

the portico, where Patrick Pearse stood ready to proclaim the purpose of the insurrection. The people were
now like an audience at a theatre, tensely waiting for
the climax of a play's first act. (*I* p. 32)

Madden's dumb soul is stirred by the drama of what he sees
and hears:

For the first time in his life, his mind had conceived an
abstract idea that lit the fire of passion in his soul.
Although the words that he heard were beyond his
comprehension, their sound evoked the memory of all
that had exalted him since childhood. Like music, they
carried him away into enchantment. (*I* p. 33)

Throughout *Insurrection* the idea of freedom is associated in
Madden's mind with a series of pastoral images, the flight of
wild geese, sailing, his mother's voice. The rebels awake his
imagination and from this point until he actually joins them
the novel dramatizes his vacillation between the 'dark rapture'
they stir in him and the reality of what he is ' . . . a peasant
soul, that yearned only for a plot of ground on which to
mate and breed his kind in peace.' He is conscience-stricken
by the words of Pearse. Is it not a mortal sin to listen to
those who preach revolt? In an extraordinary episode a line
of priests with locked arms attempt to clear O'Connell Street.
Madden is prevented by them from joining the insurgents.
'The idea was overwhelmed by contact with the power of the
Church.' (*I* p. 36) This scene is a good example of both the
method and unsubtlety of *Insurrection*. A man with the
sound of the 'whirring wings of wild geese' in his head is
prevented from reaching the G.P.O. garrison (which in full
voice is singing 'The Soldier's Song') by a line of black-
robed symbolic clerics. (It is worth remarking at this point –
and it is an indication of the kind of history with which
O'Flaherty has to deal – that a row of clerics with linked
arms *did* in actual fact try to clear O'Connell Street shortly
after the occupation of the G.P.O.). The different elements,
symbolic geese and priests, the singing soldiers and eager
peasant, fail to cohere, and have more the quality of dream

than reality.

Madden is taken charge of by a Mrs Colgan who has a young son in the G.P.O. She urges him to join the insurgents and holds up an image of future glory to him. He has relapsed into a purely selfish attitude, bewailing the loss of his money and hence his prospects in Connemara. The heroic image of himself is further reinforced when Madden carries a rifle through the streets of Dublin (he has stolen the rifle, in a totally unbelievable sequence of events, from a fallen Lancer after the cavalry charge down O'Connell Street). There is something almost obscene in his fondling of the rifle and the significance it holds for him. The following is a representative passage. The words in italics (mine) will be commented on at greater length:

> ... his whole being was intensely conscious of the weapon that he carried. Its touch gave him a marvellous sense of power and dignity. A soldier's rifle. He was carrying a soldier's rifle through the streets of Dublin, without having to wear the hated uniform of the imperial oppressor that had kept his kindred disarmed and enslaved for centuries. There in front of him lay the Nelson Pillar, the towering symbol of imperial power. He was marching straight towards it, carryign this beautiful weapon that he had taken from an imperial soldier. *Such an astounding and glorious fact was beyond the realm of thought. It could only be felt through the blood, like the sensual possession of a beloved one. It was more intoxicating than the strongest liquor.* (*I* p. 68)

In this passage possession of a gun is almost a token of entry into full manhood, a symbol of male potency. Repeatedly in *Insurrection* the language of sexual love is applied to Madden's contact with the volunteers and his gun battles with the English troops. The one inspires in him, in the words of the novel, 'rapture', 'enchantment', 'divine ecstasy'. He joins the volunteers 'like a lover in the first flush of a newborn passion'. His relationship with the captain of the Volunteers under whom he serves is that of a lover towards his mistress. He worships him; he is 'his chosen one'; after the battle 'He wanted to kneel down and kiss his captain's feet, in order to express his tender joy.' The frequent gun battles of the novel become mystical experiences that draw on the language of love. Even the English troops undergo a similar transformation. If the collective image for the insurgents is the Pure Maiden, the image for the imperial troops is the Whore, with Madden's 'gun' dealing death rather than life to them:

> Like a man bedded with an insatiable wanton, he became enraged with these yellow creatures (the khak-clad troops) whom he could not master, while waiting idly on his mattress after the attack had been repelled. Yet when they charged again and he began to fire his rifle at them, his rage changed into a mysterious and satisfying feeling of unity with these men, on whom he spent his passion. (*I* p. 134)

How is this peculiar set of images to be understood? The following theory will be supported by a further examination of *Insurrection* and *The Martyr* and would apply not just to these books but to the great bulk of literature, songs and ballads centred on Ireland's struggle for freedom. It is this: that the themes of love and death which form a nexus in so many treatments of the Irish struggle are a sublimation of the traditional *liebestod* theme as we see it in other literatures. The theme of death-in-love as it is revealed in *Tristan and Iseuld,* in *Romeo and Juliet,* in *Heloise and Abelard* has to do with personal relationships, in the fate of lovers who refuse to live except by the best they have known and choose death rather than a diminution of their great passion (an Anglo-Irish example would be Synge's *Deirdre of the Sorrows*). An Ireland variously personified as Kathleen Ni Houlihan, Roisin Dubh, Banba, seems to inspire in her devotees a similar dark passion. The young girl with the walk of a queen has led many young men in Irish literature away from their mundane sweethearts to a more 'glorious' consummation. It is part of the impenetrable quality of much nationalist rhetoric, whether in the writings of Pearse or the imaginative

works of O'Flaherty, that what is said is not couched in
political terms, often not even nationalistic, but mystical. It
would take us too far from our present purpose to explore
this theme more generally. Sufficient to notice our main
point, that the images and the terminology of sexual love are
here displaced from their more normal personal context to a
public one, often with grotesque effect.

Madden joins the insurgents because, as Mrs Colgan
explains to the local commander, Captain Kinsella, he has
'the fighting drop in him'. Kinsella grows in Madden's imagination to be a symbol of all he desires:

> The Idea had now found a leader for him to worship.
> The vague mystical longings inspired in him by the
> poet's (i.e. Pearse's) words had taken flesh, in this lean
> man with the ascetic face and the mysterious eyes of a
> monk. He felt taut from head to foot like a drawn bow,
> as he waited to establish contact with his chosen one.
> (*I* p. 84)

As the description of Kinsella suggests, he is the monk of
O'Flaherty's trinity. Indeed every extended reference to
Kinsella compares him at some point to a monk. More
factually, he is a chemist who cut short a brilliant career in
order to help his brother become a priest. His brother died
before ordination and Kinsella was left with a humdrum life
until the Revolution broke out. In the course of *Insurrection*
he has a dream in which he tries to reach a huge flower with a
black stem and scarlet petals. His friend Stapleton interprets
the dream for him:—

> You tried to kill the poet in you, in an attempt to
> become a saint; but the poet remains, still wanting to
> continue that glorious journey towards the horizon of
> the unknown, where the black and scarlet flower. . . . .
> (*I* p. 205)

Like Fr Francis of *Land* he is obviously meant to contain
within himself the threefold qualities of monk, poet and
soldier but equally obviously these are only gestures in the

direction of a theory. He is realized on the level of action as a soldier, a charismatic leader in whom his followers place implicit trust. Madden is enthralled with him:

> His faith was not placed in God but in Kinsella, upon whom he had seized as a symbol and embodiment of all the strange raptures that had ebbed and flowed through his being since noon. These raptures had now been made constant and unchangeable by his act of faith. The Idea had become a component part of his living substances. He had been liberated from his torments by a complete surrender of himself to the authority of a leader. He no longer regretted the loss of his money, or felt any concern for his future. The farm of land and the 'girl that went with it' had vanished from his mind, thrust out as irrelevant by his unique passion. He no longer had to think. That was now the affair of the sombre pale-faced man with the mysterious eyes of a monk, that marched with such dignity in front of him. (*I* p. 97)

The action of the remainder of the novel recounts Madden's gradual internalization of the qualities represented by Kinsella until, in the end, he is able to stand alone and think for himself. In summary Kinsella proposes, and is the image of, an heroic ideal. He realizes, and makes his men realize, that they have no chance of surviving the Rebellion. 'Courageous men fight best when they have no illusions.' (*I* p. 106) Their sacrifice will be an example to the Irish nation.

What meaning does O'Flaherty ascribe to the Rebellion? What is its peculiar significance for him? The third major character of the book — Volunteer Stapleton — goes some way to answer these questions. He is a poet, given to romantic reverie:

> I am a poet and all poets are pantheists like Shelley. At least they should be, for to be a poet is to be supremely capable of love. . . . Surely you will admit that Shelley was one of us? He once threw down pamphlets from his hotel window into this very street outside, urging the people to revolt. . . . I believe that the whole universe is

God and that He is equally present in all creatures and
in all things whose existence has absolutely no purpose,
other than to serve as an expression of His will to love.
(*I* p. 26)

His beliefs issue in rather odd emotions: watching with
Madden the death agony of British soldiers shot by both of
them at Mount Street Bridge, he dwells on the beauty of it
all, 'like listening to music'. A faint suspicion grows that
Stapleton's aesthetic is derived not from Shelley but from
Keats, and a Keats horribly misunderstood. Keats, we
remember, found a 'quarrel in the street' beautiful because of
'the fine energies displayed' but Mount Street Bridge with,
according to the narrator, hundreds of dead and dying bodies
strewn on the road is rather a different matter. At any rate it
is left to Stapleton to clarify the meaning of the Insurrection.
We can best come to grips with what he has to say by bringing together the scattered fragments of his thoughts on the
subject:

We have now reached what the Spaniards call '*la hora de
la verdad*' the supreme moment of passion when the
whole of life is expressed in a single gesture; when the
soul is stripped naked and its real nature is exposed.
again:
At this hour one feels the exaltation of fulfilment if one
has done and is doing what one was born to do. If not
one suffers the agony of despair and the shame of having lived in a lie, of having allowed oneself to be
regarded as a hero while one was really a mountebank;
for the lie is then mercilessly laid bare.
Finally, on the insurrection itself:
This is a poetic gesture. It can only end in death, like
the dance of love performed by those scarlet insects that
whirl in the sunlight above a shining stream, for a few
hours of their existence. (*I* pp. 201, 203, 173)

Stapleton, then, sees the revolution not in political or social
terms, but as 'a moment of truth', something which provokes
the ultimate poetic gesture. It is a refining fire that burns

away the dross of the ordinary and everyday and leaves the essence — in the case of the three main characters of *Insurrection*, their roles as poet, monk, and soldier. Any event, whether it is famine, land agitation or insurrection, is significant if it evokes a passionate response. The reviewer of *Insurrection* in the *Bell* made the essential point about this rather desperate attempt to tack on a meaning to the violence of the novel:

> It might be said that only readers who know nothing about Easter Week could get the best value out of *Insurrection;* and that is, perhaps as it should be. But will even such readers take as a matter of course those few brief passages in which Mr. O'Flaherty attempts to find philosophical meaning for the desperate act of violence by lifting particular events from the plane on which they have vividness at least to a plane where they are coloured clouds of abstraction?[16]

Then as now our answer must be — no. Even within the novel itself Stapleton's theorizing has little or no impact on the protagonist Madden. He is the first of the three to die, he does so, as we might expect, nobly. It is Kinsella, rather, who exercises a continuing pressure on Madden's imagination. When he in turn is shot, Madden momentarily looses faith. Again the comparison with Christy Mahon is opportune. Just as Christy almost fails at the last moment when the dream and actuality are about to become one and is moved to effective action by the taunts and jeers of those who previously praised him, so too is Madden. He carries the dead body of his captain into a butcher's shop where he is once again accosted by Mrs Colgan:

> He had again become a penniless vagabond, standing between two pillars of the portico, not knowing where to go or what to do, without a heroic purpose to glorify his life. (*I* p. 233)

Mrs Colgan and her friends present him with the image of what he was:

> I'm going to tell you what I think of the Maddens

before I stop. Ye are a scum of tinkers and sheep-stealers
and informers, that should be driven out of the west by
bell, book and candlelight. (*I* p. 245)

Madden is roused to fury, rejects their image of him and
remains loyal to his dead captain's concept of the heroic
soldier. Pearse and the G.P.O. Garrison surrender, but
Madden, alone with his 'Idea' refuses to give in. The last
scene is another Wild West shoot out. Madden, two guns in
hand, stalks down the street blazing away at three soldiers.
Naturally, he kills all three but is himself shot in the process:
'All round the little square, people stared in silence from
doors and windows at the dead body that lay prone, with a
rifle slung across its back and each outstretched hand gripping a pistol.' (*I* p. 254)

One further point is worthy of comment in *Insurrection*.
One set of images drawn from sexual love has been dealt
with, but there is another, more pervasive series of images in
the novel. City life and the events narrated are frequently
presented in terms of rural life. Mrs Colgan is 'like a hobbled
hen', the city mob moves 'like a herd of frightened cattle',
Madden in pursuit of the soldiers is 'like a setter dog lapsing
into immobility with infinite caution, before spotting game.'
The sounds of the city in the evening are 'like sounds of
unseen life heard at night in a forest' and so on. One could
justify this recurring imagery on the grounds, firstly, that it is
an effort somehow to 'humanize' the city by making it like
the countryside, or, secondly, since the central intelligence
('ignorance' might be more apt) in *Insurrection* is a simple-
minded countryman, there is a certain justice in using pastoral imagery. At any rate the attempt fails, the reader is
constantly aware more of the differences than the similarities
in these metaphors and similes. Indeed one is tempted at
times to see the animal imagery as an unconscious indictment
of the mindless world O'Flaherty portrays.

He (Madden) ground his teeth in impotent rage against
this form of combat that had hitherto been unknown to
him; like a bull that issues from his dark pen and clears

aspect of Irish life. Yet, when he comes to treat of the theme imaginatively, his best powers are reserved for the martyrdom of Crosbie; indeed his imagination very frequently goes dead when treating of more mundane matters. A warning from D.H. Lawrence's preface to *Studies in Classic American Literature* is opportune: 'The artist usually set out — or used to — to point a moral and adorn a tale. The tale, however, points the other way, as a rule. Two blankly opposing morals, the artist's and the tale's. Never trust the artist. Trust the tale. The proper function of a critic is to save the tale from the artist who created it.'[21]

The action of *The Martyr* takes place in a small town in Kerry, called Sallytown, in the autumn of 1922. The Civil War is in progress and the Irregulars (or Republicans) have occupied the town under the command of Commandant Brian Cosbie. The Regulars (or Free Staters) under Colonel Hunt and Major Tyson are closing in to liquidate this last pocket of resistance to the new government. They succeed. The action of the novel in which Crosbie is taken prisoner, his assistant, Captain Jack Tracy, takes to the hills ('on the run' is the classic phrase) and the Staters are everywhere successful is merely designed to demonstrate the utter incompetence of the Republicans in practical affairs and the dull competence of the Staters. However, with William Blake's *The Black Boy,* the Republicans might exclaim 'But oh! my soul is white.' The opposing groups fall into the familiar O'Flaherty categories — Innocence versus Experience, Soul versus Body, Action versus Contemplation. The central conflict of the book is that between Commandant Crosbie and Major Tyson, the one a spokesman for idealism and sacrifice, the other a practical men whose God is the state and its smooth functioning. There is a third figure, not as completely developed as these two, who is in conflict with both parties, though officially on Crosbie's side. This is one of James Connolly's men, the socialist Captain Jack Tracy. His God is the machine and he does at least manage to combine his idealism with practical competence as a soldier. These three figures, Crosbie, Tyson, Tracy, have the lineaments of the tripartite hero announced by Raoul St George in *Land* thirteen years later. Commandant Crosbie is the monk:

I have no talent for fighting. Prayer and contemplation and suffering are what appear to me most capable of purifying the souls of our people, and of making our country free and noble. (*M* p. 66)

He wishes to establish a Gaelic Catholic Republic. The struggle against 'pagan England' from 1916 forward was a holy war, 'a fulfilment of our Divine mission to Christianise Europe for a second time.' The Free Staters, by coming to terms with England, have frustrated that mission:

We (i.e. the Republicans) are a handful of the faithful, making a gesture of protest against the national betrayal. We can't prove to the people that they're wrong by killing a few of the enemy here and there. What we're aiming at is a purification of the national soul, and in order to achieve that we must keep our own souls pure. That is the important thing. The soul cannot be purified by blood letting, but by martyrdom. (*M* p. 24)

Crosbie, in short, is Pearse writ smaller. Captain Jack Tracy, late of the G.P.O. and Connolly's Citizen Army, is a much more vigorous character. He is second in command to Crosbie at Sallytown and is the soldier of O'Flaherty's scheme. As the action progresses he takes command of the ragged garrison and gives them something to do. O'Flaherty also provides him with a mistress, a dark haired, earthy creature. It is to this lady — Kate McCarthy — that he haltingly explains his view of life. Handing her his gun he explains:

That's a machine Kate. That's the new God. That's my God. Not because it's a gun, but because it's a machine. This is a machine to kill, but there are others to till the earth an' to make things in factories, an' to drive ships and aeroplanes. . . I love machines. They are my God sure enough, if ye like to put it that way, steel and combustion. Jay! If I had a proper education, Kate, I could explain it to ye. (*M* p. 91)

We are to understand that he is a Socialist but this is mainly realized at the level of Tracy verbally abusing the religious susceptibilities of Crosbie.

Major Joe Tyson is the poet, though here we have to stretch the meaning of the term a long way indeed. He is a sinister and elusive figure who reads Voltaire's *Charles XII* as he plots the crucifixion of Crosbie. At the simplest level, he is a melodramatic villain, properly garbed in dark hat and coat. At another he is the embodiment of Fascism, a candidate, if he lives, for General O'Duffy's 'Blue Shirts': 'That's what we must learn to do in Ireland. To kill in cold blood whoever stands in the way of our progress. To own no God above the state.' (*M* p. 282) More significantly, he is a surrogate for O'Flaherty as artist. The last sentence of the book contains a revealing comparison. Kate McCarthy, nursing the wounded Tracy, hears a scream in the night. She looks out to see a flaming cross hurtling over a precipice (this is, in fact, Crosbie who has just been crucified by Tyson). Unwilling to upset her patient, she tells him 'It's only a rabbit caught by a weasel.' In the autobiographies, and especially in *Shame the Devil,* O'Flaherty frequently draws on the image of the rabbit and weasal to typify the relationship between the man and the artist. The timid heart and blustering progress of one, the cool calculation and deadly accuracy of the other are the qualities which, for him, justify the comparison. It is also part of popular folklore that the weasel mesmerizes its victim, exercises a deadly fascination over him. Again O'Flaherty would claim a parallel with the relationship between the man who suffers and the man who creates.

Crosbie's expression of his beliefs employs the metaphors of martyrdom and sacrifice. There is even, in the vicinity of Sallytown, a 'holy mountain' with Stations of the Cross up its side, rather like Croagh Patrick. The very landscape is a metaphor. Tyson as artist enables Crosbie actually to enact his metaphor. It is noticeable that he does not force him to it, indeed he offers him many ways of escaping his chosen end. But so completely is Crosbie immersed in his role that he can regard Tyson's offers as temptations of the devil. His metaphors are impervious to attack:

'Don't crucify me,' said Crosbie in a womanish tone.

'Why not?'
'I'm not worthy of that,' said Crosbie. (*M* p. 273)

In a sense, Tyson/O'Flaherty is 'purifying the language of the tribe.' Men of Crosbie's kind have surrounded themselves with a metaphoric system which can only be broken by forcing them to enact their metaphors (a distant parallel might be found in the asinine Bottom of *A Midsummer Night's Dream* changed into an ass or, a more recent example, the great insect of Kafka's *Metamorphosis*). Imprison, torture such men and they will be called martyrs, praise them, save them, and they will say they are not worthy. But crucify them? On their way up the holy mountain Tyson recalls the pilgrims who once climbed there, performing the Stations of the Cross: 'What were they doing? Longing to be crucified. All enslaved people worship this fetish of the crucifixion. . . . I'll crucify that fetish in your person.' (*M* p. 275)

Tyson too is aware of the other great metaphor which binds men such as Crosbie — their love for Ireland idealized as the courtly service of Dark Rosaleen. The metaphor, in his terms, is no longer serviceable:

Why not make friends with me and become a good citizen? I remember how you said this morning that you loved Ireland. Then why do you want to die when she is just beginning her career? Or did you only love her poor and subject? Some lovers are like that. They are content only when their love is in rags and misery. They get raging jealous of bright garments and gay smiles. (*M* p. 277)

To appreciate the full force of what Tyson has to say we must revert to the scenes in *The Martyr* where Dark Rosaleen actually makes her appearance in the guise of Angela Fitzgibbon, otherwise Countess Markievicz. Her appearance in the beleagured town resembles nothing so much as the figure in the ghostly ship of Coleridge's *Ancient Mariner:*

Her lips were red, her looks were free
Her locks were yellow as gold:

Her skin was white as leprosy,
The Night-mare Life-in-Death was she,
Who thickens men's blood with cold.

O'Flaherty's description of Dark Rosaleen will be quoted at some length as it offers additional evidence for the contention, sketched earlier that the manichean love-death theme adheres to idealized images of Ireland.

Angela Fitzgibbon confronts the dreaming Commandant Crosbie prior to the Free Staters' assault:

Framed in the narrow doorway, in the gathering dusk, she looked like a ghost. She was very tall and she wore a loose, dark dress that reached to her ankles. A dark silk scarf lay loose about her throat and shoulders. She wore black gloves and wide-brimmed black hat. Even her white face increased the impression of ghostliness.

Her face was very beautiful. Great yellow eyes slanted upwards slightly towards her temples and her cheekbones were high as if she had Mongolian blood. The expression of her eyes was sleepy and mysterious, passionate, yet cold and cruel, in the irresponsible way that the eyes of a tigress are cruel; its merely being their nature to devour. Her eyelashes were very long and of the same colour as her auburn hair, which lay in thick plaits at the nape of her neck. Her mouth was wide, with large, sensitive lips. There was no trace of colour in her countenance and the skin was unblemished like pure snow. A radiance emanated from it, the effect of which was startling; the essence of unfathomable and unattainable beauty ...

It was indeed no other than the famous Angela Fitzgibbon who stood before him. The daughter of a wealthy landowner called Colonel Fitzgibbon, she had created a scandal by taking part in the rebellion of 1916, being captured in a volunteer's uniform with a smoking revolver in her hand, her tunic bloody from a wound in her side. Since then she had become a legendary figure in Irish political life. An outcast from her own class, she was regarded by the revolutionary mass of the people as a living symbol of their insurrection. To them she was the fairy queen of whom the poets had sung, the Dark Rosaleen who was the spirit of the enslaved motherland, now walking the earth to urge on the risen warriors to victory.

Yet victory never seemed to follow in the tracks of this dark angel. Instead, she seemed to be the harbinger of death. Up and down the land she went, enslaving by her beauty whatever leader she imagined for the moment to be pregnant with the nation's destiny. And death came to whomsoever she influenced. (*M* pp. 62-63)

One cannot but recall Yeats's lines on the ladies of Lisadell: 'Two girls in silk kimonos, both beautiful,/One a gazelle.'[22] and the other, according to O'Flaherty, a tigress.

Crosbie is in love — has been for years — with Angela (Angel, 'Dark Angel'). He is under no illusion as to why she has come to him now — to make sure that he dies for her. In a moment of fury and insight he realizes the dark side of her nature: 'A murderess! That's what you are. You take pleasure in sending men to their death. It's you who are mad. You are a demon.' (*M* p. 169) O'Flaherty goes on to deride the image of Dark Rosaleen even further and even more cruelly than Joyce with his image of the sow that eats her farrow. Crosbie, overcome with weariness, falls asleep and Angela paces the room. The narrator moves into her mind to reveal that she is essentially a *rouee,* bored with life. Revolution and the lovers she enticed to their deaths were merely ways of escaping from herself. Physical intimacy with men has become repulsive. Like a drug addict she can no longer react to such mild stimulants. She is in search of a new and greater excitement:

She thought of Tyson and a queer brilliance shone in her yellow eyes. He was devil enough, she thought, to dare kill her if she could rouse him. In any case, it would be exciting to try. (*M* p. 171)

Tyson, aware that if he even arrests her she will become a

martyr in the popular imagination, sends her off like a naughty schoolgirl. There is a fine absurdity in the final image of Roisin Dubh trying to get herself arrested by the forces of the Irish Government in order to regain her proper, mythical status.

The figure of Angela Fitzgibbon is balanced in the book by her dark-haired and dark-skinned counterpart, Kate McCarthy. Kate is a simple girl, loyal to the man she loves, passionate and beautiful. In the end all she wants is to get her man, the socialist Tracy. But in this land of Poets, Monks and Soldiers the menfolk are in flight from the simple verities of ordinary, everyday life:

> Now she suffered the greatest torture of a woman in love; fear that her lover had grown indifferent to her, attracted by a stronger passion; that he was caught up in some wild torrent of male passion into which no woman could enter and that her encircling arms, her tears, even her heart's blood could not draw him back. Now she loathed bitterly these damned religions of patriotism and revolution that made men senseless of what was real in life, love and mating. (*M* p. 156)

Kate and Tracy do come to a precarious union but there is little doubt at the end of the book that she will be a widow ere long. Incidentally, there is a marvellously ironic moment when Tracy is trying to put a little discipline into the Irregular garrison and catches sight of Crosbie in deep conversation with Dark Rosaleen. 'What the hell time,' he asks, 'is this for passin' the time o' night with a girl?' (*M* p. 76) For him Dark Rosaleen is 'an old bitch'.

The Martyr is, all in all, a more powerful and compelling book than either *Land* or *Insurrection*. More than any other quality what impresses the reader is the sheer *daring* of the thing. It is, as Yeats said 'very mad in the end', but it possesses something of the inspired madness of his own 'Crazy Jane' sequence. Again and again in *The Martyr* one is conscious that it is Crosbie who speaks for O'Flaherty's deepest longings. What, asks Tyson, does he love in their common motherland? It is perhaps not too fanciful to read Crosbie's reply as a description of the basic impulse behind the historical romances. He loves:

> Her wild earth and the air above her, sweetened by her fragrance. The wondering eyes of God shining through the sun and moon and stars upon His loveliest child. Her night-gowns of pale mist and the sun-lit dew in which she bathes her green cheeks on awakening. The great seas that frolic on her shores, or proudly mount on her topmost cliffs, throwing their great shawls of foam into the air for joy in their lover's kiss. I love to be alone on her hills in the evening, listening to the soft music of the wind that plays her lullabies. Oh! Tyson, all of her is sacred to me, and that any of her sons, born on her sap, should sell this dear love to a pagan king .... (*M* p. 198)

CHAPTER 11

THE DUBLIN THRILLERS

This concluding section deals with four 'thrillers' — *The Informer, The Assassin, Mr. Gilhooley* and *The Puritan* — all of which are set in post-revolutionary Dublin. They have many features in common which allow them to be considered as a group, distinct from the main body of O'Flaherty's fiction. All are concerned, in some way, with violent death, with a central alienated individual, with the city and the grotesque creatures who inhabit its 'under-world', all are heavily — and disastrously — influenced by the fiction of Dostoyevsky. The point must be made at the outset that these novels are the least interesting and least satisfactory of all O'Flaherty's works. They are frequently badly written, poorly constructed and repetitive. The reader has the impression that all would have made excellent short stories but instead they have been padded out to make bad novels. (In the case of *The Assassin* we have the short story — called *The Terrorist* — from which the novel grew). *The Assassin* and *The Puritan* repeat situations and characters from *The Informer* and *Mr. Gilhooley* respectively, and hence we have grouped these novels together in our analysis. Crude, often plainly inept, in style, construction and characterization - yet a nagging doubt remains about these works. They *do* capture a time and a facet of Irish life in a way that no other fiction has succeeded in doing.

It is part of current folklore that the late 1920s in Irish history were a sad anti-climax to the lofty dreams which had

animated the early decades of the century. The violence,
puritanism, disillusionment, the *greyness* of these years is
proverbial. This, of course, is not the whole story but it is the
popular image. If one were asked to point to the picture of
the 20s and 30s which best embodies the popular conception,
one could hardly do better than to indicate these novels, with
all their glaring faults and, in some respects, because of their
faults. They are — nasty, brutish but alas! not short — both
the product and embodiment of their time. The hunted,
obsessed creatures of *The Informer, The Puritan* and *Mr.
Gilhooley* seem *sui generis* to the period that produced the
Censorship of Publications Act (1929), the hysteria about
communism (The 'red scare', Professor James Hogan's
pamphlet, *Could Ireland become Communist?*) and the
Public Safety Bill (1931). The disjointed, awkward prose
with the frequent lapses into a series of dots . . . gestures in
the direction of some large, inexpressible meaning . . . the
recurring capitalization of KEY words which seems at once
silly and a straining away from the limitations of the printed
page, are, at one level, metaphors for the soul's plight in a
difficult time. It is just this suspicion which holds our
attention: despite the obvious crudities, something important, one feels, is struggling to be said. The relationship of
these fictions to their time parallels the relationship of the
popular novel to our own:

> Though our world of today is one of extreme violence,
> it is not true that people living the everyday routine
> lives of our society are either given to or are the subjects
> of violent acts. Though it would be insane to deny the
> abundance of rape, murder, mayhem, manslaughter,
> suicide, torture, assault, arson, enslavement everyday
> everywhere, still, considering the density of modern
> society, there is not as much actual overt violence as one
> would suppose from the evidence of motion pictures,
> comic books, radio, and cheap fiction. On the other
> hand there is universal inner violence, fear, and
> treachery. It is the great inner conflicts and tensions
> that modern story-telling describes; and it is the trans-
> lation of fiction's outward beatings, stranglings, stabbings,

and shootings into our own inner struggles that we make when we read or listen.

Since the tempest within will not submit to description in words of exact reference, the tempest without must serve as metaphor to tell about the soul's life. Modern fiction has chosen the device of hyperbole with which to show forth the inner life — all the shocks the spirit's heir to in our time — the insults, the humiliation, the sacrifice, the moral corrosion. For the most part, the modern story teller chooses to deal with the extraordinary incident. Being more dramatic, it is more immediately understandable, reflects more directly the conflicts of everyday life. The violence and the fear of violence that is in us and so much a part of our psychological life are amplified many times in the metaphor of melodrama. The terror of the cinema screen and the ferocity of, for example, *Sanctuary* are mirrors held up to the terror and rage of our inner lives. Thus, the age of anxiety gives away its inner tensions in the works of popular writers like Graham Greene, James M. Cain, Dashiel Hammett, Mickey Spillane; in the cartoons of Charles Addams; in the plays of Tennessee Williams and Arthur Miller; in the operas of Carlo Menotti; in the films of Alfred Hitchcock, Billy Wilder, Raoul Walsh, Carol Reed, and Roberto Rossellini. Not that violent death does not occur in daily life, still it occurs but seldom to the 13,000,000 people who read the fiction of Mickey Spillane. Modern novels and motion pictures express our fears, our desires, our anxieties, our hate, all that troubles inwardly — frustration, fear of poverty, of spinsterhood, of losing status, of loneliness, discrimination, humiliation, shame, heartache, of being sacrificed, of slavery, and of tyranny.[1]

The world of O'Flaherty's four novels is a hostile city, a paranoic universe of deadly plots and complex intrigues. The four protagonists react to their various situation with violence, directed against others where possible and where not, against themselves. All are, in some degree, insane or, as in the case of the Informer, so unthinking as to be scarcely

human. The basic myth at work in all four books is the dual
one of flight and pursuit, guilt and punishment. What
emerges is the figure of the hunted man, a figure we can
relate directly to O'Flaherty himself who tells us in *Shame
the Devil* of his own paranoia and how, ' . . . sometimes this
mania of being pursued by assassins had been so intense that
I sat up in bed for hours, my revolver in my hand, listening
and watching.' (p. 40) In these books he exploits, to excess,
the melodramatic possibilities of the theme of pursuit.

The most immediately obvious characteristic of *The
Informer, The Assassin, Mr. Gilhooley* and *The Puritan* is
their common grotesqueness — grotesque characters, backgrounds and situations. A closer study of this aspect may
yield a clue to the world O'Flaherty creates in these books.

Arthur Clayborough in his study of *The Grotesque in
English Fiction*[2] reviews a number of theories on the nature
and function of the grotesque and then goes on to evaluate
them. One of the more valuable aspects of his book is the
attempt to state as accurately and objectively as possible the
various theories reviewed. Among them is that of the German
scholar, Wolfgang Kayser, who offers an interpretation of the
grotesque which seems both illuminating and particularly
relevant to our reading of this group of novels. (Clayborough
disagrees with Kayser, but that is another matter). In Clayborough's summary the theory goes as follows:

i.   The grotesque is the alienated word. Kayser insists
     that in genuinely grotesque art the everyday world
     is *suddenly* changed into a strange and unpleasant
     place, into a world in which we do not wish to live.
     The grotesque arouses in us not fear of death but
     anxiety about life. A merely alien world, one which
     is completely strange to us from the outset, as in the
     fairy tale, is not grotesque; it is not a transformation
     of our own world.

ii. The grotesque is created by an impersonal force
     associated with the 'id' of psychological theory.

iii. The creations of the grotesque are a game with the
     absurd. It gives a habitation and a name to our
     secret fears.

iv. The creation of the grotesque is the attempt to banish and exorcise the demonic element in the world.

The first of these definitions will be examined in this introduction. The other points raised by Kayser — as Clayborough shows — are concerned with the artist's point of view rather than the representative aspect of grotesque art and are best integrated with a discussion of the individual novels.

The 'everyday world' of these books is the Dublin of the middle and late twenties. They all begin with a detailed statement of time and place and resemble, in their opening paragraphs, a police or newspaper report (e.g. *The Informer,* 'it was three minutes to six o'clock in the evening of the 15th of March, 192-'). The movements of the characters round Dublin are carefully plotted — often tediously so — with relation to streets, public buildings and, inevitably, McDaid's Public House. With the brief exception of *Mr. Gilhooley* (he emerges in the first paragraph from 'The Bailey restaurant in Duke Street'). O'Flaherty's Dublin lies north of the Liffey in the slum area around Mountjoy Square. The tall, eighteenth century houses, once fashionable residences are, in the 1920s, the tenements of the poor. O'Flaherty's Dublin is seen by night, or through the half-night of fog or rain a grey grim place.

> It was the slum district which he knew so well, the district that enclosed Titt Street, the brothels, the Bogey Hole, tenement houses, churches, pawnshops, public-houses, ruins, filth, crime, beautiful women, resplendent idealism in damp cellars, saints starving in garrets, the most lurid examples of debauchery and vice, all living thigh to thigh, breast to breast, in that foetid morass on the north bank of the Liffey. He ran through narrow streets and great, wide, yawning streets, lanes and archways, streets patched and buttressed, with banks of earth from fallen houses almost damning them in places, pavements strewn with offal, soddened by the rain. (*TI* pp. 242-43)

Again:

> It was a dreary sight. It almost shouted its experience,
> and if it had shouted, it would have talked in that end-
> less, loud, babbling scream in which maniacs and
> demented creatures utter their words. It was alive in
> that peculiar way in which ruins are alive at night, when
> the earth is covered with darkness and the living sleep.
> (*TI* pp. 134-35)

The city is very much an Eliotesque Wasteland, an image of
spiritual desiccation. Its greyness enters the soul. Mr Gilhooley,
loitering by 'the gloomy whitish building' of University
College, Dublin, feels his consciousness invaded by the
gloom:

> There were merely shadows in the neighbourhood and
> dark lines, winding, sharply curving and stiff, angular
> lines. There were colours too, although everything had a
> superficial contour of gloom. Whitish colours and brown
> colours and pitch-black colours stood out distinctly.
> The roads were white, if contrasted with the mouths of
> lanes. And the hulks of streets, whole rows of houses,
> were brown, standing above the white roads. He con-
> templated these colours and sounds and shadows with
> great interest inwardly. And they seemed to press in on
> him, surrounding him, the colours, the sounds and the
> shadows. (*Mr.G* pp. 44-45)

Out of this twilight world will come the shadowy girl, the
bitch-goddess, who will drive him to murder and suicide.
McDara, the assassin in the novel of the same name, delights in
the slums ('the foetid air reeked with disease') because
'everything here excited a savage hatred of society in him.'
(*A* p. 21) The locals of the various novels are represented as
being outside society, an alien world whose population is
hardly human. Each of the novels contains a vignette of some
aspect of Dublin's underworld which illuminates the whole.
In *The Informer* it is the brothels and cheap eating-houses (to
get the full force of the term, one must pronounce 'eat' as
'ate' — thus 'atin'-houses'). The *Assassin* reads, at times, like a

conducted tour of the haunts of the secret organizations of the 20s, 'the flotsam and jetsam of the revolution'. One of the best things in all O'Flaherty's works is the description, in *Mr. Gilhooley,* of the Lodging House ('digs') from which Mr Gilhooley is, ceremoniously, thrown out. *The Puritan* by a circuitous route, via middle-class Rathmines, brings us back to the brothels and shebeens of *The Informer.* This aspect of O'Flaherty's thrillers is best summed up in the words of an *Irish Statesman* review (10 October 1925, p. 148):

O'Flaherty is an instinctive creator; the figures that surge into being under his hand produce their own effect on us, inexplicable, perhaps, by him. What figures they are! They carry their own warranty for existence, even when they seem to us most monstrous. Carleton found such figures in rural Ireland and made them dance to his grim piping; O'Casey and O'Flaherty find them in the slime of the Dublin slums. They were always there, inert, but the last ten years in Ireland have not only torn off the top spit of our civilization but have objectivised this life that bred in the subsoil. Beings like Gype, Mulholland, Gallagher, had heaved their obscene forms in our underworld without much apparent stirring of the crust that separates them from us. Our troubles drew them to the surface and we put weapons into hands that had scarcely attained the human. They began to mingle their wild life with our conventional one, battling for self-expression in the only way they understood. They grow as gigantically under O'Casey's hand as under O'Flaherty's but O'Casey has breathed into them a humour that brings them a shade nearer humanity than O'Flaherty in whom this quality is entirely absent. O'Casey's characters dwindle into futility; they cannot act; human consciousness has entered into them just so far as to make them hesitant. O'Flaherty's characters act, and with violence, having little human consciousness, but an animal force and cunning. A gorilla drumming on his chest to express terrible emotions that he cannot translate into mind is nearly as close to humanity as Gypo can get after Frankie McPhilip is killed.

For all the main characters of these novels life in the city's underworld is presented as a descent into hell. None of them belong there, they are all country men or women for whom heaven is a pastoral dream. In *Mr. Gilhooley*, Macaward, the poet, tells Gilhooley:

> 'You'll rot here. Living in a lie. You can't deceive me. You aren't fit for it, no more than me. Only where there are green fields and birds and life, growing and dying and growing and dying, all the year round. Not corruption like this. We were made for the hillsides and the fields . . . and the sea. That's our life.' (*Mr.G* p. 138)

McDara of *The Assassin* is possessed by a similar nostalgia:

> He began to strip off his clothes, uttering fierce words. And he now transformed himself into a wild fisherman from his native village, a man without subtle thought to disturb and emasculate his virility, dashing his strength against the barbarous cruelty of nature. He forgot his skinny legs, his sunken eyes, his pallid, nervous cheeks, the softness of his muscles, and he felt himself towering over the angry sea in a boat, with god-like power, yelling defiance at the gale. He saw, from the rock-bound coast, civilized man afar off and spat at him with contempt. (*A* p. 213)

O'Flaherty's characters are doubly alienated, both from their own background and from the city which they can scarcely be said to inhabit.

The grammar of these stories has two leading terms, both verbs, both in the passive voice — 'to be pursued' and 'to be transformed'. It is the latter term we are concerned with here. Because of their instability, their lack of connections with anything around them, the characters and their environment are subject to a bewildering series of transformations. Their crimes or meditated crimes both elate and drive them to despair, and the city through which they slink changes accordingly. Francis Ferriter of *The Puritan* murders a prostitute. It is, on one level, a sordid act of jealousy, at

another, transformed by his fanatical imagination, a blood
sacrifice designed to cleanse the nation of corruption. Gypo
Nolan informs on a former comrade and '... the dark,
sombre mean street that had been familiar to him until now,
suddenly appeared strange, as if he had never seen it before,
as it if had suddenly become inhabited by dread monsters
that were intent on devouring him: It appeared to him rather,
that he had wandered, through a foolish error of judgement,
into a strange and hostile foreign country where he did not
know the language.' (*TI* p. 50) McDara of *The Assassin*
meditates on his 'IDEA' *(sic)* which involves the murder of a
government minister and '... He passed into a state of
ecstasy. The city became transformed in his mind. Although
he walked along the sordid, commonplace thoroughfare of
O'Connell Street, surrounded by noise, mud, ragged people
and ugly buildings, his inward gazing thoughts fashioned a
thrilling and romantic panorama.' (*A* pp. 50-51)

All of the protagonists, whether because of madness,
nervous tension or drunkenness, exhibit similar violent fluc-
tuations between elation and depression. The psychological
terms, however, hardly describe the mental states dramatized
by O'Flaherty. They convey a sense of the normally abnor-
mal which is completely lacking in these works. If we follow
McDara a little further down O'Connell Street — past the
Nelson monument in fact — his elation is portrayed in the
following grotesque images:

> Now the houses of the city, the dark waters of the foul,
> sewage bearing river and the people who passed, loomed
> large in his vision and became transformed, signalling to
> his imagination a myriad speechless signs. From all
> corners of the land came peasants marching, with blood
> on their waving banners, into the capital, into the fort-
> ress of the tyrant, who had been struck down in death,
> by the hand and brain of Michael McDara. A head! THE
> HEAD! With blood stained, yellow lips and a scattered
> brain. As he walked, gazing at the ground, thinking thus
> exultantly, his terrified humanity babbled a ceaseless
> stream of weird suggestions, overwhelmed by the size
> of the load it carried. But his mind scoffed at these

fears. (*A* pp. 51-52)

Similarly, in *Mr. Gilhooley,* the title character passes, in the
space of a few paragraphs, through at least six distinct
moods, ending up with a vision of God ' . . . a being with a
white surplice around his body, girdled at the waist with a
gold band, with enormous soft white limbs and a square head,
smiling benignantly.' (*Mr.G* p. 36) There is a hallucinatory,
obsessive quality about O'Flaherty's images that reminds one
of surrealist paintings.

It would require impossible detail to chart the sudden
transformations that take place in these novels. Sufficient to
note that it is a characteristic of all of them. There is first
the transformation of the city and its people into a hostile,
grimacing world as a result of a criminal act and then the
further transformations at the characters grow in isolation
and madness. O'Flaherty's technique − as is no doubt
obvious from our quotations − is too crude to deal adequate-
ly with these mental and physical chinese boxes.

The Informer[3]

There are, from O'Flaherty's own pen two separate, and
contradictory, accounts of the making and purpose of *The
Informer.* Such reflections on his work are so rare that it is
worth dwelling on the very few occasions when he does allow
us into his workshop.

In *Shame the Devil* O'Flaherty relates the genesis of *The
Informer.* He was living in Oxfordshire, in a cottage belonging
to A.E. Coppard, with J.B. Priestley and Gerald Bullett as
near neighbours. All were concerned with the difficulties of
making a living by writing. Coppard subsisted on vegetables
and canned soup to permit him to live on fifty pounds a year
and devote his life to serious work. Priestley, because of the
fierce competition to which writers were subjected, argued
for another way out. The writer must do something spec-
tacular to draw attention to himself. 'The mountain, (popular
opinion) even if it wanted to go to Mahomet, sees a horde of
Mahomets claiming its visit, so it stays put and the Mahomets

have to crawl up its sides the best way they can.' (p. 188)
Coppard was understandably annoyed, and condemned those
who had schemes 'for tickling the mountain's rump'.
O'Flaherty agreed with him but decided to 'cast about for a
trick' (p. 187) to make money and win popular approval. He
returned to Dublin to work out the details of *The Informer*,

> ... determined that it would be a sort of high-brow
> detective story and that its style based on the technique
> of the cinema. It should have all the appearance of a
> realistic novel and yet the material should have hardly
> any connection with real life. I would treat my readers
> as a mob orator treats his audience and toy with their
> emotions, making them finally pity a character whom
> they began by considering a monster. (*SD* pp. 189-190)

The trick worked:

> Its publication proved that I was right. The literary
> critics, almost to a man, hailed it as a brilliant piece of
> work and talked pompously about having at last been
> given inside knowledge of the Irish revolution and the
> secret organizations that had brought it about. This
> amused me intensely, as whatever 'facts' were used in
> the book were taken from happenings in a Saxon town,
> during the sporadic Communist insurrection of about
> nineteen twenty-two or three. My trick had succeeded
> and those who had paid little attention to my previous
> work, much of it vastly superior, from the point of view
> of literature, to *The Informer*, now hailed me as a writer
> of considerable importance. In other words, the mount-
> ain had moved. And yet, perhaps Powys (with whom he
> had also discussed the problem of a writer's relationship
> to his readers) was right and that it would have been
> better for me if the mountain had not moved. If it
> moves too near one, there is a danger of being over-
> whelmed by its mass. (*SD* pp. 190-91)

This is one version of the book's origin and purpose and one
which, by and large, the critics have, probably rightly,
followed. Another version, which was recently made the
occasion of a plea for a revaluation of *The Informer*, is to be

fcund in several letters from O'Flaherty to his editor and
friend, Edward Garnett. These letters are now deposited in
the University of Texas Library. The recently published
study by John Zneimer, *The Literary Vision of Liam
O'Flaherty*, however, contains an account of the relevant
material (pp. 68-69):

O'Flaherty's account of *The Informer* to Garnett is not
at all cynical, and his predictions for its reception not at
all optimistic. In a letter of April, 1924, he tells of starting on a Dublin story, 'The Vendetta', which will be a
'shocker' and a 'thriller'. In July of that year he is
deeply engaged in the story and tells Garnett about his
character, Gypo, his 'beautiful monstrosity' (July 28,
1924). By September the plans of the book are complete, and in a long letter to Garnett on September 18,
1924, O'Flaherty lays out the entire plan and asks
Garnett to judge it 'not so much for what it is by itself'
as for what he has 'set out to make' and what he has
'succeeded in making'. O'Flaherty believes that 'the
mob', the mass of readers, who 'never know anyway'
will bring all sorts of 'eccentric things into the scales —
morals, god, politics, etc.'. But he wants Garnett to
trace out the development of the book from the initial
dream:

'It is on these lines, following from an initial dream
through its changing fortunes as other circumstances
mould and redirect it to a conclusion in a way unexpected from such beginnings that I have tried to build The
Informer. I have envisaged a brutal, immensely strong,
stupid character, a man built by nature to be a tool for
evil-minded intelligence. The style is brutal at that stage,
without finesse, without deviation, without any sweetness, short and curt like a police report. Then as other
characters appear on the scene the character of the man
changes gradually. Elements of cunning, of fear, of
struggle that is born of thought, appear in him. The

style changes to suit this, almost imperceptibly. More and more characters appear. The character is no longer brutal. Sympathy veers around and stands in the balance, for him or against him. He is now a soul in torment struggling with evil influences. At this point the style becomes definitely sympathetic, lengthens itself out, softens, strikes a note of joy in the eternity of nature. Scenes of horror and sin present themselves.

Then with gathering speed The Informer is enmeshed by his enemies. His vast strength crumbles up overwhelmed by the gathering waves of unconquerable intelligence. He stands alone, without the guidance of a mind to succour him, seeking an outlet for his useless strength, finding that it is no longer strength but a helpless thing, a target for the beings that press around to harass it. Intelligence is dominant and supreme, civilization conquers the first beginnings of man upwards.

The Informer makes a last effort to escape. Here the style completely changes and becomes like a wild storm, cascading, abandoned, poetic.'

From there, O'Flaherty says, the style rises to a climax, and he quotes what will be the beginning of the last chapter, a vision of horror, of 'endless wandering through space'. Then he says he strikes a note of pity and finishes it. He does not know what success he has had in his execution of the plan, but he has hopes.

(Reading through the letter we might remind ourselves of Kayser's association of the grotesque with the 'Id' and its function as an exorcism of demonic forces.)

How well does O'Flaherty realize his intentions outlined in this letter? In the end, the novel does seem closer to 'mob oratory' than to the subtlety implied by the letter. We might give as an example the passage where 'the style completely changes and becomes like a wild storm, cascading, abandoned, poetic':

Shapeless figures dancing on tremendous stilts, on the brink of an abyss, to the sounds of rocks being tumbled about below, in the darkness, everything immense and

> dark and resounding, everything, everything without
> shape or meaning, gloom and preponderance, yawning,
> yawning abysses full of frozen fog, cliffs gliding away
> when touched, leaving no foundation, an endless wand-
> ering through space, through screeching winds and . . .
> crash. (*TI* p. 267)

The 'note of pity' which follows and on which the book
closes is evoked — if at all — by the protagonist, Gypo Nolan,
stumbling into a church, mortally wounded, where, as luck
would have it, the mother of the man he informed on is
attending Mass. He begs forgiveness. 'Then with a gurgling
sound he fell forward on his face. His hat rolled off. Blood
gushed from his mouth. He stretched out his limbs in the
shape of a cross. He shivered and lay still.' (*TI* p. 272)
O'Flaherty spoke of 'toying' with his reader's emotions. This
is, rather, crude manipulation.

The action of *The Informer* takes place soon after the Civil
War. Gypo Nolan, a huge brute with little or no intelligence,
informs on his fellow revolutionary, Frankie McPhillip, in
exchange for twenty pounds. They both belong to a mysterious organization, probably Communist, of which Commandant Dan Gallagher is the ruthless, super-efficient head.
McPhillip is cornered and killed. Gypo, having committed the
quintessential Irish crime tries to save himself from the
revenge of the 'Organization' *(sic)* by accusing Rat Mulligan
of the deed. Terrified, he goes on a wild orgy of drink and
debauchery and gives away what is left of the blood money.
Commandant Gallagher suspects Gypo, and calls a court of
enquiry where Gypo is exposed. He is sentenced to death but
escapes. There follows a lengthy account of Gypo's wandering through the city in an effort to reach the mountains. The
city streets are a labyrinth and they return him, whichever
way he turns, to his starting point. He seeks refuge in the
lodgings of his occasional mistress, Katie Fox. Katie betrays
him, while he sleeps, to Gallagher. Gypo dies, riddled with
bullets but forgiven by the dead man's mother.

We first meet Gypo in the 'Dunboy Lodging House' where
he is devouring a meal of bacon and cabbage. The sordid ugly
surroundings (one senses behind the description of the house,

The Tavern of the opening chapters of *Crime and Punishment*)
are only matched by the grotesque figure of Gypo himself:

> The man was dressed in a suit of blue dungarees with a
> white muffler wound round and round his neck. He had
> a close-cropped bullet-shaped head, fair hair and dark
> eyebrows. The eyebrows were just single tufts, one over
> the centre of each eye. They grew long and narrowed to
> a single hair, like the ends of waxed moustaches. They
> were just like ominous snouts, and they had more ex-
> pression than the dim little blue eyes that were hidden
> away behind their scowling shadow. The face was
> bronzed red and it was covered by swellings that looked
> like lumps at a distance. These lumps came out on the
> forehead, on the cheekbones, on the chin and on either
> side of the neck below the ears. On closer observation,
> however, they almost disappeared in the general glossy
> colour of the brownish red skin, that looked as if there
> were several tiers of taut skin covering the face. The
> nose was short and bulbous. The mouth was large. The
> lips were thick and they fitted together in such a manner
> that the mouth gave the face an expression of being
> perpetually asleep. His body was immense, with massive
> limbs and bulging muscles pushing out here and there,
> like excrescences of the earth breaking the expected
> regularity of a country-side. He sat upright in his seat,
> with large square head bolted to his squat neck, like an
> iron stanchion riveted to a deck. (*TI* pp. 13-14)

Many of the descriptive passages in *The Informer* are of this
order and it is quoted at length to show some of the ways in
which O'Flaherty achieves his grotesque effects. There is first
the isolation of some detail which is then enlarged — rather as
horror films frequently focus on the human eye. Here it is
the eyebrows, 'ominous snouts', which occur again and again
throughout the book. Later in the same passage he employs
the cinematic techniques of long-shot and close-up, often in
successive sentences as if to further distort and fragment the
image. Finally the similes of the last two sentences draw for
their comparisons, first on the natural world, then on the

mechanical world. (One is reminded of Dali's image of the
mechanical, bolted monster clutching a flower). The images
fail to cohere — indeed they are only connected by occuring
in successive sentences and by referring to the same object —
products, in Coleridgian terms, of fancy rather than imagination. Throughout the novel O'Flaherty employs a great
number of such images. Gypo is an 'uncouth ogre', his head is
likened to a badly shorn sheep, 'his jaws set like the teeth of
a bear trap', he is a 'pig'. All the favourite animals of grotesque
artists occur at some point by way of comparison — insects,
vermin, snails, bulls, cats.

In the first chapter the omniscient narrator betrays no
sympathy for Gypo. He is, simply, the Informer of legend,
though presented as a great deal more stupid than one imagines most of them to have been. Indeed there is a certain
sleight-of-hand involved in making Gypo so unthinking. It
absolves him from the responsibility of what he has done.
There is also a technical problem involved here — Gypo must
think, and be shown to think, even though he is portrayed as
almost incapable of thought. O'Flaherty tries to solve this
problem in two ways. The first is to treat Gypo's mind as an
unwieldly machine (e.g., 'The cumbersome mechanism of his
mind had been put in motion'). It is awkward and un-
convincing:

> Slowly he began to remember recent events. Fact after
> fact came prowling into his brain. Soon the whole series
> of events stood piled there in a crazy heap. Everything
> rushed towards that heap with increasing rapidity, but
> nothing could be abstracted from it. It was just as if the
> facts were sinking in a puddle and disappearing. It was
> utterly impossible for him to reason out a plan of action.
> "I must make a plan", he murmured aloud. In answer to
> this exhortation came a vision of Gallagher's glittering
> eyes. They fascinated him. He forgot about a plan. A
> horde of things crashed together in his brain, making an
> infernal buzzing. He lost control of himself and ran
> about under the archway, striking out with his hands
> and feet madly, trying to fight the cargo of things that
> were jammed together in his brain. It was that insensate

rage that overcomes strong men at times, when they have nothing upon which to vent their fury, no physical opponent. (*TI* pp. 245-46)

O'Flaherty also tries to circumvent the difficulty by portraying mental processes through physical reactions. This is a feature of all these novels — the major characters are given to performing dumb shows. We might instance the occasion when Gypo first becomes aware that he intends to inform on his friend:

He was looking at a pair of bright spurs and his face contorted suddenly. His eyes bulged as if he were taken with a fit of terror. He looked about him suspiciously, as if he were about to steal something for the first time. Then he rushed away hurriedly. . . . Now and again he looked around him with a kind of panting noise. He snorted and smelled the air and screwed up his eyes. Then he leaned over the wall again and rested his chin on his crossed hands. He was that way for half an hour. Then at last he drew himself up straight. He stretched his arms above his head. He yawned. He stuck his hands in his trousers pockets. He stared at the ground. Then with his eyes on the ground he walked away at the same slouching pace as before. (*TI* pp. 27-28)

Gypo informs and we are unsure of the motive for his act — it is similar to Raskalnikov's murder of the old woman in *Crime and Punishment.* Essentially O'Flaherty is not interested in his character *qua* informer but as the perpetrator of an act which cuts him off, irreversibly, from society. 'How strange! Within the course of ninety minutes the customary sound of a human footstep had, by some evil miracle, become menacing.' (*TI* p. 30) From this point forward the narrator proceeds to transform Gypo into a character for whom the *narrator* feels concern and sympathy. What is important to realize here is that the transformation takes place, not through any change in Gypo's character but through technical and mechanical manipulation of the distance between narrator and protagonist. Thus in O'Flaherty's letter to Garnett, he has confused narrative manipulation of character with character change. The reader is expected to identify with the narrator's attitude and, if he once questions this attitude, the effect is lost. The really essential demand that this book makes is that it be read quickly. The nearest equivalent we can find for the style of the whole is not the cinema but its predecessor, the kaleidoscope. This machine consisted of a series of photographic stills mounted on a circular drum. When one revolved the drum quickly the stills gave the effect of a motion picture. O'Flaherty's sentences are the stills, and read quickly, his characters seem to move (e.g., 'He began to shift about in his seat. First he uncrossed his legs. Then he crossed them again. He began to tap his knee with his right hand. He sighed.' (*TI* p. 25) The swiftness of narrative pace is all: in this sense *The Informer* is radically unsuited to the kind of analysis we brought to bear on the earlier novels. We can however, make a connection with the regional romances – particularly *The Black Soul* – in terms of the theme of *The Informer* and still remain true to the kind of novel this is. Their common concern is the conflict between intellect and nature: in *The Informer* the conflict is portrayed by the narrator varying the distance, along a moral axis of value, between himself and the various characters. Thus Commandant Gallagher (intellect) and his Organization are at one pole while Connemara Maggie and her fellow prostitutes (the body) are at the other:

> The narrator's total opposition to the intellectual cast of Gallagher's mind is apparent in the distance between the narrator and Gallagher implied in the ironic description of Gallagher's thoughts and the ironic scenes that dramatize Gallagher's actions. At the point of inter-section where the moral axis of value crosses the intellectual axis of value the reader is expected to accept the narrator's compassionate moral empathic response to the plight of Gypo, while becoming antagonistic to the intellectual values represented by Gallagher.[4]

We will conclude our analysis of the novel by examining Gypo's relationship to the two worlds symbolized by Gallagher

and Connemara Maggie. Shortly after Gypo has informed to
the police, the narrator introduces Commandant Gallagher
by way of what purport to be extracts from newspaper
articles and a secret report from the files of the Communist
International. The first report is a *pastiche* of an *Irish Times*
leading article. ('His brand of Communism is of the type that
appeals most to the Irish nature. It is a mixture of Roman
Catholicism, Nationalist Republicanism and Bolshevism. Its
chief rallying cries are: "Loot and Murder" ' *TI* p. 76)
Gallagher emerges as a figure remarkably similar to Liam
O'Flaherty. There follows another *pastiche* — this time of
'the official organ of the American Revolutionary Organization', where Comrade Gallagher is hailed as a sturdy fighter
'who rules the workers of Dublin with greater power than is
wielded by the Irish bourgeoisie.' (*TI* p. 78) (O'Flaherty, it
should be remembered, during his short-lived struggle for the
'Irish Soviet Republic' gave himself the title of 'Chairman of
the Council of the Unemployed'). Finally the 'secret report'
of the International expresses reservations about the ideological purity of Gallagher's organization ' . . . the working class
(is) in the grip of a romantic love of conspiracy, a strong
religious and bourgeois-nationalist outlook . . . ' (*TI* p. 80) It
is plainly inaccurate for O'Flaherty to claim that the events
of *The Informer* had nothing to do with events in Dublin in
which he was a prime instigator. There is a remarkable similarity too between the theoretical discussions on society and
property indulged in by Gallagher and the views put forward
by O'Flaherty in his autobiographical volume *Two Years*.
Here the views expressed by Gallagher are hedged round with
irony — we are meant to read them as neurotic intellectualism. His lengthy monologues all end lamely with the phrase
' . . . I haven't worked that out fully yet. Its only in the
theoretical stage yet.' The one term that is conspicuously
excluded from his philosophy of revolution is the one that
the narrator invokes on behalf of Gypo — pity:

> 'No,' he said, 'I believe in nothing fundamentally. And I
> don't feel pity. Nothing fundamental that has conscious-
> ness capable of being understood by a human being
> exists, so I don't believe in anything, since an intelligent

person can only believe in something that is fundamental. If I could believe in something fundamental, then the
whole superstructure of life would be capable of being
comprehended by me. Life would resolve itself into a
period of intense contemplation. Action would be
impossible. There would be no inducement for action.
There would be some definite measurement for explaining everything. Men seek only that which offers no
explanation of itself. But wait a minute. I haven't
worked out that fully yet. It's only in the theoretical
stage yet. I have no time. 'But you spoke of pity. Pity?
Pity is a ridiculous sensation for a man of my nature.
We are incapable of it. A revolutionary is incapable of
feeling pity. Listen. The philosophy of a revolutionary is
this. Civilization is a process in the development of the
human species. I am an atom of the human species,
groping in advance, impelled by a force over which
neither I nor the human species have any control. I am
impelled by the Universal Law to thrust forward the
human species from one phase of its development to
another. I am at war with the remainder of the species.
I am a Christ beating them with rods. I have no mercy. I
have no pity. I have no beliefs. I am not master of
myself. I am an automaton. I am a revolutionary. And
there is no reward for me but the satisfaction of one
lust, the lust for the achievement of my mission, for
power maybe, but I haven't worked out that yet.'
(*TI* pp. 108-109)

Gallagher in his first encounter with Gypo is portrayed as a
villain whose glittering eyes hyponotize the mindless informer.
Their major confrontation takes place at the Court of Inquiry
where, in a blatantly rhetorical fashion, the narrator tries to
enlist the reader's sympathy for Gypo. Gallagher's face is
covered with a diabolic smile and under his probing Gypo
blunders and reveals the truth, 'the dreadful fascination of
Gallagher's cold eyes sucked his passion clean out of him.'
The narrator proceeds to pull out all the stops:

The sight was fearsome even to the callous men that

surrounded him. Even THEIR hardened souls saw a
vision of a strange life just then, an unknown and unexpected phantom that comes to some once in their
lives and never comes to many, the phantom of a human
soul stripped naked of the covering of civilization, lying
naked and horror stricken, without help, without hope
of mercy. They forgot for the moment their hatred of
him . . . . . They only knew . . . . . that he was a poor,
weak human being like themselves, a human soul, weak
and helpless in suffering, shivering in the toils of the
eternal struggle of the human soul . . . (*TI* pp. 199-200)

Gypo is rescued from this *impasse* by his instinct for survival.
In a scene worthy of Mickey Spillane he escapes from the
room where he is imprisoned. Gallagher promptly collapses
with fear of what will happen if Gypo goes to the police a
second time. His babbling idiocy is meant to contrast with
the stern, unflinching revolutionary pose adopted earlier on.
In this nightmare world the hunter and hunted, the strong
and the weak, exchange roles.

The contrast between Gypo and Gallagher is further
elaborated by the dramatization of their respective love
affairs — though this is hardly the term to describe their
involvements with Connemara Maggie and Mary McPhillip
respectively. The Gallagher-McPhillip affair is banal in the
extreme and we need not go into it except to remark that
what little social satire the novel contains is centered on the
McPhillip family. They are doing their best to rise in the
social scale from proletariat to lower middle-class and their
efforts are spearheaded by Mary. Gallagher's intellectualism
despises passion and he attempts instead to convert Mary into
a tool for his revolutionary programme. Gypo's revelling in
the stews of Dublin is something else again:

Gypo picked up two women and perched them one on
each shoulder. Then he seized two others round the waist,
raised them from the ground under his arms and began
to jump into the air, yelling like a bull with each jump
while his fluttering, half-naked cargo of women laughed
hysterically as they dangled about him. (*TI* p. 145)

His casual encounter with Connemara Maggie ('soft eyes
swollen and gentle like the eyes of a heifer') is invested, by
the narrator, with a sweet innocence ' . . . she busied herself
tending her man, just as if she had never left the purity of her
Connemara hills and she were tending her peasant spouse
after a hard day's work in the fields: instead of tending a
casual lover in the sordid environment of a brothel. There
was no hint of vice or of libidinous pleasure in her face or in
her movements. She seemed to be, like Gypo himself, a
daughter of the earth, unconscious of the artificial sins that
are the handiwork of the city.' (*TI* p. 160) At this point the
distance between narrator and protagonist is at a minimum,
and because of the insistent rhetoric, between reader and
narrator it is at a maximum.

Apart from this episode the description of Gypo's rampage
through the brothels of Dublin is something of a *tour de
force*. It remains in the mind long after all else has faded, as a
chamber of horrors where diseased, emaciated faces swim to
the surface. The following passage exemplifies the most
perversely rewarding aspect of *The Informer* — its grotesqueness:

> The bed was so huge that it might be mistaken for
> anything, were it not supported by four thick, wooden
> posts and had a canopy over it, at the head, after the
> fashion of those beds that are called in Irish country
> places 'Archbishops Beds'. The bed-clothes were indes-
> cribable. Everything was pitched on to the bed and
> everything stayed there. Louisa Cummins lived in the
> bed most of the day. She had done so for eight years,
> since she became 'bedridden' as a result of 'injuries'
> received from the police, one night she was arrested on
> a charge of trafficking in immorality. She was quite
> strong and healthy. She did all her work in bed. The
> blankets were gathered about her bulky person in the
> far corner, near the wall. In the other corner, Katie
> Fox's corner, there was a couple or so of tattered
> blankets. The foot of the bed was heaped with junk of
> all sorts, from a notched mug, out of which the old lady
> drank her tea, to a statue of Saint Joseph that hung on
> the bed-post, suspended from a thick nail by a rough,

knotted cord.

The cord was around the statue's neck, in a noose. The statue was not suspended there out of crude respect, as might be supposed. It was hung there as a blasphemous protest against the incompetence of the saint. Four years before she had made a Novena to Saint Joseph, requesting a cure for muscular rheumatism, and because her request was not granted she hung up the statue by the neck. (*TI* p. 251)

The Assassin[5]

In June 1927 Kevin O'Higgins, Vice-President of the Executive Council of the Irish Free State and Minister for Justice, was mysteriously assassinated on his way home from Mass. One year later O'Flaherty's *The Assassin* appeared, plainly an attempt to make literary capital out of the event. The thriller is dedicated 'To my Creditors' which may go some way to explain the poor quality of the book.

The protagonist, Michael McDara, has returned to Dublin from America accompanied by one Daniel McFetterich ('Gutty Fetch') with the intention of murdering HIM. (Higgins is nowhere mentioned directly in the text. O'Flaherty adopts this rather silly device of capitalizing indirect references to the Minister — THE HEAD, THE IDEA etc.). McDara involves two other disgruntled Republicans — Kitty Mellett, an 'old flame', and Frank Tumulty — in his scheme. The plot details the steps taken by the group of assassins to shoot HIM, the event itself, and the subsequent dissension among the conspirators. McDara escapes to England where he intends to commit suicide. This summary may imply a greater variety than the book actually contains: in essence it is a psychological analysis of the central figure, McDara. All the rest is a backset for the melodrama of his tortured soul.

The central problem that the book raises for the reader is: why does McDara want to assassinate anybody? In short, the motive for the whole creaking plot is unclear, and this has given rise to a number of interpretations of the novel. McDara himself provides several reasons for carrying out the deed. These will be examined shortly. Real complexity, whether in life or letters, is always interesting and stimulating. Here, however, the impression is that O'Flaherty has, as it were, worked up the complexity (confusion) by making large, clumsy gestures in the direction of the philosophies of Nietzsche and Dostoyevski. The different reasons put forward at various points by McDara for his intended assassination do not, really, enrich our understanding of the deed or of McDara himself. This reading of the novel is opposed to, say, John Zneimer's who discovers a significance in this work which seems as vapid as the work itself: 'The Assassin strikes out in violence. He kills not for a cause or a reason but from the terror of his soul, to find meaning, to make meaning, to define himself against the lack of meaning, to do anything in a positive gesture, to relate himself to something that is fundamental, to defy God, to challenge God, to determine if there is a God'.[6]

All this, in a sense, is true (of what modern novel is it not true?) and one can find a warrant in the text for all of Zneimer's statements. It is certainly what O'Flaherty intended. Yet it seems that there is a complete failure to realize these ideas in terms of action or character, except in the most simplistic way. The sententious philosophizing of McDara protrudes from the text. One is reminded of some modern films where the catch-phrases of existentialist philosophy ('Hell is other people') are introduced to give a pseudo-significance to the whole. McDara explains his IDEA *(sic)* to his fellow conspirators in the following terms. (The capitalization is a good indication of how uneasily the idea matches with the surrounding text):

> 'Well!' said McDara. 'In the first place, our business is not to cripple England but to create a superior type of human being here. That is the objective of the revolutionary, to create a superior type of being. Most revolutionary movements make the mistake of aiming at a change of government, seizing political power and that sort of thing. That is not revolution. It is merely a transposition of the material wealth in a community.' Tumulty contracted his eyebrows. His underlip closed

over his upper lip, in a gesture of violent contempt.
McDara paused and then continued gloomily: 'Power
should always be in the hands of inferior types, because
power has a demoralizing influence. When a strong man
seizes power, he should be cut down at once. Because
the mass feels inferior to a strong man. Each individual
loses his initiative. The strong man sucks all power into
his own being. The mass become slaves. No progress is
made. Until the head is chopped off. Then the mass is
free to grope about again. Each individual becomes a
living force, groping forward, unimpeded. Do you see?'
Tumulty rubbed his large palms, one against the other,
slowly. He opened his lips and looked at McDara suspiciously. Then he shook his head. 'Listen,' said McDara
excitedly. 'There are never more than a handful of
revolutionary minds in any country. They therefore
must stand apart and make no attempt to direct the
Government, actually. If they take part in the adminis-
tration of the Government, they either become tyrants
because they are strong, or corrupt because they desire
money or strike down whatever individual tries to arrest
the progress of the community. There is only one way
to do that.' He paused and looked at Tumulty. His eyes
glittered. Tumulty suddenly sat erect and put his closed
fists on his widespread knees. 'What way is that?' he said.
McDara whispered, almost inaudibly, with a sibilant
sound: 'Assassination'. Very slowly, Tumulty leaned
forward until his elbows reached his knees. Then again
he rubbed his large palms together. 'Eh?' said McDara in
a querulous tone. (*A* pp. 98—99)

The lengthy discussion ends in a rather disarming fashion: 'I
had almost forgotten that, Frank. This act must be directed
against the idea of God.'
    In the first paragraph McDara sets himself a Nietzschean
objective — the creation of a race of Supermen. This gives
way, in the second paragraph, to the anarchist ideal, the
'propaganda of the deed'. A group of dedicated Anarchists
will ensure weak leadership of the state by violence. Finally,
an almost forgotten Dostoyevskian purpose is introduced.

Later in the novel McDara confesses to yet another motive — again the thought is Dostoyevskian — 'I am doing this because I want to be free. To cut every cord. It's only when a man cuts every cord that he approaches nearest to being a God. Suppose then, a man arises, who is far beyond the comprehension of his mates, in fearlessness, in bru-' (*A* p. 142), and again the thought tails off into incoherence. What becomes more and more obvious is that O'Flaherty's intellectual powers are in excess and often hostile to his creative power. *The Assassin,* though a bad novel, is revealing in a number of ways. In this connection it is interesting to note the way in which O'Flaherty identifies almost completely with McDara. The narrator maintains a neutral attitude to his protagonist throughout. All the irony of the novel is directed against the revolutionaries who surround him. O'Flaherty and McDara are the same age and their histories are the same. McDara, we are told, has been shell-shocked in World War 1, and after his discharge from the army he has gone round the world as a seaman. Most important of all he comes from peasant stock. There is an odd moment in the novel when McDara remembers 'his young manhood, that had been lashed by a shameful sense of inferiority':

> His mouth opened wide. His fury left him and he became sad. Gradually, his lips closed again, his face shut up, his eyes became locked doors concealing his mind. Once more, he stood aloft, looking down with equanimity on life, on his sordid birth, on his youth, when he had been drawn away from primitive, peasant thoughtlessness by a thirst for knowledge, on his young manhood, when the primitive man in him, timid in its strange atmosphere of complex thought, grew morbid with a sense of inferiority and injustice onwards towards the chaos of unbelief. (*A* p. 165)

This corresponds with what older residents of the Aran Islands have said about O'Flaherty — that he was, as a youth, despised because of his inability to perform the ordinary, everyday work of the islanders.

More important than any of the evidence offered so far in

support of the claim that O'Flaherty identifies with his character is the kind of consciousness with which he endows him. It is exactly similar to the divided — almost schizophrenic — consciousness which he claims as his own in *Shame the Devil*. McDara is 'aware of being two people'. The first — and the dominant one — is described as feminine. 'It had a feminine attribute, because he was negative, hysterical and cunning, preying on his other personality, just like a woman preys on her mate.' (*A* p. 50) This aspect of McDara is like a red, raw nerve, making him sensitive to the slightest tremulation in the air around him. The other personality is, appropriately, masculine. 'With a bold, callous will, it caught and crushed every idea and suggestion that was offered to it, rummaged through it, plundered what was useful and cast out the remainder. This personality existed in his body like a foreigner. It despised his body.' (*A* p. 50) The masculine personality rises to the heights of Nietzschean gaiety, the laughter of the Superman, the feminine descends to the depths of Dostoyevskian despair. And yet O'Flaherty, in *The Assassin*, captures only the most superficial aspects of both. The shabby, misshapen creatures, absurdly dressed in outsize garments, with 'their pallor, their deep eyes, their habit of gazing vacantly into the distance', are the most tangible results of his study of *Crime and Punishment*. *Thus Spoke Zarathustra* has yielded up McDara's version of ' . . . man with a shining body, stalking the firmament, with the conquered earth on his back, seeking other spheres to loot.' (*A* p. 147)

Apart from the purely revelatory aspects of the book, what can be said on the credit side? The account of the actual assassination is gripping. It is viewed objectively, as if through the impersonal eye of a camera and ends on a wildly grotesque episode:

> Then a little man with yellow face, wearing large spectacles, crawled in through the crowd on his hands and knees, until he got to the pool of dark-red blood. He dipped his hand in it. It had curdled and the blood-froth reached to his wrist. The little fellow stood up and raised his frenzied face to the sky.

'Make way, make way,' he cried to the people. 'Make
way for the Sign of the Lord'. They stepped back and
he walked through them, with his knees trembling, to
the corner of the grey orchard wall. He reached the wall.
Then with a grotesque gesture, he struck his chest,
twisted his body, held out his gory hand and made the
Sign of the Cross with the blood, on the wall. Then he
pointed to the crooked bloody cross he had made and
burst into a peal of hysterical laughter. (*A* pp. 215-16)

Again, the occasional descriptions of people and places
connected with the Republican movements of the 1920s is
savagely ironical. Read in the light of events today one has
the impression of threading through the breeding ground of
our present violence and hatred.

Mr. Gilhooley[7]

The Informer, The Assassin, Mr. Gilhooley and *The Puritan* —
the third title is the odd man out in that it refers to a character rather than to a character type. (O'Flaherty originally
intended to call this work *The Firebrand,* and from the
evidence of the text might just as easily have called it *The
Voluptuary*). The difference in nomenclature reflects something of the difference between *Mr. Gilhooley* and the other
Dublin novels. There is a thinness, an abstract quality about
these others which, though not wholly lacking in *Mr.
Gilhooley,* is less in evidence. The character of Gilhooley
himself is a much more credible, more rounded one than
that of any of the protagonists we have seen so far. We must
qualify this by saying, however, that he is credible only up to
a certain point. Towards the end of the novel he goes mad.
This seems to be one of those damning failures of nerve on
O'Flaherty's behalf — a failure to follow through the
implications of the character and story he has created.
Dublin, both in its physical aspect and as a grim monster
which maims the 'innocent' country folk who come within its
reach, is powerfully present in the book. Gilhooley is
supported by a host of minor characters who reveal different

aspects of the city's life and the wounds it inflicts. There is, too, a strain of grotesque humour which is wholly lacking in the other novels and which, to some extent, relieves the gloom and despair that are at the heart of the book.

Mr Gilhooley (a hybrid character, a cross between Gypo Nolan and McSharry of *Thy Neighbour's Wife*) is a retired civil engineer who has returned from South America to Ireland. The first few chapters present him as a bored sensualist, given to drink and his own particular brand of debauchery — interfering with women in cinemas.

An early episode describes him exploring the thigh of a middle-aged woman in the Grafton Cinema. She leaves her seat in annoyance and the omniscient narrator uses his privilege to show us Gilhooley's self disgust and the conventional 'respectable' cast of his mind. He wanders the streets in search of his drinking companions and is accosted by a young woman, Nelly Fitzpatrick, who agrees to sleep with him. Their relationship develops and they set up house together. Gilhooley, desperate for affection, falls in love with the girl but, as becomes more and more obvious, she is using her 'Uncle' as she calls him for her own ends — to win back her former lover. Nelly is promiscuous and gives herself, with abandon, to one of Gilhooley's friends. Madly jealous, Gilhooley murders her. The narrative falls to pieces at this point. An insane Gilhooley runs through the streets of Dublin chased by imaginary pursuers. He takes his own life by jumping into the Grand Canal. As the dark water closes over his bald head the narrator concludes with two questions meant to convey the absurdity and futility of it all — 'Whither? Whence?'

There is a strong naturalistic strain in the novel — all of the characters are both the products and victims of circumstances. They exist in a society for which their rural background has not prepared them. These people are to be found in the public houses and cheap lodging-houses of the city and it is there, in their unnatural habitats, that O'Flaherty discovers them. In this examination attention will be focussed on his portrayal of the denizens ('species permanently established but not native of a place') of what is, unmistakably, McDaid's Public House and Davin's Lodging House.

The long shadow of Dostoyevski's St Petersburg casts its gloom over Dublin:

> He halted when he entered Grafton Street. He surveyed the street. In spite of the mist, the gloomy yellow lamps, the wet pavements and the dull, hurried business-men, the street appeared very gay to him. The gloomy appearance of the street merely enhanced the feeling of romantic sin that lurked there at that time of day. And for a bored man, gloom, under certain conditions, is more attractive than light and healthy gaiety. He watched the courtesans, swaying their full haunches as they ambled past, arching their shoulders and beckoning with their eyes. He recognized them all by their gay stockings, their rakish hats and by the peculiar look in their never-smiling eyes. That look of mingled avarice, suspicion and fear, which the eyes of courtesans share with the eyes of peasants who have come to the fair to sell something. (*Mr.G* pp. 12-13)

As Gilhooley grows in boredom and isolation the 'mist wrought gloom' thickens and the 'unreal city' of Eliot's poem takes on its now familiar linaments

> The streets were becoming long empty tunnels instead of streets and a human being going along a street looked very queer and small. The electric lights in the big shops had been turned off and the hats perched on stands in the drapery shops looked very tawdry in this gloom. A strange silence was falling over the city, and every sound, no matter how loud, appeared to be very far off.... A ship's siren screamed in the docks at a great distance. Around corners there was an icy current of air without the noise of any wind to say where it came from. A very still night, very cold and forbidding. (*Mr.G* pp. 38-39)

The way in which Gilhooley's consciousness is invaded by the shops and colours and sounds of the city has already been described (p. 264) Indeed the recurring image in the novel of the gas lamps glimmering through the all-pervading gloom

('...they seemed to be transfixed in empty space. Gloomy
yellow moons.') is a fit metaphor for Gilhooley's own
consciousness.

The public house where he goes to relieve his boredom
('distracted from distraction by distraction') is an extension of
this twilight world where there are only a few dull flickerings
of life:

> The public-house bar was a long narrow room, with a
> sawdust-covered floor and a bar counter formed of a
> broad deal board, three feet wide, unpainted, four
> inches thick, with a wainscotting of the same colour and
> material. Behind the counter, at regular intervals, stood
> one fat proprietor, with his enormous bare arms crossed
> on his chest, and two other attendants. There were
> several customers scattered at intervals in groups along
> the counter, and near the door, perched on his custom-
> ary high stool, sat a drunken old racing tout with three
> yellow teeth in his upper jaw, who was always to be
> seen there from six o'clock in the evening until closing
> time. At the far end of the room, where the bar counter
> curved inwards, Mr. Gilhooley's two friends were stand-
> ing. They were drunk and creating a scene . . . (*Mr.G*
> pp. 14-15)

Gilhooley's two friends are Sean Macaward, a drunken poet,
and a cashiered army officer, Shemus Hanrahan. Both are
emblematic figures, one of the fag end of the Celtic Revival,
the other of the Nationalist Revolution. Their drunken
conversation is laden with blasphemous references to the
Mass and the sacraments: when Gilhooley enters they are
busily baptizing a stray puppy with a glass of port. We are
not far from the world of *Ulysses,* the Citizen and *his* dog.
Yet, here, even emblematic dogs have gone down in the
world. 'I baptize thee, mangy cur, fleabitten, lop-eared cur,
homeless, destitute cur, fatherless, manyfathered cur, blear-
eyed, cowardly cur, whining, grovelling cur, symbol of
servitude. I call thee all the names of pot-bellied, yellow-
livered publicans, shopkeepers, gombeen men and plaster
saints, of which O Lord our unfortunate country has a

multitude.' (*Mr.G* pp. 17-18) The Poet Maudit is a grotesque figure compared to the Citizen Triumphant. His main claims to distinction seems to be that he has collected thirty-seven summonses for pulling the alarm cords on trains:

> He was a very small fellow, with a triangularly-shaped head, an enormous skull and a chin which, although it was not pointed, was very narrow compared to his broad forehead. His face was probably not sallow originally, but owing to drink and lack of washing, looked quite dark. His little extraordinary eyes had hardly any lashes. They were red around the rims and within the red rims there was a white line right around them. They were of a dim blue colour. His face was wrinkled like that of an old man. It continually changed its expression, at one moment having an ecstatic look of extreme and exalted intelligence, and the next moment looking devilish, at the next moment looking quite stupid and innocent, like the face of a peasant who is asked a question by a police officer.
>
> This extraordinary man was dressed from head to foot in a woman's bath-robe, which was the colour of unwashed linen, with black and yellow vertical stripes. From the ends of the robe, the toes of two heavy army boots appeared, twisted and yellowish, as if they had been thrown on some refuse heap for a long time. His head was bare, still with all its hair, of a darkish colour. A small grey cloth hat, such as lunatics in asylums and children at the seaside wear, was stuck on a blackthorn stick against the counter. Both the stick and the hat belonged to Macaward. (*Mr.G* pp. 16-17)

Hanrahan, his companion in distress, is equally grotesque. The warfare of the previous decade provided an outlet for his crude energy. In times of peace he is reduced to futile plotting and conspiracy, an effort to recapture the vanished glory:

> A man without any evil in his nature and yet without a capacity for making any effective use of the good in his nature. A man to be pitied by artists and women and

looked upon with suspicion by all efficient citizens, who
used him on occasion for rough work like warfare, but
cast him aside when there was nothing of the sort
needed. . . . Yet in spite of his shabbiness, . . . he had a
military cut about him, that curious air of desperate
gallantry which the born soldier of fortune retains even
to the end of his career. (*Mr.G* p. 16)

Despite their degeneration, better, because of it, both
Hanrahan and Macaward pose the vital question which *Mr.
Gilhooley* raises (Hanrahan: 'How can we love in the midst of
all this ugliness?') and attempt an answer (Macaward: 'We're
Irish. We were made for the hillsides and the fields . . . and
the sea. That's our life.'): a pastoral dream, their childhood
Eden, haunts their imaginations and unfits them for their
place in the normal human world while not fitting them for
any other. One imagines that, if they were all back on the
Aran Islands where they so obviously belong, they would
dream of another world elsewhere, Hy Brasil, just over the
horizon.

One of the best things in the novel is the description of Mr
Gilhooley's boarding house. Chapter V could almost stand on
its own as a fine short story. Mr Gilhooley brings Nelly
Fitzpatrick home with him, surreptitiously, as it is against the
rules of the house. (Chapter IV contains an amusing description of Gilhooley carrying his boots and Nelly on his back up
the stairs to his room). Chapter V opens at six o'clock the
following morning with Cissy, the household slave, preparing
breakfast. The narrator's voice, edged with a barely suppress-
ed *saeva indignatio* begins his account of the household with
the lower depths and works up to the top floor where the
landlord and landlady are asleep. Cissy is barely human and
there is a quite terrifying description of the drudgery of her
daily life. She is another victim of the city, brutalized beyond
redemption:

Cissy had never the cunning to become a courtesan, nor
indeed the wisdom. For there is some variety in a life of
sin. There is danger too. But in Cissy's life there was the
horror of sin without variety or pleasurable danger. She

surrendered her virtue to the first comer long ago. She wept and was horrified afterwards. But again she sinned and again. She had two children that suckled at her flabby breasts. They were both dead. One died in the workhouse. The other died in the care of a harpy on the south side of the city. The harpy offered to rear him — it was a boy — for five pounds. And it promptly died. Cissy lost her job after each child was born, for no honest matron is willing to keep a fallen woman in her house, even though her son or husband may be the father of the child; or perhaps just because of that. Anyway, these falls and these misfortunes wrought a savage change in the mind and body of Cissy.

We see a playful animal in the first joy of youth, frolic at its mother's side, romp over fields and gambol fearlessly towards a stranger. And we see the same animal, reared brutally by a brutal master, become brutal, timorous and snarling. So, like a constantly beaten brute, Cissy's mind and soul had become brutal and pitiless. (*Mr. G* pp. 76-77)

On her early morning rounds she calls the medical student who goes to Mass every morning, the two grocer's curates who eat in the kitchen, because they are regarded as socially inferior, her great enemy, the landlady's daughter, and finally Mr Gilhooley whom she overhears talking to his bed mate. The dreadful news spreads through the house. O'Flaherty, quite brilliantly, evokes from the different lodgers different responses that have a quality in common, what D.H. Lawrence called a combination of calico purity and underwear excitement. Cissy uses the news to take revenge on the landlady's daughter who is secretly in love with Gilhooley, the landlady uses it as a weapon in her long struggle with her husband, the grocer's curates make it an occasion for a row about the respective merits of Socialism and Catholicism. Peace is restored by the landlord. 'Mr. Davin belonged to that class of man with whom it is a pleasure to converse, who are loved by all except their wives, . . . who are always happy because their natures are unable to contemplate a difficulty of any kind for more than a moment.' With great tact he clears the house of all the lodgers, has Gilhooley's breakfast sent up to his room and slips the bill under the door. When Gilhooley and his girl leave 'by common instinct the four of them rushed to Mr. Gilhooley's room, and such was the common excitement to see where "she" had spent the night that nobody turned Cissy away.' This episode represents O'Flaherty at his happiest – a combination of grotesque humour and savage irony.

We turn now to consider the central characters of the book, Gilhooley and Nelly Fitzpatrick. Nelly is the first of the 'country girls' whom Edna O'Brien was to make her own – indeed she might be taken as the prototype of all those imaginary girls from Galway and Clare who come to ruin in Dublin, Paris and London. She has all the social qualifications (short spell in convent as an orphan, etc.) but in *Mr. Gilhooley* her existence is as much on the level of the mythical as the actual. She is the fatal woman of legend, vicious, unappeasable but fascinating – a younger, lapsed Catholic sister to the ladies of the Big House whom we have seen earlier. (There is a curious connection here: Nelly has first been led astray by a son of the Big House and there is a hint of a lesbian relationship between her and the feckless boy's mother). We will first examine her 'real' existence and then observe how Gilhooley mythologizes her.

Nelly tells her story to an inattentive and drunken Gilhooley. This 'background information', though lengthy, is dramatically acceptable, in that the telling emphasizes the unease and incompatibility of the two. Nelly is the country girl *par excellence* whose story will be repeated again and again. An orphan, she was 'taken in' by the nuns in Galway and later removed from the convent by a lady who wished at one stroke to exercise her charity and gain some cheap labour. Her guardian intends to return her to the convent later on as a nun. Nelly does not want to be a nun:

'Can you blame me? What did I know? There she was, with a black band around her throat, wearing the same black dress day after day. God! How I hated that black band and that black dress and the holy way she had with customers. She kept a little hat-shop . . . She used

to beat me, though, with her holy books, and drink
too . . . on the quiet.' (*Mr.G* p. 66)

In short, the classical Irish guardian. Her first lover is equally
conventional. He is one Matt Considine, a richly romantic
figure in the prosaic world of Galway. Son of a local landowner and a 'genius' to boot, he has been thrown out of
several public schools. When the war breaks out he is in
Trinity College, which he leaves to join the Flying Corps.
After many adventures he returns to Galway where he meets
Nelly. In 1919 the Republicans give him twenty-four hours
to leave the country. He joins the Auxiliary Cadets – otherwise the Black and Tans. Later still Nelly runs off to London
with him where they live together for two years and have a
child who dies. Matt, at the time of the novel's opening, is
married to a widow. Nelly is in hot pursuit of him still but
because of her obsession with her lost lover it seems more
that she is pursued by Matt. The unfortunate Mr Gilhooley
tries to cope with this difficult situation.

He is, on the whole, rather a simple soul. In the opening
chapter he goes to the cinema because ' . . . there was an air
of mystery about it. An air of romance and of remoteness
from actual life.' His ideal world, the life he would like to
lead, is as remote from his actual life as the flickering
shadows on the screen. 'Something simple, an innocent
country wife, children, a house in the country, pigs, cows,
ploughed land, the music of a river, birds, new-mown hay,
everything. He thought of the rabbit-farm which he had
contemplated recently during similar fits of penitence. He
thought of a bee-farm. "Anything at all . . . provided it's
simple and useful and . . . and healthy" '. (*Mr.G* pp. 34-35)
Later in the same chapter we are made aware of the kind of
love he seeks – ' . . . not sensual love, but that ideal, pure
love of which even the most degraded human beings are
aware, which they treasure in their inmost hearts, perhaps
unknown to themselves, their conception of that ultimate
good which man calls God . . . . ' These, then, are the two
imaginary worlds which collide throughout the remainder of
the book – Nelly's phantasmagoria where she is pursued by
Matt who wants to kill her (though it is really she who is

pursuing him) and Gilhooley's pastoral dream of useful, simple toil, blessed by a conception of ideal love.

At their first encounter Nelly is shown to be an ambiguous figure. She is a waif, one of the derelicts of the city, knowing nobody; she has walked the streets for four nights. Yet in her first smile to Gilhooley there is 'some precocious knowledge, a knowledge of bacchanalian joy and of feminine subtlety.' In this world of sudden transformations 'an astonishing sight' meets Gilhooley's eyes when he brings her to a cheap cafe for a meal:

> The girl was transformed. Instead of the miserable waif, with a skimpy body, a shabby raincoat, with a safety-pin at her throat, he saw a charming, impish, smiling face, crowned with a thick mass of golden curls. They shone in the light. Suddenly released from the close pressure of the black cap, they bubbled up in little hillocks, disentwining like writhing snakes, sparkling and trembling. Beneath them the white face had now taken a different light. The short white teeth and the brilliant, blue, laughing, big eyes mocked him, as if they suddenly disclosed a secret they had been hiding. They mocked with the same look of gaiety, as when she smiled before, but now it was different, for the sparkling yellow curls, like a golden treasure, stood above them explaining this gay madness. (*Mr.G* p. 55)

The 'golden girl' seems to be an obsessive image with O'Flaherty (notice that, like Nora of *The House of Gold,* her hair is compared to 'writhing snakes'). Apart from its connection with folklore and legend the image also connects with a commercial metaphor – this girl, like all his golden girls, sells herself for money. The subsequent action of the novel also makes another familiar connection, that between love and death. Gilhooley, driving with Nelly in a taxi to his lodging house, is reminded of another significant event in his life – his father's funeral. Once in his room the girl undergoes a further series of transformations – ' . . . she seemed a different person . . . she carried herself like a woman who is used to interiors', and later the 'bacchanalian look' returns to

her eyes. Gilhooley, like the Stranger of *The Black Soul*
experiences violent sexual remorse after his night of love. The
extremes of emotion which the novel portrays is a product of
that same Manichaean flight from the body that we have
noted so frequently in O'Flaherty's works:

> The events of the night, during which he had abandoned
> himself to her devilish charms, now evoked horror in his
> mind. For how could such vitality be possessed by a
> slim frail creature, unless it were some charm of an evil
> spirit? When he awoke in the morning, a frenzy of
> hatred made him lean over, with his hand clawed,
> desiring to choke her . . .
>
> For it was this insane passion for her, for the memory
> of that drunken excitement of the night, . . . that filled
> his mind with terror. He was slipping over the brink of
> the precipice, over the edge of which he had been hang-
> ing for three years. He had now lost the last hold, his
> respectability. He was unmoored, in her possession.
> Where was he going? (*Mr. G* p. 98)

In short, O'Flaherty now has his character where he wants
him — removed from society and plagued by the devil.
Gilhooley's bewilderment increases as Nelly oscillates in his
imagination between an angelic figure and an emissary of
Satan. Their love-making is an attempt to escape 'from the
consciousness of existence and the fear of death through lust
and drunkenness.' The more she becomes necessary to his
existence the less she needs him. His love is half hatred,
hatred that she has awakened his dormant passions, hatred of
her youth and vitality. In the climactic scene of their passion,
Nelly dances naked before a stupified Gilhooley. She begins
to hate him because she has sold herself for food and shelter,
Gilhooley is enraged 'at the impossibility of crushing her
body, making it limp with satiety.' Thereafter Nelly proposes
to put their relationship on its proper business footing — 'I'll
give you a good time. See the idea?' For her, love is a game.
Gilhooley, as he realizes, is too old to play the game and
besides he has his pastoral dream. 'He seemed to be very far
away, among the wise old men, who brooded over proverbs

on the Irish hills. A distant, slender root, withering in barren
soil, yearning for the mother sap.' (*Mr.G* p. 187) Up to this
point (Chapter XIII) the novel is credible enough — a sometimes searing portrait of disharmony. From now on, with
rare intervals of lucidity, O'Flaherty seems to loose control
of characters and situation. Gilhooley goes mad, murders the
girl, drowns himself. There is, really, nothing very much one
can say about this, except to remark that O'Flaherty is avoid-
ing the implications raised by his story. (It would be possible
to read the final chapters as somehow a portrayal of the
absurdity of life but this would be a further avoidance of
responsibility — by the critic).

The Puritan[8]

The Puritan is the last of the Dublin thrillers and much that
has been said of the earlier books applies here too — despite
the fact that, as Joseph Holloway records in his diary
(Sunday, 18 September, 1932), Yeats hailed the book as a
masterpiece. Its central character, Francis Ferriter (the
Puritan of the title) is pathological, and O'Flaherty does little
or nothing to inspire sympathy or understanding for him in
the reader. Quite the contrary: the distance between the
narrator and Ferriter is one of total opposition and hostility.
One experiences, reading the book, a growing sense of boredom and alienation from both the narrator and the uninterest-
ing main character. Again, this work is heavily influenced by
Crime and Punishment, particularly in those scenes where
Ferriter is followed by an indefatigable detective and the
confession scene where he reveals the real motive for his
crime. As in *The Assassin* there is some confusion as to why
the murder is committed — there is a similar (Dostoyevskian)
association between murder and the problem of the existence
of God. In *The Puritan,* however, O'Flaherty maintains a
firmer grip on his material: what seemed merely grafted on
from the outside in the one is more organic in the other.
Finally, by way of introduction, *The Puritan* demonstrates
very clearly that O'Flaherty cannot admit violence into his
fictional world without becoming violent. Violence lends the

tone to the whole and it is both sudden and largely inexplicable. Francis Ferriter, a Dublin journalist, murders Theresa
Burke, a prostitute who lodges in the same boarding house.
He does this from motives of religious fanaticism which are
explained in a confession entitled 'The Sacrifice of Blood'
written prior to the murder. He so plans the murder that
suspicion is cast on the woman's lover, Dr O'Leary, who is
the son of a prominent member of the vigilance society to
which Ferriter belongs. Ferriter believes that not only should
the prostitute be punished for her sins but so also should her
male clients. He hopes, in his professional capacity as a
journalist, to seize on the event and gain publicity for his
plans to have puritanical law reforms introduced in the Irish
Parliament. The police officer in charge of investigating the
crime, Chief Supt. Lavan, suspects Ferriter immediately. In
what is, for O'Flaherty, an extraordinary *volte face,* all the
reader's sympathy and concern is directed towards the chief
superintendent. Ferriter's defences are gradually broken
down as he fails to find sympathy for his cause from the
editor of his newspaper, the *Morning Star,* or from the pious
though fascist editor of the *Catholic Vanguard,* Fr Moran. A
visit to his bourgeois relatives in Rathmines proves even more
debilitating — they regard him, with his meagre talents, as a
failure. Subsequently he finds himself where all the protagonists of these novels at some point find themselves — in a
church. He confesses his crime under the seal of confession
and in the process comes to realize that he has murdered the
woman because of sexual jealousy. The priest refuses him
absolution on the grounds that murder is a reserved sin and
Ferriter runs out of the church. In this world of extremes it is
not surprising that he goes straight to a brothel-cum-shebeen
where the remainder of the night is spent in drunkeness and
debauchery. He is arrested with one of the whores and signs a
confession of his guilt. In the final scene, Ferriter beholds a
vision that symbolizes his loss of faith in God. 'There is no
God, but man has a divine destiny.' (*P* p. 326) As we might
expect from our reading of the previous work he is, at this
stage, stark, staring, raving mad.

This condensation of the plot demonstrates the sheer
incredibility of the story and indeed the incredibility of the

central character. There is, however, some good incidental satire on the *nouveaux riches* who have come to wealth and power after the revolution. The main target, is, of course, the Church and those who support it, particularly the Catholic editor of the *Morning Star:*

> When Dr. Johnson said that patriotism was the last refuge of a scoundrel he could not have meant his words to apply to Ireland; for in our country that last refuge is religion. Mr. Corish and the proprietors of his newspaper fell back on religion in an attempt to retain their circulation and to prevent the masses from buying the English newspapers that began again to become popular. They joined hands with the Catholic clergy, who were then starting their great campaign to consolidate their power under the new government by completely destroying the remnants of the old Protestant middle class. The *Morning Star* became the official organ of the new Puritanism which began to sweep the country. (*P* pp. 77-78)

Much else in the book is hackneyed — the girl who is murdered is a reworking of Nelly Fitzpatrick from *Mr. Gilhooley.* The city is the same, shabby Dostoyevskian one as we have met before. There are the same sudden transformations and the prolonged *angst* of the leading character. Ferriter shares with McDara of *The Assassin* and others a split personality and a vision of his life in the city as a descent into Hell. There is an occasional lift to the narrative, especially when 'Hairy' Maggie Considine comes on the scene to explain the murdered girl's background:

> . . . she was my sister's child, my youngest sister Mary, who worked for Sir George Bodkin of Killuragh Castle. A rip he was that got eight women into trouble . . . and Mary was the last of them. He was as old as I am at the time. He married her to his under-gardner. . . . They opened an hotel and then Burke died. Teresa was about five at the time. Mary was well over forty and then she put her foot in it by marrying a poxy peeler. She's dead

now, and God forgive me for speaking bad of the dead, but it was fitter for her to start saving her soul than fiddle under the blankets with a bodach like that . . . . Now look at the result of it. She and her child are dead an' gone, . . . while that bould criminal Finnerty (the under-gardner) is going up for the County Council at the next election. God's curse on the country that hasn't a gunman in it to put a streak o' lead in through his cowardly guts. (*P* p. 176)

More generally the novel is of interest because in it that puritanical, Manichaean streak which we have noted in many of O'Flaherty's works is to the fore. It is interesting to speculate that O'Flaherty writes his imaginative condemnation of this condition in such a melodramatic fashion, precisely because he shares it himself.

CHAPTER 12

CONCLUSION

Liam O'Flaherty's best work is to be found in those novels which have been grouped together under the heading 'Regional Romances', and after these come *Famine, The Martyr* and *Mr. Gilhooley*. All of these books — bleak and crude as they often are — offer an unmatched imaginative portrayal of the contradictions and disharmonies that have at once enriched and impoverished our culture and society. O'Flaherty's best work occurs at the fracture point of a broken world; Irish and English, oral and written, folk culture and 'civilization'. Increasingly, he will probably be seen as a key figure in the development of Anglo-Irish literature if and when the emphasis falls on the 'Irish' rather than the 'Anglo' part of that troublesome hybrid. He is not a novelist of the first rank; he lives more in the mind for what he tried to do rather than for what he actually accomplished.

O'Flaherty, man and artist, is something of an enigma. Perhaps the final word has been said on both by Francis Stuart in his fictional autobiography *Black List Section H,* where O'Flaherty becomes the hero of another man's fiction:

O'Flaherty was enjoying a successful phase. He'd shown H the proof of an advertisement his publisher — who was also H's — was putting in one of the papers that devoted several pages to literature the coming Sunday. It consisted of a good half-column of carefully selected quotations from reviews, and was headed: 'Triumph for a great Novelist'. Although O'Flaherty's novels struck H as stark and gloomy, he respected the untamable spirit both in them and his friend, and rejoiced in his increasing renown, whose tangible fruits were lavish entertaining.[1]

ABBREVIATIONS

A	The Assassin	Mr G	Mr. Gilhooley
BS	The Black Soul	P	The Puritan
F	Famine	S	Skerrett
HG	House of Gold	SD	Shame the Devil
I	Insurrection	TGI	Tourist's Guide to Ireland
IWR	I Went to Russia	TI	The Informer
L	Land	TNW	Thy Neighbour's Wife
M	The Martyr	W	Wilderness

NOTES

PART I: CHAPTERS 1 − 8

1   Liam O'Flaherty, *Shame the Devil* (London, 1934).

2   Liam O'Flaherty, *Two Years* (London, 1930).

3   Liam O'Flaherty, *I Went to Russia* (London, 1931).

4   Roderick O'Flaherty, *A Chorographical Description of West or H-Iar Connaught,* ed. James Hardiman (Dublin, 1846), pp. 65 - 69.

5   A.C. Haddon and C.R. Browne, 'The Ethnography of the Aran Islands, County Galway', *Proceedings of the Royal Irish Academy,* 3rd series, XVIII (Dublin, 1891-93) 768 - 830.

6   J.M. Synge, *Collected Works,* ed. Alan Price, Vol. II,

Prose, (London, 1966), p. 47.

7   Tom O'Flaherty, *Aranmen-All* (Dublin, 1934).

8   Michael O'Donovan, 'Aran Island, County Galway'. In the *Galway Vindicator*, 12 February 1892.

9   'The Aran Island Atrocities', *Daily Independent*, 14 April 1894.

10   See *Galway Vindicator*, 19 May 1894.

11   *Galway Express*, 14 June 1913.

12   Ibid.

13   Tom O'Flaherty, *Aranmen-All*.

14   Ibid.

15   William Stokes, *The Life and Labours in Art and Archaeology of George Petrie* (London, 1868).

16   *Shame the Devil*, p. 17.

17   William Carleton, *The Life of William Carleton: being his Autobiography and Letters: and an account of his life and writings from the point at which the Autobiography breaks off.* by David I. O'Donoghue, Vol. I (London, 1896), p. 94.

18   *Shame the Devil*, pp. 17 - 18.

19   *Galway Vindicator*, 4 January 1892.

20   Stephen Gwynn, *To-day and To-morrow in Ireland: Essays on Irish Subjects* (Dublin, 1903).

21   *Galway Vindicator*, 9 April 1892.

22   *Shame the Devil*, p. 64.

23   Ibid.

24   *Galway Express*, 5 March 1898.

25   Tom O'Flaherty, *Aranmen-All*, p. 163.

26   *Two Years*, p. 327.

27   E.W. Lynam, 'The O'Flaherty Country'. *Studies* III (1914).

28   'An Craoibhin', 'Sgeal faoi O Flaithbheartaigh', *Bealoideas* I (Meitheamh 1927).

29   John T. O'Flaherty, *A sketch of the History and Antiquities of the Southern Islands of Aran* (Dublin 1824) p. 13.

30   Stokes, 'Aran — Character of the Islanders', in *The Life and Labours in Art and Archaeology of George Petrie* p. 52.

31   Ibid., p. 376.

32   Ibid.
33   Synge, 'The Aran Islands', in *Collected Works: Prose.*
34   Haddon and Browne, 'The Ethnography of the Aran Islands', p. 811.
35   P.A. O Siochain, *Aran, Islands of Legend.* Third Edition (Dublin, 1967).
36   *Shame the Devil*, p. 58.
37   'Folklore in Literature: A Symposium', *Journal of American Folklore,* LXX (1957).
38   John Messenger, 'Man of Aran Revisited. An Anthropological Critique', *University Review* III No.9 (1966).
39   *Galway Express,* 7 September 1910.
40   Arthur Symons, *Cities and Sea-Coasts and Islands* (London, 1918).
41   Ibid.
42   Synge, *The Aran Islands.*
43   Benedict Kiely, 'Liam O'Flaherty: A Story of Discontent'. *The Month* NS II (September 1949).
44   *Joseph Conrad: An Appreciation.* Blue Moon Booklets No.1 (London, 1930).
45   Emily Lawless, *Grania: The Story of an Island* (London, 1892).
46   *Two Years,* p. 247.
47   Quoted in Synge, *Collected Prose,* p. 283.
48   Ibid.
49   *Connaught Tribune,* 1 December 1934.
50   Quoted in the *Galway Express,* 15 April 1911.
51   W.B. Yeats, 'The Irish Dramatic Movement 1901 - 1919', *Explorations* (London, 1962) pp. 203 - 204.
52   Synge, *The Aran Islands,* p. 150.
53   Ibid., p. 115.
54   In the *Irish Statesman,* IX (1927).
55   Tom O'Flaherty, *Aranmen-All,* p. 158.
56   Haddon and Browne, 'The Ethnography of the Aran Islands', p. 816.
57   Lady Augusta Gregory, *Visions and Beliefs in the West of Ireland* (first published London, 1920; Coole Edition, London, 1970).
58   J.H. Delargy, *The Gaelic Story-Teller, with some*

notes on *Gaelic Folk-Tales* (London, 1947) p. 6.

59   *Shame the Devil*, p. 18.

60   Delargy, *The Gaelic Story-Teller*, p. 6.

61   Elizabeth Rivers, *Stranger in Aran* (Dublin, 1946).

62   Sean O Suilleabhain and Reidar Christiansen, *The Types of the Irish Folktale* (Oslo: F.F. Cummunications, 1963).

63   Synge, *The Aran Islands*, p. 54.

64   Haddon and Browne, 'The Ethnography of the Aran Islands', p. 819.

65   B.N. Hedderman, *Glimpses of my Life in Aran. Some experiences of a district nurse in these remote islands off the west coast of Ireland.* (Bristol, 1917) p. 104.

66   Haddon and Browne, 'The Ethnography of the Aran Islands', p. 812.

67   Monsignor D'Alton, *History of the Archdiocese of Tuam,* Vol. II (Dublin, 1928) p. 112.

68   Ibid., p. 123.

69   Liam O'Flaherty, 'Autobiographical Note' in *Ten Contemporaries: Notes towards their Definitive Bibliography,* second series, ed. John Gawsworth (London, 1933) p. 139.

70   *Shame the Devil*, p. 19.

71   Ibid., p. 19.

72   *Rockwell Annual* (Dublin, 1928) p. 2

73   *Shame the Devil*, p. 20.

74   *Report of the Examiners, Board of Intermediate Education, 1903-11.*

75   *Rockwell Annual,* (Dublin, 1966) p. 23.

76   'Autobiographical Note', p. 140.

77   I am indebted to Fr. John Ryan, official historian of Blackrock College, Dublin, for this information.

78   *Shame the Devil*, p. 21.

79   Ibid. p. 21.

80   *Two Years, p. 161.*

81   *Shame the Devil*, p. 83.

82   *Two Years*, p. 161.

83   *Shame the Devil*, p. 83.

84   Ibid., p. 239.

85   *Two Years*, p. 74.

86   Ibid., p. 12.
87   Ibid., p. 13.
88   Ibid., p. 59.
89   Ibid., p. 102.
90   Ibid., p. 128.
91   Ibid., p. 225.
92   Ibid., p. 350.
93   Gerald Griffin, *The Wild Geese* (London, 1938) pp. 191 - 92.
94   Ibid., p. 192.
95   *Shame the Devil*, p. 35 - 36.
96   Ibid., p. 38.
97   'Autobiographic Note', p. 143.
98   H.E. Bates, *Edward Garnett* (London, 1950).
99   Ibid.
100   Ibid.
101   *Irish Statesman*, 3 May 1924.
102   Letter to Edward Garnett, 6 September 1925.
103   Sean O'Casey, *Autobiographies* II (New York, 1949).
104   Ibid.
105   *To-morrow* II, August 1924.
106   *Irish Statesman*, 18 October 1924.
107   Ibid., 1 November 1924.
108   Ibid., 18 October 1924.
109   Ibid., 1 November 1924.
110   Ibid., 4 June 1929.
111   Letter to Edward Garnett, 1926.
112   *Irish Statesman*, 17 December 1927.
113   *I Went to Russia*, p. 51.
114   Ibid., pp. 298 - 99.
115   Letters to Edward Garnett, 29 February 1932.
116   *New Age*, 25 December 1913.
117   Anthony Canedo, 'Liam O'Flaherty: Introduction and Analysis', (Ph. D. dissertation, University of Washington, 1965).
118   *The Bell*, June 1941, pp. 28 - 29.
119   *Shame the Devil*, p. 145.
120   Ibid., p. 11.
121   Ibid., p. 23.

122   Ibid., p. 198.

123   Ibid., p. 101.

124   *I Went to Russia*, p. 188.

125   *Irish Statesman*, 18 October 1924.

126   *I Went to Russia*, p. 62.

127   *Shame the Devil*, p. 216.

128   Ibid., p. 217.

129   Ibid., p. 230.

130   Ibid., p. 85.

131   Quoted in *John Keats* by Robert Gittings (London, 1968) p. 11.

132   *I Went to Russia*, pp. 82 - 83.

133   *Shame the Devil*, p. 16.

134   Liam O'Flaherty, *A Tourist's Guide to Ireland* (London, 1929).

135   Ibid., pp. 20 - 21.

136   Ibid., p. 38.

137   Ibid., p. 49.

138   Ibid., p. 50.

139   Ibid., p. 71.

140   Ibid., p. 81.

141   Ibid., p. 83.

142   Ibid., p. 86.

143   Ibid., pp. 88 - 89.

144   Ibid., p. 109.

145   Ibid., p. 116.

146   Ibid., p. 132.

147   John Broderick, 'Liam O'Flaherty: A Partial View', *Hibernia*, 19 December 1969.

148   'A. de B.', *The Irish Statesman*, 1 December 1923.

149   'A. de B.', *The Irish Statesman*, 3 May 1924.

150   John Broderick in *Hibernia*, 19 December 1969.

151   *Irish Statesman*, 10 October 1925.

152   *Irish Statesman*, 27 November 1926.

153   William Troy, 'The Position of Liam O'Flaherty', *The Bookman*, March 1929.

154   Ibid.

155   C. Henry Warren, 'The Bookman Gallery: Liam O'Flaherty', *The Bookman*, January 1930.

156   L. Paul-Dubois, 'Un Romancier Realiste en Erin',

Revue des Deux Mondes, 15 June.

157   Benedict Kiely in _The Month,_ September 1949.

158   Vivian Mercier, 'Man Against Nature: The Novels of Liam O'Flaherty', _Wascana Review,_ I, 1966, pp. 37 - 46.

159   Ibid.

160   John N. Zneimar, _The Literary Vision of Liam O'Flaherty_ (New York, 1970).

PART II: CHAPTER 9

1   D.H. Lawrence, _Studies in Classic American Literature_ (London 1964) pp. 5 - 6.

2   Eudora Welty, 'Place in Fiction', _South Atlantic Quarterly_ LO (1965): 62 - 63.

3   Phyllis Bentley, _The English Regional Novel_ (London, 1941).

4   Royal Commission on Congestion in Ireland. Appendix to the Tenth Report, (Dublin, 1908) pp. 16 - 17.

5   Bentley, _The English Regional Novel,_ p. 26.

6   Vivian Mercier, 'The Irish Short Story and Oral Tradition', in _The Celtic Cross,_ ed. Roy B. Browne, William John Roscelli and John Loftus (Indiana, 1964) p. 105.

7   Liam O'Flaherty, _Thy Neighbour's Wife_ (London, 1923).

8   Conor Cruise O'Brien, '1891 - 1916' in _The Shaping of Modern Ireland,_ ed. Conor Cruise O'Brien, (London, 1960) p. 13.

9   RTE Guide, 30 April 1971.

10   Liam O'Flaherty, _The Black Soul_ (London, 1924).

11   James Joyce, _A Portrait of the Artist as a Young Man_ (New York, 1916).

12   W.J. Harvey, _Character and the Novel_ (London, 1966).

13   A.N. Kaul, _The American Vision_ (New York, 1956).

14   Liam O'Flaherty, _The House of Gold_ (London,

(1929).

15   Thomas Flanagan, *The Irish Novelists 1800 - 1850* (New York, 1959), p. 138.

16   Douglas Hyde, *Sgealta Thomais Ui Chathasaigh* (Dublin, 1939).

17   Dorothy Van Ghent, *The English Novel: Form and Function* (Harper Torchbook edition, New York, 1961) p. 165.

18   Flanagan, *The Irish Novelists 1800 - 1850,* p. 93.

19   Liam O'Flaherty, *Skerrett* (London, 1932).

20   *Galway Express,* March/April 1912.

21   Ibid., 6 June 1908.

22   Ibid., 23 March 1912.

23   Liam O'Flaherty, *The Wilderness* (serialized in the *Humanist,* February — June 1927. As there is no pagination in the original text, a chapter and page reference has been provided here.)

24   Angeline O'Kelly, 'O'Flaherty on the Shelf', *Hibernia,* 20 November 1970.

25   J.E. Cirlot, *A Dictionary of Symbols,* trans. Jack Sage (London, 1962).

26   Leslie Fiedler, *Love and Death in the American Novel* (London, 1970 edition) p. 7.

PART II: CHAPTER 10

1   R. Dudley Edwards and T. Desmond Williams, eds., *The Great Famine, Studies in Irish History 1845 - 52* (Dublin, 1956) p. vii.

2   Ibid., p. 396.

3   Ibid., p. 436.

4   Rev. J. O'Rourke, *The History of the Great Irish Famine of 1847 with Notices of Earlier Irish Famines* (Dublin, 1875).

5   James Connolly, *Labour in Irish History* (first published Dublin, 1910.) Republished with *The Re-Conquest of Ireland* under the general title *Labour in Ireland* (Dublin, n.d.).

6   George Lucaks, *The Historical Novel*, trans. Hannah and Stanley Mitchell (London, 1962).

7   *Labour in Irish History*, p. 6.

8   Ibid., p. 8.

9   Zneimar, *The Literary Vision of Liam O'Flaherty*, p. 135.

10   Liam O'Flaherty, *Famine* (London, 1937. References are to the Reader's Union edition, London, 1938).

11   T.S. Eliot, *Collected Poems 1909 - 1962* (London, 1963) p. 197.

12   W.B. Yeats, *Essays and Introductions* (London, 1916) pp. 215 - 16.

13   Liam O'Flaherty, *Land* (London, 1946).

14   Fiedler, *Love and Death in the American Novel*, p. 28.

15   Liam O'Flaherty, *Insurrection* (London, 1950).

16   *The Bell*, January 1961 (Dublin, 1961).

17   Yeats, *Collected Poems*, p. 375.

18   Liam O'Flaherty, *The Martyr* (London, 1933).

19   P. H. Pearse, *Collected Works: Plays, Stories, Poems* (Dublin, 1924).

20   W.B. Yeats, *Letters*, ed. Alan Wade (London, 1954) p. 809.

21   D.H. Lawrence, *Studies in Classical American Literature*. Phoenix edition (London, 1964).

22   Yeats, *Collected Poems*, p. 263.

PART II: CHAPTER 11

1   Weller Embler, 'The Novel as Metaphor', *ETC* X, Autumn 1952.

2   Arthur Clayborough, *The Grotesque in English Fiction* (London, 1965).

3   Liam O'Flaherty, *The Informer* (London, 1925).

4   Harold J. O'Brien, 'The Representation of Religion in the Fiction of Francis Stuart and Liam O'Flaherty (dissertation, Trinity College, Dublin, 1967).

5   Liam O'Flaherty, *The Assassin* (London, 1928).

6   Zneimar, *The Literary Vision of Liam O'Flaherty*.

7   Liam O'Flaherty, *Mr. Gilhooley* (London, 1926).

8   Liam O'Flaherty, *The Puritan* (London, 1932).

PART II: CHAPTER 12

1   Francis Stuart, *Black List Section H,* (Southern
       Illinois University Press; Carbondale and Edwardsville,
       1971).

BIBLIOGRAPHY OF WORKS BY LIAM O'FLAHERTY

I. BOOKS AND BOOKLETS

(Arranged in order of publication)

Thy Neighbour's Wife. London, 1923; New York, 1924.
The Black Soul. London, 1924; New York, 1925.
Spring Sowing. London, 1924; New York, 1926.
The Informer. London, 1925; New York, 1925.
Civil War. London, 1925.
The Terrorist. London, 1926.
Darkness: A Tragedy in Three Acts. London, 1926.
The Tent. London, 1926.
Mr. Gilhooley. London, 1926; New York, 1927.
The Child of God. London, 1926.
The Life of Tim Healy. London, 1927; New York, 1927.
'The Wilderness' in *The Humanist,* February-June, 1927.
The Fairy-Goose and Two Other Stories. London, 1927, New York, 1927.
The Assassin. London, 1928; New York, 1928.
Red Barbara and Other Stories: The Mountain Tavern, Prey, The Oar. London, 1928; New York, 1928.
The Mountain Tavern and Other Stories. London, 1929; New York, 1929.
A Tourist's Guide to Ireland. London, 1929.
The House of Gold. London, 1929; New York, 1929.
The Return of the Brute. London, 1929; New York, 1930.
Joseph Conrad: An Appreciation. London, 1930.
Two Years. London, 1930; New York, 1930.
The Ecstasy of Angus. London, 1931.
A Cure for Unemployment. London, 1931.

I Went to Russia. London, 1931; New York, 1931.
The Puritan. London, 1932; New York, 1932.
The Wild Swan and Other Stories. London, 1932.
Skerrett. London, 1932; New York, 1933.
The Martyr. London, 1933; New York, 1933.
Shame the Devil. London, 1934.
Hollywood Cemetery. London, 1935.
Famine. London, 1937; New York, 1937.
The Short Stories of Liam O'Flaherty. London, 1937.
Land. London, 1946; New York, 1946.
Two Lovely Beasts and Other Stories. London, 1948; New York, 1950.
Insurrection. London, 1950; Boston, 1951.
Duil. Baile Atha Cliath, 1953.
The Stories of Liam O'Flaherty. New York, 1956.
The Pedlar's Revenge and Other Stories (Wolfhound Press) Dublin, 1976

II. ESSAYS

'National Energy', *Irish Statesman,* III (1924): 171.
'Mr. Tasker's Gods', *Irish Statesman,* III (1925): 828.
'A View of Irish Culture', *Irish Statesman,* IV (1925): 460-61.
'The Plough and the Stars', *Irish Statesman,* V (1926): 739.
'Literary Criticism in Ireland', *Irish Statesman,* VI (1926): 711.
'Facism or *Communism'*, *Irish Statesman,* VI (1926): 231.
'Art Criticism', *Irish Statesman,* IX (1927): 83.
Introduction to *Six Cartoons by Alfred Lowe* (sketches of Barrie, Bennett Chesterton, Kipling, Shaw and Wells). London, 1930.
'Foreword', Rhys Davies, *The Stars, The World, and The Women.* London, 1930.
'Red Ship', *New Republic,* LXVIII (23 September 1931): 147-50.
'Kingdom of Kerry', *Fortnightly Review* CXXXVIII (August 1932): 212-18.
'The Irish Censorship', *American Spectator,* I (November 1932): 2.
'Autobiographical Note' in *Ten Contemporaries, Second Series,* J. Gawsworth, ed. London, 1933.

III. POEMS

'Smaointe i gcein', *Dublin Magazine,'* II (December 1924): 330.

'Na Blatha Craige' in *Nuabhearsaiocht,* Sean O Tuama, ed. Dublin 1951.

Letters to Edward Garnett, 5 May 1923 — 3 March 1932. In the manuscript collection of the Academic Center Library, University of Texas, Austin, Texas.

Correspondence of F.R. Higgins. National Library of Ireland. MS. 10, 864.

INDEX

Inishmore Aran Islands Co Galway

(Inverara or *Nara* of the novels)*

The Fictional Geography of Liam O'Flaherty's Regional Novels
Fictional names are shown in italics

Rooruck
Bungowla

*Firbolg's
Point* ■ *Hill of Fate*

Coill Namhan
Kilchreest House ■

Kilmurve

Coillnamhan Fort
Head of Crom
Dun Aengus